Charismatic Bureaucrat

CHARISMATIC BUREAUCRAT
*A Political Biography of
Matsudaira Sadanobu
1758-1829*

HERMAN OOMS

*The University of Chicago Press
Chicago and London*

HERMAN OOMS is assistant professor of history at the Chicago Circle
Campus of the University of Illinois.

*Grateful acknowledgment is made to the Committee on Japanese Studies, Center
for Far Eastern Studies, at the University of Chicago, for their support of the
publication of this book.*

THE UNIVERSITY OF CHICAGO PRESS, CHICAGO 60637
THE UNIVERSITY OF CHICAGO PRESS, LTD., LONDON

Library of Congress Cataloging in Publication Data

Ooms, Herman
    Charismatic Bureaucrat.

    Bibliography: p.
    1. Matsudaira, Sadanobu, 1759–1829. I. Title.
DS872.M32065   952'.025'0924 [B]   74–10342
ISBN 0–226–63031–5

Contents

List of Tables

Dankbaar opgedragen
aan mijn ouders, Jozef en Maria Ooms.

Introduction

Matsudaira Sadanobu is famous in Japanese history as the leader of the Kansei Reform (1787-c.1800). He was the author of the second of the three Tokugawa reforms (the others being the Kyōhō Reform of the 1720s and the Tempō Reform of the 1830s) that bolstered the *bakufu* regime during critical periods in its history (1600-1868).

Historians, however, have not always agreed on how to evaluate his achievements as reformer. Traditional prewar Japanese historians celebrated Matsudaira Sadanobu as a model statesman, and often portrayed him as an example for their contemporary leaders. They spared no words of praise from the rich Japanese Confucian vocabulary for the ethical character of his leadership and reform. In the present day, few remember Matsudaira Sadanobu as a great political figure. Now it is more fashionable to consider him a political reactionary, lacking imaginative policies.

This fluctuation of historical interest in Matsudaira Sadanobu has more to do with changing attitudes of Japanese historians concerning the ethical and even religious quality of Sadanobu's regime than with his historical significance in his own time. Sadanobu's moralistic and edifying writings and his frugal policies were perfectly in tune with the political attitudes and convictions of many prewar Japanese leaders and some intellectuals as well. But postwar historians reject them as feudalistic and oppressive.

Yet even without the emotional response his name once commanded, Matsudaira Sadanobu is worth major attention because he revitalized the bakufu bureaucracy—the complex and sophisticated administrative apparatus that dominated Japan until the Meiji Restoration of 1868. The renovation of the bakufu's bureaucratic ethos was the most lasting aspect of Sadanobu's reform, surviving his short term in office and even the bakufu regime itself. The quasi-religious dedication which Sadanobu brought to bureaucratic performance persists as the hallmark of Japanese bureaucracy.

The present study seeks not merely to reexamine in detail the bureaucratic, political, and economic aspects of Matsudaira Sadanobu's Kansei Reform, but also to understand the mind of the man who was the driving force behind that reform. It focuses on the style of Matsudaira Sadanobu's statesmanship as well as on the substance of his decrees and policies. The policies received summary treatment in various general Western works on the period. The style of his statesmanship, however, although touched upon in a number of traditional Japanese studies, has never been granted the importance it deserves for a full understanding of the political personality of Matsudaira Sadanobu. And yet an insight into his psychological make-up is indispensable for an adequate evaluation of his leadership in a crisis situation calling for reform, when additional powers were entrusted to one man.

To rescue a premodern Japanese personality from history poses some serious methodological problems related to both the nature of the material and its interpretation. Personalities from a Confucian or Neo-Confucian tradition usually do not leave personal letters, notes, diaries, or autobiographies. Moreover, in the exceptional case that firsthand material is available, it is predominantly oblique in character. Almost invariably, the nature of such personal material is more expressive of role expectations than self-consciously confessional. Cross-checking with testimonies of contemporary witnesses does not help either, because they belong to the same literary tradition. Hence, reports of what a prominent historical figure actually did are always obscured by descriptions of what he is supposed to have done, or intended to do. Intentions and achievements blur under standardized Confucian rhetoric.

If the actual deeds of great men lie thus hidden behind the offical record, it becomes all the more difficult to discern their individual personalities and psychologies from their socially prescribed roles. It is hard to imagine men of flesh and blood, given to drives and ambition, behind the exemplary portrayal by their biographers. Under such historiographical conditions, how can one come to understand a historical personality? Did he act out of pure Confucian motives, and should we thus accept at face value the moralizing biographers? Or should we psychologize and thus pretend to discover the man behind his role?

These problems apply to Matsudaira Sadanobu, but with a difference. Matsudaira Sadanobu was an extraordinarily introspective and self-conscious man. In this respect we are fortunate, because his high esteem for the importance of his role and his charismatic self-perception of his leadership inspired two autobiographical works. The existence of these works made it possible to analyze the interaction between Sadanobu and his times.

Serious methodological questions, however, confront the historian who relies on a psychohistorical frame of reference. Traditionally, psychoanalysis seeks to explain behavior solely through an analysis in libidinal or drive terms of an individual's psychological makeup, which is assumed to have been fixed at an early age. It provides no theoretical link, except in reductionist terms, between the individual and his culture or society at large beyond his intimate familial relationships of childhood. In the case of Sadanobu such early data are not available, but Freudian speculation with elements such as emulation of his father, preoccupation with death, and suppression of his sex drive during his adolescent years is obviously tempting. Yet an explanation of the spirit behind the Kansei Reform in terms of a Freudian interpretation of Matsudaira Sadanobu's psychology would be highly unsatisfactory to a historian. It would surely limit our understanding of many aspects both of Sadanobu's life and of his political achievements, and it would neglect the formative influence of the cultural and social milieu on his personality.

Erik Erikson has bridged to some extent the gap between the individual and society by stressing the contribution of the environment beyond the nuclear family to the continuing formation of an individual's identity. This approach is akin to the attention traditionally given by historians to cultural and social factors. Yet psychohistorical studies, by closely applying specific personality theories to historical figures, have often turned into clinical case studies. Psychological interpretive categories can contribute to the understanding of past personalities, but only insofar as the specific conclusions they underpin are warranted by the historical data. The present study is not a mere historical embroidery on a personality theory. It offers a historical interpretation that takes account of certain psychosocial dimensions in character formation and makes use of several relevant interpretive categories of human behavior.

Because psychosocial (political, social, and cultural) factors are even more important than psychological ones for understanding Matsudaira Sadanobu's personality, this study examines Sadanobu's environment before tracing his psychological development. Furthermore, in order to establish the leading themes that shape Sadanobu's personality, I have not confined myself to a single theory of personality, but have made use of several relevant works of psychology and social and cultural anthropology. I have relied on Weberian categories and Edward Shils's refinement of them, Erik Erikson's theories on personality, and Clifford Geertz's writings on religion and ideology as cultural systems.

The charisma of Sadanobu's statesmanship offers the key to his political personality. Charisma, as defined by Max Weber, is a certain exceptional individual quality which sets a personality apart from ordinary men. Others see him—or he sees himself—as being endowed with unusual spiritual powers. Charisma always constitutes a "mission" or "spiritual duty."[1] In Weber's typology of authority this irrational, religious quality of charismatic leadership is antithetical to bureaucratic authority.[2] Recent theoretical developments by Edward Shils, however, have revealed a much more intricate and far from mutually exclusive relationship between these two types of authority.[3] Matsudaira Sadanobu reflects this newer understanding of charisma. Although a great bureaucrat, Sadanobu must be understood in the light of the religious mode of his behavior.

Charisma, an overworked concept in Western historiography, has until now found little place in the study of Japanese political figures. Some scholars, like the anthropoligist Nakane Chie, have even spoken of a conspicuous absence of charismatic leaders in Japanese history. It is undeniable, however, that charisma, as defined above, explains Sadanobu's political style and his fame as a model ruler even until the recent past.

During Sadanobu's lifetime the political system of the bakufu faced a profound crisis that affected all aspects of society—financial, economic, political, and moral. A study of the political career of Matsudaira thus offers a cross-sectional analysis of Tokugawa political society at a crucial point in its history.

Chapter 1 traces the crisis of the Tokugawa political order until Sadanobu's accession to power and examines the political dimension of his upbringing. Sadanobu's intellectual views and his psychology form the subject of the second chapter. In chapter 3 we study Sadanobu's career before he came to the bakufu: his rule in his domain and his political activity in Edo. Sadanobu's performance in both these areas reveals the transposition of his ideas, often clouded in ambiguous rhetoric, into concrete action. During these years he laid the foundation for his bakufu tenure as chief councillor. His reforms are examined in the chapters 4 through 6: first his bureaucratic renovation, then his restoration of bakufu prestige and authority, and finally his creation of a fitting ideology to give durability to his reform. Continued attention is given to Sadanobu's political style, to the particular leadership he provided, and to the common assumptions about the relation between politics and ethics that underlay all his measures. His regime can best be typified as the rule of a bureaucrat who understood how to channel his sense of mission into the renewal of a complex bureaucracy.

For the more intimate aspect of Matsudaira Sadanobu's psychology and for his perception of his political role, I have consulted his own writings, both published and unpublished. For the content of his Kansei Reform, I was able to draw upon the works of a number of Japanese historians who wrote before the Second World War. And for the earlier political and economic reform that Sadanobu carried out in his own *han* or domain of Shirakawa, I was able to use both very recently published primary sources and local histories, and some unpublished material still available in Shirakawa.

It is further my pleasant duty to express my gratitude for the continuous encouragement I received during the course of my research and writing from Professor Tetsuo Najita of the University of Chicago. I am also greatly indebted to the various institutions and libraries in Japan which made their material available. Special thanks go to Mrs. Yasuda Hisako from the Shiryō Hensanjo of Tokyo University for her patient assistance in reading manuscript materials. And I am particularly indebted to Sukama Zenkatsu, local historian from Shirakawa, who communicated to me his cherished knowledge of the history of his region—his birthplace—and led me as well to some untapped sources.

Charismatic Bureaucrat

1 *Political Legacy*

Matsudaira Sadanobu grew up in the latter half of the eighteenth century, a time of unprecedented social upheaval for the Tokugawa period. The legacy that was left him was one of great political complexity and uncertainty: the bakufu bureaucracy, whose highest post of chief councillor he filled in 1787, was in political disarray; the Shirakawa domain, where four years earlier he had started his career as daimyo, faced one of the direst famines of the entire Tokugawa period; and the Tayasu house, into which he was born in 1758, had had an unfortunate history of thwarted political ambition. Nevertheless Sadanobu succeeded in assuring himself a firm place in Japanese history. When he retired from his bakufu office in 1793, at the early age of thirty-four,* he had inaugurated a new era. Viewed as a model ruler in his own day, he continued to attract admirers well into modern times.

As with other political leaders who leave their mark upon society, Sadanobu possessed the ability both to achieve tangible results and to give his rule a distinctive political style. The Kansei Reform was Sadanobu's work, and in defining and implementing its policies, he showed a great pragmatic sense of statesmanship. He had a clear conception of his goals, understood which forces to use to realize them, and took the proper measures to make his achievements survive his term in office. But in his determined efforts to improve the quality of government, Sadanobu perhaps suffered from an overoptimistic view of human nature and, hence, of what he could expect from his subjects.

During his first four years as daimyo, and during his subsequent six years as chief councillor, Sadanobu developed a political style that consisted of two seemingly contradictory qualities, which may be characterized as the charismatic and the bureaucratic. Although historians often view these two styles as mutually exclusive, in the

*Matsudaira Sadanobu was born on 1758/12/27. (Dates will be indicated in the year/month/day order, following Japan's traditional lunar reckoning.) In 1783 he was thus twenty-four and, according to Western calculation, turned twenty-five only at the very end of the year. This way of speaking of Sadanobu's age, which will be followed here, reflects more accurately his age than the Japanese way of computing, by which Sadanobu turned two on the first of January, five days after his birth. Therefore, any checking of ages mentioned here with Japanese sources or studies has to take into account a discrepancy of two years.

manner described by Max Weber, they can be seen as intermingled elements in Sadanobu's exercise of authority. Sadanobu was convinced that the example of the virtuous ruler was an indispensable tool of government. At the same time, he had the ability to renovate the bakufu bureaucracy, and to create new institutions to further solidify it.

THE BAKUFU

Three names dominate the political history of the bakufu in the eighteenth century: Yoshimune, the eighth shogun (in office: 1716–45; in retirement: 1745–51) and author of the Kyōhō Reform; Tanuma Okitsugu (1719–88), who rose from an obscure post in the shogunal household to the offices of grand chamberlain and senior councillor, and who gave his name to a period of weak shogunal rule and official corruption (the 1770s and '80s); and Matsudaira Sadanobu, Yoshimune's grandson.[1]

Sadanobu grew up at a time when the bakufu's administrative system had begun to show signs of serious strain. Financial distress and political tension at the top, and agricultural instability at the bottom, failed to respond to piecemeal remedial measures. When in 1786 the bakufu leader Tanuma Okitsugu fell from official grace, a concensus concerning the need for overall reform and firm leadership had developed in the responsible leading circles of the bakufu. The families collateral to the shogun decided to give Matsudaira Sadanobu a mandate to emulate Yoshimune's Kyōhō Reform.

The intention of the collaterals and of Sadanobu was clear: to restore the bakufu's strength through an overall reform. But the task was much more difficult, for, since Yoshimune's time, the problems had grown in size and complexity and were, in fact, partially the result of certain of Yoshimune's measures. During the intervening regime of Tanuma Okitsugu, corruption and unorthodox policies, provoking the ire of the collaterals and other leading daimyo, had led to placing the blame for all the ills of the time on Tanuma. His regime was discredited, although it was in many respects a continuation and further development of policies and trends initiated by Yoshimune. Hence a mere reapplication of his grandfather's solutions would not do for Sadanobu.

Yoshimune, as Sadanobu was to do later, had aimed directly at restoring the bakufu's deteriorating finances. Financial distress had resulted from the separation of the warriors from the land—a political measure taken by Tokugawa Ieyasu (1542–1616), the founder of the shogunal house. The warriors were concentrated in Edo and the regional castle towns, where they were cut off from their immediate source of income, and thus from a potential independent base of power. They had to depend completely upon stipends from the bakufu or daimyo. This shrewd political arrangement, however, had unhealthy consequences for the government's financial autonomy. City life made increasing financial demands upon the lords and their stipended warrior-administrators, who therefore grew dependent upon the capital of money dealers and merchants.

The role Yoshimune assigned to the merchants in the solution of the bakufu's financial needs had far-reaching consequences. His solution laid the basis for the subsequent troubles Sadanobu had with the merchants and for which he had to devise new answers, despite his slogan "Return to the Kyōhō Reform." Yoshimune failed in his initial attempt to suppress merchant capital or to sap its power through monetary reforms and the cancelation of debts.[2] Through monopolistic licenses granted against a fee, Yoshimune accommodated the merchants' economic power, prudently and profitably, but he did not break the dependency of the bakufu on merchant capital.[3]

Yoshimune thus succeeded in finding a place for merchant capital in the bakufu's overall administrative system. Yet he was reluctant about the measure. The license fee was not a tax, commensurate to the merchants' profits. The merchants were allowed, under bakufu supervision, to continue capital-building on the increased rural output, which the government did not attempt to tax directly. They therefore became a solid part of the Tokugawa social edifice. Their new importance altered Tokugawa society significantly: to the earlier dual structure of rulers and tax-paying subjects, they had added a new economic power center, only partially subject to political control. Thus, the Japan of the Kyōhō era failed to "return to the ways of Ieyasu" as Yoshimune had intended. On the contrary, the reform had merely neutralized momentarily and accommodated within limits a new socioeconomic force. Further encouraged by Tanuma, that force had, by Sadanobu's time, more seriously undermined the bakufu's financial solvency than had been the case under Yoshimune.

Another problem area common to both reform periods was the bureaucracy. Initially Yoshimune sought to reestablish a more direct rule, conducting the business of government from the Interior (his personal court), and relying more upon his personal lieutenants than upon bakufu officials of the Exterior (the bakufu's administrative organs). But the government had become too complex to be conducted by one man. Its growing dependence upon merchant capital, for instance, resulted in the increased importance of the new office of superintendent of finances.[4] Delegation of power had become unavoidable, but in the following decades power became concentrated in the Interior, with all the open corruption and crude politicking for which Tanuma's years are notorious.[5] Sadanobu's foremost political concern was to restore power to the Senior Council where it traditionally belonged.

For Yoshimune, the problem with the bakufu's growing bureaucracy was one less of corruption than of routinization, which he tried to fight by reviving the warrior's military ethos. Yoshimune thus encouraged the martial arts and frugal virtues, aiming to create a spirit of militancy and service rather than to restore the military character of the bakufu administration itself. "Moral rearmament," however, also prominent in Sadanobu's revitalization of the bureaucracy, proved to be the most short-lived aspect of Yoshimune's reform.

There is thus a certain cyclical nature to the reforms of the Tokugawa period. Murdoch speaks of "intermittent spasms of virtue."[6] To use another image, historians traditionally have viewed Yoshimune's Kyōhō Reform and Sadanobu's Kansei Reform as the two reactionary wings of a triptych, the central panel being filled by the corrupt but expansive Tanuma regime. The two reform periods are thus characterized by retrenchment policies and sumptuary laws, while in the intermediary period mercantilism flourished in the midst of social and political decay.

As already pointed out, however, the break between Yoshimune's policies and Tanuma's rule was not as great as official historiography leads one to believe. Tanuma's mercantilist policies, although relatively rewarding to the government, failed to balance the budget and led to the bakufu's increasing dependency upon the merchant class.[7] The bakufu suffered indirectly from these policies in two ways. First, the increased importance of merchant capital developed into a threat to the political culture. Not that powerful central merchants were growning politically ambitious; but the lure of wealth and the ethos of profit accumulation were subversive of the warrior's style of life. Many contemporaries, including Matsudaira Sadanobu, expressed concern about the bakufu's spiritual fate by condemning the Tanuma regime for its corruption. This judgment, however, though shared by most historians, merely denies the applicability of merchant values to the operation of politics. Politics, it is contended, is based upon a status system, and is the province of warriors, who are subject to the different and nobler code of mutual loyalties and obligations.

Second, the inroads of the merchants into the countryside under the bakufu's reluctant blessing had an adverse effect upon the land base of the bakufu's income. Merchant monopolies depressed the producer's price and therefore deprived the peasants of their surplus profits, greatly adding to their hardships.[8] Cash crops, moreover, increased the peasants' vulnerability to the hazards of weather conditions, because a bad year now often meant a total loss of income. In the middle of the eighteenth century the peasants started responding to these pressures by abandoning the land and reducing the number of their dependents by practicing abortion and infanticide. The resulting labor shortage in agriculture was viewed with great alarm by the bakufu because it seriously imperiled the stability of the peasant class and, ultimately, the bakufu's land tax revenues.

The warning by Sadanobu and a number of other writers that the agricultural base of the country (as a source of government income) was falling asunder was not an exaggeration. The entire blame, however, could not be put on Tanuma. The Tanuma years were beset with successive natural disasters that gave rise to great social unrest. In 1772 Edo suffered the second largest fire in its history, reducing to ashes 127 official daimyo residences, 878 nonofficial residences, over 8,000 houses of bannermen (*hatamoto*), and 600 blocks of merchant dwellings.[9] Throughout the decade, the country was plagued by drought, reducing yields and preventing storage to stave off other disasters: in 1770 the bakufu's land tax revenues, usually above 2 million *koku*, fell to 1.5 million for the first time in thirty years. They wavered slightly above that level until 1780, but were below 1.5 million for the next fourteen years.[10] Almost every year there were tempests, droughts, floods, and epidemics, causing unprecedented loss of life and property.

In the summer of 1783, the Asama volcano (some eighty miles northwest of Edo) erupted, raining ashes upon the crops of three provinces. In the autumn of that same year, the country was afflicted with a widespread crop failure. Japan's backward northern region, including Shirakawa han, where Sadanobu was on the point of assuming rule of the domain, was hit hardest. Hundreds of thousands died; there were even tales of cannibalism. This dark year was preceded by two partial crop failures and followed by three more, caused this time not by drought but by prolonged rains.[11] Rice became scarce. Its price and the general cost of living rose steeply. Since Yoshimune, the price of rice had been subject to bakufu regulation, and had usually fluctuated between forty-five and seventy *momme* per koku. But during the Tenmei famines it soared to unprecedented heights: 98.3 in 1783; 111.2 in 1784, and 167.9 in 1787.[12]

During these years of financial distress and natural disasters, peasant uprisings and city riots became the most effective means for the populace to express its discontent. Although the mobs did not aim directly at overthrowing the political system, their riots were not simply meaningless and diffuse explosions of anger. In their selection of targets (wealthy land-owning peasants, merchants, money lenders, or local administrators), the rioters singled out in each case the local sources of the abuses.

The bakufu, which justified its existence through its role as pre-server of the peace, was seriously upset by the high incidence of these disturbances. Between 1781 and 1788 (the Tenmei era), there was an average of twenty-six riots a year, a number that was more than three times the previous all-time peak of 8.8 riots per year during the Kyōhō era (1716-36). A breakdown of the Tokugawa period per decade offers the same picture. The decade of the 1780s witnessed almost twice as many riots as the previous record decade of the 1740s: 229 versus 130.[13] Moreover, from the middle of the eighteenth century, peasant uprisings were more extensive than in the past, when they were distinguished by groups of villages dramatizing their demands through mass protest. The uprisings since the middle of the eighteenth century encompassed entire domains, sometimes several, and involved tens of thousands of protestors. In 1786-87, when Sadanobu was becoming chief councillor, practically the entire country was in continuous turmoil.[14]

Initially, the bakufu tried to steer a middle course between total suppression of social unrest and maintenance of the good will of the peasants, but as uprisings became more numerous, more violent, and wider in scope, the authorities resorted to more oppressive and forceful means to keep the peace. The bakufu issued orders instructing neighboring daimyo to rescue pressured bakufu deputies without awaiting specific pleas for help. Edicts forbade local officials to compromise on peasant demands, and enjoined them to apply random punishments of villagers if the leaders of the riots were unknown. Rewards were offered to informers of rebel leaders. Finally, the bakufu permitted the use of firearms to quell the riots.[15] These bakufu directives, however, were not confined to its own territories. Recognizing the nationwide character of the problems, the bakufu in the 1760s and 1770s took the unprecedented step of interfering in the internal affairs of the domains through repetitive directives to all daimyo on how to deal with the disturbances.

Law and order was only one issue on which the bakufu asserted its authority over the domains; it was part of a new pattern in bakufu policy, which seriously disturbed the daimyo. Increasingly, bakufu directives had national ramifications. Thus the bakufu was encroaching more and more upon the daimyo's range of idependent action, which had increased since the establishment of the *bakuhan* system.[16] The most ominous expression of this new trend was the bakufu's effort to regulate and control a greater share of the national economy according to its own needs. Through various arrangements and restrictions concerning domain monopolies, the bakufu was threatening the commercial interests of the daimyo. In 1767, for example, the bakufu attempted to monopolize the cotton production of the Kanto area; in 1780 it established an iron monopoly; and in 1785 it dispatched an official to the Aizu domain to study its monopolistic wax-making process.[17]

What further added to the animosity of the daimyo was the fact that they had no control over these new policies. Customarily, bakufu policies were set by the Senior Council, a cabinet staffed by vassal daimyo. Now, however, only one man was responsible for this course of action—Tanuma, an arrivé who completely bypassed the Senior Council.[18]

By the end of 1783, the self-serving interests of the bakufu, which had sporadically hurt several daimyo, were publicly revealed through two measures that affected the whole country. In 1783/12, the bakufu declared a seven year frugality program, which canceled all loans during that period.[19] This decree meant an end to all assistance the bakufu customarily granted to financially pressured daimyo, who were now, in a year of great famine, left to their own resources. The reason for this retrenchment, of course, was the bakufu's own financial distress. Bakufu land revenues in kind, which for over a decade had maintained the exceptionally low level of 1.5 million koku, dropped to 1.25 million koku that year—three years later they plunged to one million.[20]

The decision to cancel all loans came one month after another measure, which had turned daimyo apprehension about bakufu intentions into firm opposition.[21] It had to do with a plan to strengthen bakufu control of the Osaka rice market by forcing the payment of all futures in the hands of Osaka merchants. In 1773, the bakufu had arranged to buy all futures from claimant merchants, and then to collect the rice directly from the storehouses of the daimyo. In 1782 Tanuma dropped this arrangement, appointed an arbiter (Gotō Nuinosuke) to ascertain the amount of debts, and forbade the daimyo in question to sell a corresponding amount of their domain's income. Twelve daimyo received such an order that same year; one of them was related by marriage to Sadanobu.[22] In 1783/11, Tanuma went a step further. He decided that all futures of the previous ten years needed the arbiter's stamp of approval, and he issued a decree to process without delay all pending cases. Those who would not comply were to go on trial. Furthermore, Tanuma requested a commission of one *bu* of silver per koku.[23] Opposition from the daimyo was firm: they declared invalid all futures that would bear the stamp of the bakufu arbiter.

The daimyo's concerted action marked the first open opposition to Tanuma. In 1784/3, four months after the daimyo's refusal to comply, Tanuma's political prestige received a more serious blow when his son Okitomo, whom Tanuma was obviously preparing as his successor, was assassinated.[24] Although there seems to have been no political plot behind the assassination, Tanuma must have become apprehensive about arousing more antagonism. At the end of 1784 he retreated in the Osaka affair, and agreed that the claimants had merely to register with the arbiter if they wished to bring their case to court. This compromise, however, did not carry the full approval of the daimyo. They finally succeeded in canceling the agreement in 1787/1, after Tanuma's resignation but at a time when his clique was still in power. (Tanuma resigned in 1786/8, and Sadanobu became chief councillor in 1787/6.)

During the last two years before his resignation, Tanuma made a belated effort to regain daimyo good will by attempting to establish a relief fund to ease their financial distress. Tanuma's two projects, however, ended in failure.[25] In 1785 he planned to float a loan among the Osaka merchants. The loan was to be operated by the bakufu who would guarantee with its authority repayment by the daimyo. One-seventh of the interest was to stay with the bakufu, the rest to go to the merchants. The merchants, however, found the investment too risky, and most of them refused to cooperate.

Tanuma's second scheme was more daring and ultimately cost him his career. In 1786/6 he made plans to requisition a nationwide loan on all property of temples, shrines, peasants, merchants, and artisans, in the bakufu territories and in all domains.[26] This loan, to be paid back by the bakufu after five years with 7 percent interest per annum, was in fact a national property tax. Allegedly meant as a plan of assistance to the daimyo, the project drew immediate opposition from all quarters. A recently discovered document called *Tenmei kōsetsu* (Rumors of the Tenmei era) shows the scope of the opposition, involving *fudai* and *tozama* lords (vassal daimyo and outside daimyo), the three collateral houses, and even two Tanuma protégés on the Senior Council, Mizuno Tadatomo and Makino Sadanaga.[27] The daimyo were convinced that the new tax would meet with great resistance from the peasants.[28] Some daimyo, like Kuroda from Fukuoka han, thought it necessary to make military preparations in anticipation of peasant uprisings if the tax was levied.[29] It was the senior councillor Makino Sadanaga who, through the lord of Mito, secretly persuaded the three Tokugawa collateral houses of Mito, Owari, and Kii to block the plan.[30] They seized their chance in the eighth month, when they were able to control access to the shogun, who was on his deathbed. From the twentieth of the eighth month they were daily with the shogun, while Tanuma, sick himself, kept to his residence.

The *Tenmei kōsetsu* sheds new light upon this unfortunate coincidence of Tanuma's illness and the shogun's death, as reported in the *Tokugawa jikki* (official records of the Tokugawa house).[31] This new historical source recounts the events as follows. On 8/19, after two new physicians recommended by Tanuma had begun to attend the shogun, the latter's condition suddenly took a turn for the worse. Rumors circulated that Tanuma was poisoning the shogun. A group of attendants and pages from the Interior (one of whom was a nephew of Tanuma), promptly formed a plot to assassinate Tanuma. In order to avoid the fate of Okitomo's assassin Sano Masakoto, who had been ordered to commit suicide, the group from the Interior involved higher functionaries in their plot by revealing their plan to Matsudaira Noritada, the lord of Okudono han, at that time head of the attendants. (After Tanuma's fall, on 11/12, he was apparently rewarded for his intentions with a promotion to superintendent of works.)[32] The plotters also pressured the senior councillor Mizuno Tadatomo, who advised Tanuma to stay away from the castle.[33] Thus, on 8/22, Tanuma excused himself from his attendance duty for "reasons of health." On the twenty-fourth, the three collaterals effected the cancelation of the floating loan scheme and other projects; three days later, Tanuma resigned.

With Tanuma's fall, the opposition had won a major battle, but their victory was far from final. Political power was still in the hands of numerous Tanuma protégés, entrenched strategically in all major bureaucratic posts. It took ten months of maneuvering and negotiating before the opposition was able to assure the appointment of its own candidate, Matsudaira Sadanobu, as the head of the new government. The legacy that befell him was in fact a multiple mandate: to restore social order, to reduce political tensions, to clean up bureaucratic corruption, and to redress the bakufu's finances.

Sadanobu's task was vastly more complex than that which Yoshimune had faced sixty years earlier. The disruption of the agricultural sector had reached greater proportions. Furthermore, the bakufu, out of financial necessity, had allied itself much more closely with merchant capital. This alliance was a very uneasy one. The merchants were as necessary to the government as its bureaucratic servants, but their public commitment was always limited and conditional; their values of unrestrained competition and profit maximization were viewed by the bakufu as countervalues to the public good. The bakufu was worried about the degree to which profitseeking had become a leading motive among the Edo officials and to what point it had eroded the public spirit of the bureaucracy. Sadanobu thus faced a completely new problem: how to restore the morale of a complex and corrupt bureaucracy. Aggravating the general situation was the closer interdependence and greater friction between the bakufu and the domains. More than ever the future of the bakufu was tied to, and limited by, the existence of the domains. Tanuma's attempts to establish a national, bakufu-centered polity had cost him his career. No matter how rational and appealing the prospect of a national polity for the bakufu, the difficulties the bakufu had encountered when venturing in that direction set limits to its early realization. Political realities were a severe check on political rationalism.

Daimyo particularism was not the only block to the bakufu's ambitions for a closer national integration under its own hegemony. Since the middle of the century, idealist thinkers like Takenouchi Shikibu (punished in the "Hōreki Incident" of 1758; exiled in 1767) and Yamagata Daini (executed in the "Meiwa Incident" of 1767) had envisioned a national order for whose realization the bakufu was not the instrument but the principal obstacle. Although their influence was limited at this point, the potential appeal of these counter-ideological thinkers could not be lightly dismissed, since they seemed to have responded to social abuses which the bakufu had not been able to get rid of.

Takenouchi was probably inspired, as Hayashi Motoi suggests, by the bakufu's impotence to deal with the large-scale riots of the late 1740s and early 1750s. The first large-scale riot (involving over 20,000 peasants) erupted in 1745 in bakufu territories of the Kōchi and Settsu provinces in the Kyoto area. The peasants took the unprecedented step of sending numerous delegates to appeal to the Imperial Court and the nobles. It is known that they also went to the residence of Bōjō Toshiyasu, one of Shikibu's disciples. Shikibu began his lectures among the nobles that very same year, making veiled suggestions to restore peace under direct imperial rule.[34]

In the light of these disturbing tendencies, vassal daimyo and the collaterals were ready by the early 1780s to support political reform from within the bakufu. They constituted the sector of society in which the sense of deprivation was organically linked with political ambition. Undoubtedly they were driven by self-interest. But they also understood that ultimately they would be better served—even if this merely meant a maintenance of the status quo—by a broader definition of national interests, including the interests of the domains and the peasants.

In order to succeed, a reformist political leadership needs a model of a social order that integrates the aspirations of the deprived, and psychological and institutional levers to generate cooperation from people attached in varying degrees to the old order. In Tokugawa Japan the most obvious model was the sociopolitical structure with which Ieyasu had given peace to the country after more than a century of civil war. The bakufu located the need for change in the bureaucratic personnel rather than in the administrative structure. For those concerned with reform, the political structure was sacrosanct, and much more than a convenient blueprint for the management of society that could be altered at will. The reformists stressed the necessary character of the structure by pointing out that the Tokugawa system was not only constitutive of society but was creative of civilization as well. They also argued that this system protected the country against the only alternative—the chaos and barbarism that preceded its establishment. This argument, of course, insofar as it was convincing, gave Ieyasu's model great motivational appeal.

It is relatively easy to mobilize emotional support when there is an external threat to the country. When the "enemy" is within, however, and takes the form of widespread corruption, the government has to find subtler means to legitimate change. Its first objective is then to restore the public's confidence that it is exclusively oriented toward the common good. This attempt usually consists of a deliberate and credible association of the government with an exemplary model of action, present or past—one which visibly embodies the central values underpinning the social order commonly considered to be just. Thus in Tokugawa Japan, political emotions were best mobilized around model rulers. Their virtue, justice, and selfless concern for the people's welfare were upheld in times of strain to generate confidence in the government.

Sadanobu made full use of this device of "exemplary politics." He chose Yoshimune as his model just as Yoshimune had legitimized his reform after the example of Ieyasu. Equally important to Sadanobu, however, was his own image of the ideal ruler, which he had carefully cultivated during his daimyo rule in Shirakawa. During these four years he had been able to shortcut the time usually needed to create the charismatic halo of a model ruler. When Sadanobu came to the bakufu in 1787, even outside his domain he was already known as an efficient and just ruler.

Shirakawa was one of the 240 domains of the Tokugawa period, all of which faced financial and economic difficulties like those of the bakufu. They responded with similar reform programs.

The natural calamities of the Tanuma era had been particularly devastating for the northern han. Shirakawa han was situated in Iwaki province (the southern part of today's Fukushima prefecture), just north of the Kanto plain, on a plateau that forms the gateway to Japan's poor northern districts. In the latter half of the eighteenth century, the domain's official annual yield was 110,000 koku of rice, with a population close to 110,000. When Sadanobu took over the domain's administration in the fall of 1783, the domain faced an unprecedented famine crisis. Over 108,000 of the 110,000 koku of rice were reported lost. The measures that Sadanobu took, which rescued his domain and acquired him lasting fame, will be described in chapter 3. Sadanobu's leadership, however, gains salience if seen against the background of earlier solutions adopted in similar, if less extreme situations.

First it is important to know that Shirakawa was a vassal daimyo domain, which determined in a very special way the relationship between the daimyo and the peasants. By the nineteenth century, and the situation was little different in the last quarter of the eighteenth century, the territory that was not directly controlled by the bakufu was divided into 151 vassal daimyo (*fudai*) domains, 21 related daimyo (*kamon*) domains, and 108 outside daimyo (*tozama*) domains.[35] The fudai domains were closely linked to the bakufu, so that most of them were subject to the bakufu's general policy of preserving its own primacy in the overall balance of power in a pacified Japan. This bakufu policy of *primus inter pares* was directed not only against the less trustworthy outside daimyo but also against its most powerful vassals. Shirakawa was one of the bakufu's twelve great vassal domains (among the others were Hikone, Takata, Odawara).[36] In order to prevent its vassals from building strength in the provinces, the bakufu frequently arranged their transfer, often accompanied by territorial adjustments as rewards or punishments, from one domain to another. Shirakawa had experienced many such transfers (for a detailed history of Shirakawa han, see Appendix A).

The units that were transferred in these territorial adjustments were taxable villages. Vassal domains, therefore, were mere agglomerations of taxable villages, easily mutable, leased by the bakufu to vassal daimyo for use at their own discretion. They were very rarely political units, like tozama domains, where the same family ruled for centuries and which had stood the test of time.

A vassal daimyo had little chance to establish roots in his territory. He often knew that his identification with a particular domain would not last. This tenuous association of a warrior house with a domain also encouraged greater exactions from the peasants, if for no other reason than that each transfer meant an additional financial burden for the domain. Hence, the relation between the tax-paying peasants and their lords tended to be especially exploitative and, from the peasants' viewpoint, fraught with distrust.

Tension in most domains was not limited to the relationship between rulers and ruled. Since the beginning of the eighteenth century, the deteriorating financial situation of the retainers had created great difficulties for the daimyo. In Shirakawa, the daimyo tried to meet this problem by paying the interest on loans contracted by the retainers, by limiting interest rates at 15 percent, by ordering postponement of payments, and by circulating paper money. These measures, however, failed to remedy the situation so that an increasing number of retainers, unable to fulfill their military duties, requested temporary exemptions from their obligations (*tsubushi*). The daimyo often had to refuse such requests, for they could not let the contingent of their militia drop below the quota set by the bakufu.[37]

Thus the daimyo were being pressured from two sides: the peasants sought to reduce the domain's tax income as much as possible, and the retainers were increasingly in need of a greater share of that income. The han administration tried to steer a middle course between a policy geared to the needs of the impoverished and discontented retainers, often banded together in factions to press their demands, and a policy of appeasement toward the peasants, overtaxed in their own eyes and ready to voice their protest in increasingly disruptive uprisings.[38] Moreover, the daimyo's power in deciding a policy was very limited. Policy making was more often than not the outcome of power struggles among domain officials. In Shirakawa too, up to Sadanobu's time, the domain's administration was determined not by the daimyo but by the officials, who were backed by one of the leading factions.

The most famous of these political struggles in Shirakawa's history was fought during the rule of the Matsudaira (Yūki) house (1692–1741) between two contending factions that identified with two separate policies.[39] The reform party, led by the councillor (*toshiyori*) Hayakawa Mozaemon, advocated in 1708 a long-range plan to increase revenues through the development of new lands. The reform

called for a tax cut for the peasants, especially reducing their corvée
duties and the numerous miscellaneous taxes which had multiplied
during the regime of the Honda (1649-81) (see Appendix A). Extraordinary levies by the bakufu, however, forced the domain to
contract new debts, which in turn forced Hayakawa, in order to save
his reform, to reduce the retainers' stipends. The elder (*karō*) Doki
Hannokyoku, who had been in charge of contracting the loans,
became spokesman for the retainers. He blamed their financial duress
on Hayakawa's policies favoring the peasants and won the daimyo
with false accusations against Hayakawa. Over a span of three years,
he ousted seventy-two officials, including Hayakawa and several
deputies (*daikan*), and reestablished the old tax system. His victory
did not last long, however, for in 1720 the peasants staged a riot,
demanding the dismissal of the three main captains of Doki's party
(the elder Doki, an inspector general and a superintendent of finances)
and a return to Hayakawa's regime. All their demands were met.[40]

Much of the data on Shirakawa han during the Matsudaira
(Hisamatsu) rule was lost. In general, the frequent transfers of fudai
families have resulted in poorer conservation of documents than in
tozama domains. In the present case there is an additional reason for
this absence of data. In the civil war of 1868, the Hisamatsu castle in
Kuwana (near Nagoya), where the family had been enfeoffed since
1823, was razed by the loyalist forces. In that same war the Shirawaka
castle also went up in flames.

Sadanobu's warnings and measures indicate the persistence of
factional disputes of the sort just described among han bureaucrats in
Shirakawa. Most assuredly, Sadanobu's effective administration of
his han bureaucracy was due to his familiarity with the history of his
house. In 1781/1, for example, he examined in detail a document
(*Bokumin kōhan*, Additional considerations on how to govern the
people) dealing with twenty-five problems of han government, written in 1649 by Sadatsuna, the founder of the Hisamatsu family. This
work inspired him to write his *Kokuhonron* (On the basis of the
country) in the eighth month of the same year—the month in which
the Chinese *kambun* text of the *Bokumin kōhan* was transcribed into
the vernacular by one of his retainers.[41]

In summary, Shirakawa han was not a very attractive domain. Its
prestige as one of the great vassal domains was offset by its geograph-
ical remoteness and lack of historical continuity, both in its territory
and in the succession of the ruling houses. Historical continuity
consisted rather in the persistent tension between peasants and
whoever were their rulers. The domain's administrative and financial
structure changed with each ruling family and, according to Sadanobu, consisted of haphazard regulations and devices rather than a

coordinated set of house laws.[42] Moreover, the daimyo showed little determination to deal with the factions that split the administration on financial policies.

When Sadanobu took over the government of Shirakawa in 1783/10, he found the domain in a state of disarray: it was on the brink of famine; cash and food reserves were extremely low; two months earlier, the peasants had staged a destructuve riot in the castle town, protesting high rice prices; and retainers' stipends had been reduced to help meet the crisis situation. Moreover, Sadanobu succeeded to a house into which he had been adopted on the bakufu's order, against his own expectations and the wishes of his native Tayasu family.

THE TAYASU HOUSE

As one of the six Tokugawa collateral houses, Tayasu ranked among the most prestigious houses of the time. The six collaterals consisted of the Three Houses (*sanke*) of Mito, Owari, and Kii, which had been created by Ieyasu, and the Three Lords (*sankyō*) established by Yoshimune (Tayasu and Hitotsubashi) and his son Ieshige (Shimizu). The Three Lords were thus junior in rank and prestige among the collaterals.

Prestige rather than political or military power was the hallmark of the Three Lords. They lacked a real autonomous basis of power. Unlike the daimyo and the Three Houses, they did not have a defined territorial area, nor did they have castles or a large vassal following. The lands from which they drew their income (parcels amounting to 100,000 koku per lord, taken from shogunal house land), the mansions, the retainers, and even the titles were not hereditary. They were bestowed only upon the living lord. The Three Lords thus resembled high-level stipended members of the shogun's extended family. Their main function was to provide potential shogunal heirs.[43]

Munetake (1715–71), Sadanobu's father, was the first lord of Tayasu, the senior house of the Three Lords (see table 1). After the death of Munemasa, his younger brother and founder of Hitotsubashi, Munetake was the only surviving uncle of the shogun Ieharu. He was thus in line for the shogunal office in case Ieharu were to have no heir.

TABLE 1 Abbreviated Genealogy of the Three Lords

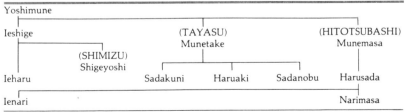

Moreover, as Yoshimune's favored son, Munetake had identified
closely with his father's policies. As founder of Tayasu, he had made
the spirit of Yoshimune's Kyōhō Reform the backbone of the family
tradition.

The Tayasu tradition was a weighty factor in shaping Sadanobu's
political outlook. It exerted its influence upon Sadanobu in three
different but closely interrelated ways: as an educational milieu, as a
cultural tradition, and as a political orientation. Life at Tayasu was
harmonized to a high degree. Educational, cultural, and political
values, stemming from the same "Kyōhō spirit," reinforced each
other, thus maximizing the formative impact of Tayasu's closely
integrated life style upon Sadanobu.

The spirit of austerity and frugality of the Kyōhō Reform was
consciously kept alive by Munetake as a precarious family legacy, and
as a guide for education. Munetake lived through two contrasting
periods in Tokugawa history: the martially austere years of the Kyōhō
Reform and the conspicuously luxurious Tanuma regime. The rampant luxury of the surrounding society during the latter period,
however, did not affect life at Tayasu.[44] Life was simple there. The
family had only a few attendants, and Munetake's offspring was
subject to strict discipline concerning food, clothing, and bathing.
Conformity to regulations was stressed, and the expression of
one's own wants or desires discouraged. Education was thus an
exercise in self-denial and a moral conquest of one's instincts. In
an obvious retrospective justification for his own frugal policies,
Sadanobu remarks in his memoirs that the restrictions of the Kansei
years were mild by comparison with the rigor to which he was
subjected during his childhood.[45] In a society where conspicuous
consumption had become a fashionable expression of social status, the strict life style at Tayasu was doubly remarkable. Their
self-imposed frugality gave the Tayasu members a sense of moral
excellence over most of Edo's officialdom.

A similar sense of austere moral elitism was also present in the
literary views of Munetake and in those of Kamo no Mabuchi
(1697-1769), one of the founders of National learning (Kokugaku). In
1746 Munetake invited Mabuchi to the Tayasu house, and together
they worked out a new theory of the development of Japanese
literature.[46] They viewed the *Manyōshū* (a collection of eighth-
century poetry) as a pure reflection of Japan's pristine culture, which
meant to them masculine and austere simplicity. They saw post-Nara
literature as weak and effeminate, the reflection of a degenerate age.
With the establishment of the Kamakura bakufu, however, Japan
returned to its own sacred spirit. As evidence, they pointed to the

Kinkaishū, a collection of *waka* poems by Minamoto Sanetomo (1192–1219), the third shogun of the Kamakura bakufu, who harked back to the *Manyōshū* tradition.[47]

It is easy to see how Munetake's literary values and their historical bedding supported the bakufu in general and, more specifically, the kind of ethos Yoshimune had tried to prescribe for the country. His analysis, therefore, did not stop at a mere summation of Japan's unique cultural values: it was at the same time a normative formulation of an ideal that indicated what Japan ought to be. Munetake, for instance, celebrates the ethos of the warrior in his praise of the manly spirit (*masuraoburi*) as against the feminine spirit (*taoyameburi*).[48] This view, of course, was as much an indictment of the post-Yoshimune mores of contemporary society as an expression of style preference with respect to Japan's literary past. Tayasu's cultural tradition rested upon the same clearly pronounced prejudices that governed the life of its members.

In the field of politics, too, Munetake had distanced himself from contemporary society. He witnessed the growing administrative decay under the rule of Ieshige (1745–60) and Ieharu (1760–86) with dismay and possibly with resentment. There was a very personal reason for this attitude, for Munetake was an eminently capable man who had been barred from the shogunal seat. In 1745, Yoshimune had retired in favor of his sick son Ieshige, against the advice of some bakufu officials who correctly saw a better candidate in the able Munetake. Yoshimune, however, had decided the succession according to the custom of primogeniture and left his office to his oldest son, the weak Ieshige. Munetake's support must have been quite considerable, because Matsudaira Norimura, who was appointed regent to Ieshige at the latter's succession in 1745/7, resigned three months later; Yoshimune, fearing a coup, ordered Munetake to live in retirement for some time.[49] By the next year, when he invited Mabuchi to Tayasu, Munetake had definitely settled for scholarly pursuits. But the political developments of the following decades were a constant reminder of Yoshimune's unfortunate decision to the once politically ambitious Munetake.[50]

Sadanobu was only twelve when Munetake died in 1771. At that age, however, members of the ruling elite had already a highly developed political consciousness: their education started around age five and quickly took on an intense "public" or political orientation. Sadanobu began by learning hiragana through the reading of the *Classic of Filial Piety;* and by nine, he writes, had already developed a keen interest in politics. At ten, he surprised his father with a short essay, composed with the help of his tutor, on Confucian precepts, the

Jikyōkan (Mirror of self-instruction) for which his father rewarded him with a set of the *Shiki* or Historical Analects, a 130-volume history of China up to the reign of Emperor Wu (140-87 B.C.) of the former Han dynasty.[51]

The location of the Tayasu house in Edo, adjacent to the shogun's Chiyoda castle, offered Sadanobu an excellent vantage point from which to observe both the splendor and the detail of Edo's political world—Tanuma's world. Sadanobu was born there in 1758, the year Tanuma became daimyo; he was thirteen when Tanuma was named senior councillor and became the undisputed master of Edo politics. Sadanobu and his contemporary biographers report how, as a young boy, he used to wander around the guard houses and offices and listen to the political and personal gossip of the day.[52] Sadanobu writes that this exposure to the political scene not only served as a confirmation of the political ethos prevalent at Tayasu but also taught him an invaluable lesson as a future ruler.

The education Munetake gave his offspring was undoubtedly inspired by his hope to see realized in one of his sons what fate had denied to him. And the one upon whom all attention in the Tayasu house was focused as the stand-by for Iemoto, the only son of the shogun Ieharu, was Sadanobu. His older brother Sadakuni had been adopted by the Matsudaira of Matsuyama han in Iyo (Shikoku) when Sadanobu was nine.[53] The half-brother Haruaki (son of the main wife) was chosen to succeed to the house. Thus Sadanobu was the only surplus male child that logically could be made available to the Tokugawa house in case the shogunal line needed a successor.

The realization of Tayasu hopes, however, did not only depend upon the hazards of shogunal succession. The house had no clear right to the shogunal office. The institutional status of the house called only for keeping its progeny at the disposition of shogunal will. In terms of seniority—a weighty factor in decisions on succession matters—Sadanobu was the most qualified candidate. Yet, despite his early training and his qualification as son of the senior of the Three Houses, in 1774 Sadanobu, as his father had been, was barred from the highest political position three years after Munetake's death.

On 1774/3/11, the shogun abruptly ordered Sadanobu, then fifteen, to become the adopted heir of the Matsudaira (Hisamatsu) house of Shirakawa, a kamon or daimyo related to the Tokugawa house.* Prestigious as it might have been, the prospect of becoming daimyo in

*Kamon daimyo were originally cadet houses of the Tokugawa. There were some twenty kamon daimyo. Shirakawa was ruled by fudai families, except for the Matsudaira Hisamatsu, a kamon family.

a 110,000 koku domain fell short of Sadanobu's anticipations for his future. His adoption precluded him from ever becoming shogun. Now the Hitotsubashi house with its multiple offspring would become the primary source for a possible shogunal heir. Furthermore there was the question of Tayasu's future: Haruaki who succeeded to the house, had no offspring of his own yet. In both respects, it was a great shock to Tayasu that Sadanobu should be adopted by another house.

The situation worsened when only four months later Haruaki, at age twenty-one, fell sick and died on 8/23. Sadanobu's stepmother immediately tried to reverse the shogunal decision and keep Sadanobu in Tayasu. Through a house elder, she approached Inaba Masaakira, one of the shogun's chamberlains. He gave her good hope. Mourning for Haruaki was postponed since it was thought that the succession problem would be settled in a matter of days. After ten days of waiting and maneuvering, however, no progress had been made, and the mourning period was finally started. The same day word came that the decision was irreversible. At Tayasu, the members felt remorse toward the founder of the house for failing to provide an heir, as well as rage toward the "wicked" politicians who had brought about this calamity. "From the beginning," writes Sadanobu, "no one agreed with my adoption into the Matsudaira family. There was nothing we could do, however, against the wicked way of politics [*shissei jaro*]."[54] (On the solution of Tayasu's succession problem in 1787, see Appendix B.)

Sadanobu gives us no further insight into the reasons for the shogun's intransigence, but historians agree that he fell victim to one of Tanuma Okitsugu's schemes to consolidate his position. During the years of Sadanobu's childhood, Tanuma had succeeded in extending his power in the Interior, and then in establishing a strong clique of his own in the Exterior. Two years before Sadanobu's adoption, he had combined his post of grand chamberlain with the office of senior councillor. In order to stay in power, however, it was of utmost importance for Tanuma to continue his control of the shogun and hence also of his successor. The shogun Ieharu had only one son, Iemoto, and if he were to die prematurely, Tanuma might face political opposition from the Three Houses, who were consulted in succession matters. Therefore, by his early neutralization of the senior of the Three Lords, he could eventually ingratiate another of the Three Lords and in that way influence the choice of an heir.[55]

Tanuma's stratagem payed off. In 1779 Iemoto died, and two years later Tanuma succeeded in bypassing the Three Houses, arranging the appointment of a young boy from the Hitotsubashi family, the future shogun Ienari, as new heir apparent. This ended for the second time in two generations the dream of the Tayasu house to produce a shogun.

On 1775/11/23, Sadanobu left Tayasu for the Edo mansion of Shirakawa in Hatchōbori. The future looked to him far less brilliant than what his status and ambition called for.

2 Intellectual Legacy and Psychological Development

Sadanobu was adopted by the Matsudaira of Shirakawa at age fifteen, but he did not succeed to the house until he was twenty-four. The nine intervening years were a period of intense preparation for his future task as daimyo.

It was during these years of study that Sadanobu did most of his reading and writing. The bulk of his political works was composed between the ages of nineteen and twenty-three, and his later occasional political writings show little further development of thought. Even Sadanobu's adolescent writings, which drew ideas from hundreds of works, show all the components of his political philosophy.

Despite his buoyant intellectual activity, Sadanobu was not a scholar. He had only one purpose in mind: to make of himself an impeccable ruler. Yet the time of waiting was long; at twenty-three he seriously despaired of ever getting the opportunity to put his ideals into practice. Frustration about his political career was an important element in Sadanobu's psychological development. It brought into sharper focus a self-image which had been with him in a nebulous way since his childhood and whose integrating force was to play a central role in shaping his political personality. Throughout this period of training, however, Sadanobu showed great perseverance in pursuing his studies on a wide variety of subjects. There is little doubt that he was intellectually the best prepared ruler of his time.

Intellectual Legacy

Sadanobu was an avid reader. He writes, for instance, that in one year, he read 400 fascicles (*maki*).[1] The list of his readings between the ages of seventeen and twenty includes well over a hundred titles in Japanese and Chinese history, classics, and literature, and he read some works several times. In 1779, for instance, in less than two weeks, he read the Analects of Confucius, the Mencius, the Great Learning, and the Doctrine of the Mean.[2] Sadanobu also studied the current ideas of his time, which provided him with sophisticated views of the social and economic problems of his day.

As a member of the elite, Sadanobu was introduced to the fine arts and belles lettres. From his early youth he displayed the same fervor in these fields that was characteristic of his later studies.

Sadanobu practiced calligraphy, painting, and verse; by the time he was fifteen, he had composed no less than seven thousand poems. In these years, Sadanobu also produced a number of purely literary works—for the most part, occasional compositions. For instance, while waiting at the Tayasu house to move to Hatchōbori, he wrote down his observations of the passing summer and autumn seasons in three scrolls of scenery descriptions (*Tokuhitsu yokyō,* Amusement with a frayed brush).[3] The next year, he presented to his new bride (the daughter of his adoptive father Matsudaira Sadakuni)[4] a short tract on feminine virtues (*Naniwa-e,* The Naniwa estuary); and he surprised his sister Tanehime, then adopted by the shogun, with a travelogue relating the impressions of his first journey to Shirakawa (*Kasumi no tomo,* Companion of the mist).[5] There exist also a number of *tanka* poems about the four seasons, written during these years and later edited by his grandson Sadakuzu as the *Genshishū* (Anthology of poems). And at twenty-three, Sadanobu produced his first work that is representative of his later literary productions, where literature serves a moralizing purpose. His *Migiri no yanagi* (Willows by the eaves-stones) consists of six descriptions of nature, each illustrating an ethical precept.

Sadanobu's first three political works, written when he was nineteen and twenty, hardly went beyond the level of note taking. In his *Kanjo ronsetsu* (A dissertation on the "Han History"), Sadanobu copied passages from Pan Ku's (A.D. 32–92) history, drawing ethico-political lessons from the reigns of Chinese emperors by meting out praise or blame. The *Kyūgen roku* (A record of the search for opinions) is an anthology in seven scrolls from the Chinese classics and histories, illustrating the single idea of the need for rulers to listen to advice from their retainers. The selection of this theme for the collation of an anthology testifies to Sadanobu's early concern with communication between rulers and subjects. Sadanobu ascribed much of the political evil of his time to a breakdown of this unhampered flow of information from the bottom to the top. This anthology was later blockprinted and distributed to the officials of the domain in an effort to promote frank reporting. The unpublished *Koshi-itsu* (Anecdotal ancient history) is a fictive exhortation to the daimyo, warning them against the evils of negligent government.[6]

Another work, which in its unstructured way resembles the above three, is the *Shiji seiyō* (Vade mecum for government), a selection of anecdotes and maxims from the Chinese classics, interspersed with short reflections and remarks. Sadanobu wrote this work at twenty-four. Around the same time, he also wrote *Shoyūhen* (Section on possession by the masses), an economic treatise on the distribution of wealth and the problem of the merchants.

The *Kokuhonron* (On the basis of the country) and the *Shūshin roku* (A record for the cultivation of the person) were written when he

was twenty-two and twenty-three. They are more organized statements of Sadanobu's political views. The former is divided in para-
graphs, and there is a clear though unsuccessful attempt to develop
one topic at a time. The organization of the *Shūshin roku*—topical,
with a title for each section—is the one he finally settled for, and
which he followed in his *Ōmu no kotoba* (Parroted words), when he
was twenty-seven, *Seigo* (Discourse on government), two years later,
and *Kagetsutei hikki* (Random notes from the pavilion of blossoms
and moonlight), when he was sixty-seven.

Two other works should be mentioned: *Tōzen manpitsu* (Stray
notes by lamplight) and *Kanko-dōri* (Birds on the admonitory drum).
The former, written during his bakufu tenure, consists of moral advice
to the daimyo. The latter, composed in 1788, is merely a list of items
Sadanobu wanted changed in the government; one of them was a
proposal to modify the system of alternate attendance by allowing the
daimyo to reside in their domains for three-year stretches after
spending three years in Edo, thus reducing the expenses of the
costly journeys.

Sadanobu includes comments on government and ethics in three
other works. These are the *Rakutei hikki* (Random notes from the
pavilion of leisure), a collation of writings and instructions written
between 1783 and 1800; the *Daigaku keibun kōgi*, (Lectures on the
classic "The Great Learning"), a series of lectures to the retainers of his
domain, delivered the year after he became daimyo in 1784; and the
Sekizen shū (Collected themes for mutual encouragement toward
good), a collection of ethical themes for discussion and self-improve-
ment for his vassals, composed in 1800.[7]

All Sadanobu's political works after the *Kokuhonron*, except for the
short *Shiji seiyō*, were written for a well-defined public. The *Ōmu no
kotoba* was addressed to a particular daimyo, and the *Kagetsutei
hikki*, which is a further expansion of the same, was written forty
years later for his grandson. All his other works were addressed to the
daimyo in general or to his retainers.

Sadanobu justified his writings in two ways. First there was the fear
that he would meet his end before succeeding to the house and hence
before getting a chance to put into practice his most ardent convictions. At twenty-three he wrote the *Shūshin roku* and the now lost
Seiji roku (Record of government), which he termed his legacy to
posterity.[8] Second, he profoundly disagreed with the type of pedantry
and pointless erudition that, in his eyes, characterized contemporary
scholarship; he undertook to make scholarship again relevant for
administrative purposes.[9] For Sadanobu, scholarship and philosophy
were not a disinterested pursuit of knowledge, nor the *ancilla theo-*

logiae, handmaiden of theology, as in medieval Europe; for him, scholarship stood in the service of politics and government.

Judging from his notes and from the composition of his political works, Sadanobu's method of study consisted of quick perusing, reading, and often rereading, combined with selective note taking.[10] In political matters, he never tried his hand at a scholarly or critical study of certain topics or problems. His aim was practical and didactic. He knew what he was looking for, and his notes were therefore aimed at backing his own views with the highest classical authorities.

Almost all his illustrative material is Chinese, and only rarely does Sadanobu turn for his examples to Japanese history. (Japanese examples show up mostly in his instructions to his retainers.) This, however, does not mean that Sadanobu was a sinophile. His examples only illustrate the practice of certain virtues, or the functioning of correct government, without necessarily extolling things Chinese. On several occasions he even castigates sinophiles as useless and unpatriotic polemicists.[11] Sadanobu's political model was Chinese only in a limited way. Chinese scholarship provided him with material by which to organize his political thinking, but his own thinking focused on the economic and political situation of his time.

This material, undigested and overwhelming, burdens his early works. But even a cursory glance at the output of his young adult years reveals how Sadanobu developed from a student of government and history into a master of practical statecraft. He lacked a clearly formulated synthesis; yet he succeeded in communicating his views with great persuasion. Sadanobu was not a philosopher, and the immediacy of his concerns with government, together with his high emotional commitment to it, impeded any attempt at a comprehensive statement of a more consistent and theoretical nature.

In treating Sadanobu's political thought, therefore, one has to gather the main tenets of his thought from a wide variety of writings, where there is much more thematic repetition than systematic exposition. Although a composite presentation may do some injustice to Sadanobu's thought because he himself never defined his ideas in a structured way, such a treatment has the advantage of disclosing the concerns, assumptions, and contradictions underlying all of Sadanobu's thinking.

The lack of philosophical consistency creates a particular problem for understanding Sadanobu's work as a whole. He himself does not seem to have been bothered by the contradictions that run through his thinking. He did not confront inconsistencies on an intellectual level but, rather, solved them in his political praxis. He was able to adjust apparent logical contradictions to the demands of his own political ambitions and programs and thus, in an eclectic manner, reconcile in practice the opposing tenets of different philosophies.

Sadanobu thought of himself as a true Neo-Confucian. And indeed, he shared the basic philosophical premises of Japan's main Neo-Confucian thinkers, such as Fujiwara Seika (1561–1619), Hayashi Razan (1583–1657), and Arai Hakuseki (1657–1725). Yet Sadanobu was undeniably influenced by Ogyū Sorai (1666-1728),[12] whose views on the function of ethics and politics were radically critical of the Neo-Confucian tradition.

With the Neo-Confucians, Sadanobu believed in the metaphysical foundation of society, which Sorai had rejected for a historicist explanation of the basic structure of society. Virtue, as the qualification for office, Sadanobu sees as a heavenly gift, which is innate; and yet he strongly hints sometimes that only the virtuous should rule and that rulers are not ipso facto virtuous. Again with Sorai, Sadanobu accepts the man-made nature of rites as regulative tools for ordering society. Underlying his emphasis on the importance of ethics for the purpose of political integration is also the functional assumption, like Sorai's, about the necessity of a consistent ethical code for the proper functioning of society. On the other hand, Sorai taught that administrative efficiency could be obtained through timely adjustments of the politico-social structure to changing historical circumstance, while Sadanobu held to the Neo-Confucian view of the inalterable and sacrosanct character of the political structure. Thus, while Sorai's view of political phenomena was unambiguously functional in conception and historicist in its explanation, the sharpness of Sadanobu's functionalist philosophy was blunted by its Neo-Confucian metaphysical legitimation and by a unique stress on ethics.

The emphasis Sadanobu placed on ethics to effect political conformity, while undoubtedly part of the Neo-Confucian world view, was especially representative of Yamazaki Ansai's version of Neo-Confucianism. Ansai (1618-82), more than any other scholar, saw the polity as a normative entity whose proper functioning could only be assured through an uncompromising enforcement of ethical compliance and through imposed ideological uniformity. In this tradition, the conformity to the demands of the political structure that is asked of the individual had a religious overtone, both in its conceptual justification of political behavior and in the actual intensity that was manifest in such behavior.

These three trains of thought were the intellectual legacy that Sadanobu inherited: Neo-Confucian metaphysics, Sorai utilitarianism, and Ansai ethics. Together they constituted the backbone of Sadanobu's political thought and practice. In his policies they were indistinguishably and effectively blended together to give strength to his political program. In his philosophy they were less perfectly integrated, and it is not always easy to determine Sadanobu's own views on a subject or to identify his philosophical affiliation.

According to the Neo-Confucians, society or the political community had two basic characteristics. Its structure, based on cosmic premises, was unchangeable, and its operation at all levels rested upon the proper enactment of ethics. In this view, then, the degree to which what one might very broadly call civil morality was practiced determined the political, social, and economic health of the nation.

Many bakufu leaders, at one time or another, have proclaimed this as their philosophy, but none equaled Sadanobu in his commitment both to the philosophy and to its operational implications. There are two reasons for his commitment. First, Sadanobu's education had sensitized him to the ethical component of problems. Second, it was only natural that in a time of crisis he should turn explicitly to the premises upon which the well-being of society was assumed to rest. Thus the intricate interaction of what today we distinguish as the political and the ethical should not come as a surprise in Sadanobu's writings.

Sadanobu's image of the world consists of three distinct parts: the cosmos (or the universe), human society (or civilization), and the animal world (or the negation of civilization, the subhuman world, or nature). The cosmos is the model after which human society is patterned, while the animal world is the counterimage of ordered society, nature in its unstructured, chaotic, and uncivilized state.

Society is cosmos-ordained. This does not mean that men had no part in its formation. Sages were responsible for establishing society's basic structure in accordance with the cosmos. Their structuring of society was not an invention but the discovery of the only proper way to order society, namely with the cosmos as model. Society was not merely likened to the universe; the cosmos simile had the force of legitimating social structure. Because there is differentiation in the cosmos, there exists unchangeable social distinction. What was thus being validated was hierarchy within society, the distinction between the rulers and the ruled.

The rulers are like the mountains or heaven, and the people are like the earth. What is above is honorable, and what is below is ignoble. As heaven and earth are clearly separated but interdependent and unchangeable, rulers and ruled should not fuse, but neither should they lead an isolated existence from each other. The rulers are also compared to the heavenly substance or ether (*tenki*), moistening the earth, and the ruled to the earthly ether (*chiki*), which in turn assists heaven; in a similar way, the land will be at peace when rulers and ruled respect each other.[13] Both are equally necessary to make up society. The rulers are necessary because the people are foolish, but the rulers need the people because the people provide them with the necessities of daily life.[14]

In his early writings, where Sadanobu composes compassionate and lyrical descriptions of the hardships of the peasants, this balance between rulers and ruled was clearly slanted in favor of the latter. Sadanobu seems to blame oppressive government for the country's economic distress. In his later years, he corrected this picture by stipulating in more detail the duties of obedience and service of the subjects toward their masters.

The distinction between rulers and ruled was established once and for all, so that by his own day, according to Sadanobu, it merely means that one's ancestors were either honorable or humble.[15] The elevated status of the rulers is no excuse for misuse of their prerogatives. They should never forget that in many respects, they are the same as their subjects, who, Sadanobu stresses, are also human beings.[16]

Moreover, although convinced of the natural necessity of this original difference, Sadanobu was intellectually aware of its man-made character, which was essentially a view of Ogyū Sorai. The opening paragraph of *Seigo*, for instance, could easily have been lifted from Sorai:[17]

> The Way was made, based on the character of the sages, and not on the nature of Heaven and Earth. All kinds of clothing, food, and shelter were also started by the sages. People think that all this is ordained naturally by Heaven and Earth, but that is because the sages made all this in accordance with the character of all things.

A careful reading of the text, however, reveals that, after a passing nod to more secular views, the contingent character of human society is subsumed under the inevitability of the inherent "character of all things"; the specific form of human society as known to Sadanobu— of the Tokugawa order—is thus posited in an absolute way. In other words, in a convoluted way, Sadanobu reconciled the metaphysical and the functional view of society, upholding nevertheless the basic hierarchical structure of society which must not be altered. Society's hierarchy was man-made but metaphysically grounded. Unless the distinctions between noble and humble, venerable and ignoble, are kept, society will revert to the realm of beasts and birds.[18]

What is it then that keeps civilization from reverting to the animal world? In answering this question, Sadanobu again blends necessary and contingent characteristics. Class distinctions and rites, he says, are man-made devices, but indispensable nevertheless, for keeping societal hierarchy from disintegrating.[19] Rites or proprieties are all-important because they regulate the use of material resources for everyone according to his status; and thus, through regulating consumption, they keep the superior and the inferior in their respective places, which is essential for the maintenance of society. In this view, civilization from the start is given a political definition. What sets man off from the animal world is that he is member of a polity, where he has a definite, unalterable place.

One should not conclude that rites make the superior and the inferior what they are. Rites merely keep the distance between the superior and the inferior, which are, by themselves, of a different quality. What intrinsically differentiates rulers and ruled is that the former possess virtue.[20] Thus the difference of ancestry, distinguishing the ruling elite from the subjects, is based on the possession or lack of virtue. And here Sadanobu is purely Neo-Confucian when he asserts that virtue is a heavenly gift[21] just as native intelligence is. Heaven dispenses it generously to founders of dynasties, so that their successors, even if they are unworthy and therefore threatened by Heaven with punishment,[22] still profit from the overflow of original virtue bestowed upon their forefathers.[23]

Here again, however, Sadanobu toys with the idea of man's intervention in the political process, this time through a radical change of the ruling (shogunal or daimial) dynasty as the result of misgovernment. It should be noted that the idea of the founder's ascriptive virtue, which works as a "saving grace" for those of his descendants who do not qualify for administering the country, is missing in the parallel text of the *Kagetsutei hikki*, which Sadanobu wrote three years before his death.[24] Although this lacuna may indicate a shift in Sadanobu's thinking, given the absence of other evidence, it is hard to say that he envisaged then the possibility of the overthrow of the Tokugawa house. In the final analysis, Sadanobu tended to affirm strongly the need for continuity, which is ascribed to the unchallengeable element of the founders' and the present rulers' "virtue."

Heavenly virtue is really what makes government possible. It is not only present in the ruler at the top and transmitted hereditarily, but it is also passed down through all the ranks of officials. Because Heaven cannot rule the whole realm alone, it governs through the Son of Heaven, who appointed the Great Lord (shogun). The size of the empire, however, made it necessary for the Great Lord to appoint different lords, and so on down the administrative ladder, so that all offices are offices of Heaven, and the people ruled are the people of

Heaven.[25] Neither the people nor the domains are thus private property of the lords; they belong to the realm.[26] The different rulers of
today are thus not autocrats. They partake in authority that comes to
them from Heaven, through the lords, and through their ancestors.[27]

If all channels of authority are thus staffed with virtue, how does it
then finally reach the masses, who, by definition, are devoid of
virtue? The gap in quality between rulers and subjects is bridged by
humane sentiment (*ninjō*), which makes the unity of the realm possible. *Ninjō* makes the people do as their lord does: they follow his
likes and dislikes, for better or for worse.[28] The people are like the
grass that bends with the blowing wind: if the lord is virtuous, the
country will be at peace.[29] Hence the importance of the rulers' exemplary role.[30]

This metaphysical view of political life cuts across familiar distinctions of modern society. There are no autonomous private or
public areas; virtue and government are indistinguishable; ethics and
politics are one. And all is subsumed in a great emanation of virtue
from Heaven down to the people.

A crucial factor in this movement is the sincere heart (*magokoro*).
The lord, just like the sages, can make mistakes, but they can be
corrected as long as he has sincerity; thus the lord should make his
words and deeds correspond. This view is explained in the following
reductive concatenation of elements: the basis of the country is the
house; the basis of the house is the body; the basis of the body is
constituted by words and deeds; and the basis of words and deeds is a
sincere heart.[31]

The primacy of virtue in Sadanobu's ideal scheme did not blind
him, however, to the imperfections of government. After all, that was
the center of his concern. So it happens, Sadanobu admits, that
between a virtuous lord and the people, officials act as obstacles
rather than as channels for the flow of virtue.[32] There are two remedies to this evil: the study and practice of the classics[33] and the
selection of talented administrators.[34] Candidates for office should be
examined and subjected to a period of observation.[35] People that only
agree with the ruler are to be avoided. In his old age, Sadanobu added
that one should know the candidate's bad points as well as his good
ones, and he clearly articulated the total trust with which one ought to
delegate responsibility to men of tested talent.[36]

Thus Sadanobu's view of government had room for rational devices. Not surprisingly, these were granted only a secondary place. In
his *Ōmu no kotoba*, after speaking briefly about different devices,
skills, and formulae, Sadanobu concludes that, no matter how much
one may speak about formulae or talent, the basis of all is virtue.[37]

Virtuous men are necessary not only for smooth administration.

They are equally important for keeping open the channels of communication from the people to the lord. As noted already, superior and
inferior, like heaven and earth, are different but should not exist in
isolation. The avenue of words should therefore be kept open. In this
way the lord will stay in touch with the sentiment of the lower.[38]
Communication is necessary because human sentiment is the field in
which the grain of good government has to take root.[39] Again, various
obstacles may prevent the lord from getting to know the sentiment of
the lower. The main cause of his ignorance is his isolated education in
the chambers of the Interior, where he is cajoled by flattery and
remains unaware of the hardships of the people.[40] Hence the need for
clear and objective remonstrance from below.[41] Information can be
obtained through special inspectors (*yokome*) who really know and
are not reluctant to report even unpleasant facts.[42] The use of in-
formants is not repulsive and does not contradict the view that a wise
ruler considers his people as his children.[43] The ruler loves his people[44]
and is like a father and mother toward them, but a parent has to know
in detail what his children are doing—without letting them know that
he knows.[45]

Although Sadanobu understood clearly the importance of institutions such as the *yokome* as a check against abuses, corruption, or
distorted information, his conviction that what really counted was the
virtue of the ruler still ran very deep. The daily personal practice of
moral principles by the ruler is what makes for good government.
And the main virtue a ruler must have is benevolence (*jin*), a heavenly
quality which Sadanobu equates with sincerity.[46] It is the basis of the
Way. The quality of benevolence also protects the warrior, whose
duty calls for the destroying of life, from being a barbarian.[47]

Thus, in his analysis of the political ills of his time, Sadanobu
locates the problem and its solution in the men that run the institutions rather than in the institutions themselves. Misgovernment does
not stem from the political system, which was established once and for
all by the sages. In the interaction between man and institution—the
interaction that constitutes the realm of politics—man is the variable:
he is malleable and should conform in his mind and behavior to the
requirements of good social order within the set framework of
the institutions.

An antithetical line of thought, prevalent among the followers of
Ogyū Sorai, declared that man is what he is, full of passionate desire
and instinct that threaten social order. In this perspective, man's
nature cannot be changed, and therefore the task of politics consists of
establishing proper institutions to prevent social chaos. Theoretically,
institutions are not sacrosanct: if they do not serve their purpose, they
should be readjusted or replaced.

Sadanobu, however, had opted for the primacy of virtue, and his emphasis on virtue should be taken as a conscious political option. In that respect, Sadanobu is consistent throughout all his writings. As purely metaphysical pronouncements, however, devoid from political intent, Sadanobu's various statements on virtue are hard to reconcile with one another. The statement that benevolence or sincerity is the basis of the Way, for instance, should not be taken literally. Elsewhere, Sadanobu stresses filial devotion (*kō*) and loyalty (*chū*) as the most central virtues. Thus in *Seigo*, filial devotion is called the basis of all virtue.[48] The purpose of his writings, as well as his mode of discourse, is moralistic persuasion, rather than systematic exposition. Each stylistic unit (be it a short essay, a chapter, a lecture, or a paragraph) is less a building block in a clearly outlined ideology than a set of favored statements to drive home to his audience, in the most persuasive way possible, his basic conviction that man ought to be perfected.

R. L. Backus has pointed out how the virtues stressed by Sadanobu, which are strong social integrating forces, become absolutes in his writings only after his experience with government.[49] Toward the end of his life, Sadanobu writes that filial duty and loyalty need no justification such as indebtedness to one's parents or lord.[50] A retainer's mode of existence should be unquestioned loyalty to the country and to one's lord: he has a country, not a house; a lord, and not a body.[51] The increased reliance, in Sadanobu's thought, upon the absolute character of ethical virtues shows again Sadanobu's fundamental option: the country's ills would be cured if men conformed more closely to the political structure.

Rulers, retainers, and officials should be devoted to public affairs. Self-interest and profit seeking are the greatest evils that lead a country to ruin. Throughout his writings, Sadanobu attacks profit (*ri*), just as he warns against the dangers of a ruler's isolation from the masses.[52] Profit seeking is directly opposed to duty (*gi*).[53] Profit and duty really belong to two different worlds: *gi*, to the public (*kō*) world of the true gentleman; *ri*, to the private and selfish (*shi*) world of the merchant.[54] The disruptive effects of profit seeking are seen foremost, but not exclusively, in the all-important agricultural sector, which constitutes the base of the country.[55]

In his early writings, Sadanobu shows a great concern for the peasants. He denounces in his *Kokuhonron* the abuses they have to suffer from excessive taxation or from the greed of local administrators who pressure the peasants into advanced payments of taxes.[56] In his instructions to the district deputies (*gundai*) of his domain, he pleads for pity, even if stern measures are necessary.[57]

Aside from humane motives, Sadanobu's concern with the pea-

santry was prompted by his sound political insight that the good will
and the welfare of the peasants were essential to run the country. His
recommendations for safeguarding a healthy base for the nation are
centered on policies to make provisions for crop failures or other
natural disasters. In *Seigo* he defines the task of government as welfare
—the duty to take measures against eventual natural disasters. He
demonstrates the need for storage of grain,[58] and spells out, using the
Chinese model, a complete system of granaries.[59] His experience as
daimyo and chief councillor, however, later led him to the conclusion
that his youthful views were too idealistic, and that government
reserves were insufficient to control famine. At most, they could serve
a psychological purpose and stimulate the people to build reserves on
their own.[60]

Welfare was only one element in a system of economic politics that
should guide the government. Again, Sadanobu sees this task of
government as not divorced from ethical concerns. According to one
of his graded reductionist schemes, economic politics consists of a
chain of factors. The government of a country rests upon economic
politics (*rizai*), which are implemented by an equitable system of
taxation. Further conditions for a healthy government are a large
(productive) population, just officials, and trustworthy inspectors.
But the whole taxation system would be pointless if no provisions
were made for disaster years through savings and storage. Therefore,
the secret of political economy is frugality. And frugality will only be
realized through the rulers' self-discipline.[61] Thus frugality, explicitly
defined as an ethical concept,[62] offers the key to the life of a nation.[63]
Frugality, however, should not be confused with stinginess, which is a
self-serving vice. It should be restrained and public-oriented. Extreme
frugality, if necessary, should be enforced only for short periods. The
enforcement of frugality necessitates, of course, the promulgation of
sumptuary laws.[64]

Sadanobu's conception of regulative economics is quite simple and
is explained with an obvious cosmological metaphor. Regulative
economy is a question of regulating one's expenditures according to
one's income:[65] "Just as the Way of Heaven is *yin-yang*, where yin is
income and yang outgo, and just as the Way of Man is inhalation and
exhalation, so income in economy means storing in storehouses, and
outgo means use of the stored goods."[66] The means by which expenditures are controlled are the rites or proprieties, which ought to be
defined according to the need for usage and the trend of the times.[67]
But proprieties are not merely an administrative device for regulating
consumption. Propriety rules are patterned on Heaven, and it is
through them that man moves toward goodness. They are the dikes

that, in times of distress, protect society.[68] According to Sadanobu, the fabric of contemporary society had been dangerously loosened by rampant luxury and conspicuous consumption.[69] The daimyo, for instance, vied with each other in the collection of dozens of time-pieces, "whereas one clock would suffice to know the time."[70]

This was, in short, Sadanobu's political philosophy. Its Neo-Confucianism was nonacademic and very practical, overweeningly moralistic, and yet it had assimilated important ideas from less ortho-dox philosophers. Sadanobu's understanding of the man-made nature of politico-ethical systems, his stress of the importance of such a "legalistic" institution as inspectors, and his rational interpretation of the social function of proprieties are all in the rationalistic tradition of Ogyū Sorai. Even his view of the political use of ethics or of the ethical intent of politics is to be attributed to Sorai's school. Sadanobu's Neo-Confucianism and Sorai's political philosophy, although contra-dictory in theory, met in their practical assumption that man, if uncontrolled and left to himself, is disruptive of the polity. For Sorai, man ought to be controlled by institutions. For Sadanobu, man ought to conform to the institutions through the proper observance of ethics. This view of ethics as a manipulative device, however, was a transpo-sition of Sorai's view of the political structure as a means to maintain social order.

It would not be correct to see the ethical component of politics as a mere expedient of an enlightened and cynical despot to facilitate his control over the ignorant masses. Such an interpretation would do injustice to the serious-mindedness with which Sadanobu, in his pri-vate life, was committed to his ethico-political world view. Sa-danobu's practical administrative measures, however, can only be properly understood as stemming from such a world view.

Sadanobu's works do not read like well-structured and dispas-sionate academic treatises. As soon as one knows the arguments and analogies, the repetitive and sermonizing character of the discourse becomes tedious. Some of his later critics also complain about the doctrinaire nature of Sadanobu's policies.* But his daimyo and retainer audiences were no doubt impressed with Sadanobu's au-thority and the sincerity of his conviction.

---

*Thus, for instance, Uezaki Kyūhachirō, a *hatamoto* who had written for Sadanobu in 1787 a memorandum, analyzing the ills of the time, turned his wit against him in 1801 in a long attack presented to the shogun. In this piece he complains about the stinginess behind the sumptuary laws, the excessively suspicious nature of the government, the priority given to doc-trine over the welfare of the people, and the colorless quality of life, if it is regulated by too many and too detailed laws (Uezaki Kyūhachirō, *Sensaku*

There was indeed an uncommon ardor and even passion to Sadanobu's intellectual activity during his pre-daimyo years. The daily
schedule which he developed then and kept throughout his whole life
was monastic in its regularity: he rose at seven and examined the
previous day's correspondence and messages; he had breakfast at
eight, followed by archery practice or study until eleven; he lunched
in the Interior and conferred with his stepfather, or later with his
officials—sometimes he read during his meals; in the afternoon from
two to four, he again studied in the Exterior; this study was followed
by practice with sword or bow, or horseback riding; he had supper at
six, and then for an hour compiled notes of the day's readings, retired
at seven to the Interior, and ended his day at nine.[71]

This discipline, hard work, and relentless effort at persuasion suggest an unusual drive, which psychologists have often recognized in
famous figures as the source of remarkable accomplishments during
their young adulthood.[72] How can one account for this psychological
drive, and what was its significance in terms of Sadanobu's political career?

PSYCHOLOGICAL DEVELOPMENT

Sadanobu was a very ambitious young man. In his memoirs he
observed that he wanted "to become famous for generations to come
and to make [my] name ring throughout China and Japan."* An
incident to which he refers in passing illustrates his political awaken-
ing as a young boy. This anecdote is important for understanding
Sadanobu's perception of himself and of the role he chose as his own.

---

zasshū, NKT, XX (1968), 507, 511, 513, 518, 529). Most famous is Ōta
Nampo's (1749-1823) epigram, ridiculing Sadanobu's revival of *bumbu* (letters and martial arts) with a pun on *ka* (this/mosquitoes) and *bumbu* ("letters and arms"/the buzz of mosquitoes): "There is nothing in all the world so
bothersome as this/mosquitoes. You can't even sleep at night with 'letters
and arms' (with their buzzing) in your ears."

Uge, p. 24. This ambition undoubtedly was further encouraged by
Sadanobu's occasional association with the shogun. From his early years, he
was well known to the shogun Ieharu. At age three, due to a fire at the Tayasu
house, he shared life at Chiyoda castle for some time (*Uge*, p. 23; Doki,
Tayasu, IV, 278). At that time, Ieharu's first son had died and the shogun's
attention to Sadanobu, who remained longer than the other Tayasu members
in the castle, might well have been inspired by an affection for his possible
future heir. The next year, however, Iemoto was born, but the special
relationship between Sadanobu and the shogun seems to have continued, for
Sadanobu writes how he used to pay a visit to the shogun once or twice a year
until he was eleven (*Uge*, p. 27). The ambitious nature of Sadanobu's
stepmother comes out very clearly in the succession problem of Tayasu. See
Appendix B.

At age twelve,[73] when reading the *Hou Han Shu* (History of the Later Han Dynasty), Sadanobu was struck by the indignant words of a certain Ch'en Fan. In checking the passage one finds the young man, replying to a reprimand by a guest of his father, asserting that he could not occupy himself with weeding the courtyard because it was his task to clean the empire. Men of great worth, Ch'en added, deal with the world and cannot busy themselves with household trivia.[74]

Struck by the bravura of these words, Sadanobu slapped his knee in a moment of sudden sympathy and insight. Ch'en Fan was fourteen, almost the same age as Sadanobu, and his reply betrays a proud sense of election, of being set apart for an uncommon mission. One can detect the same logic in the answer of the twelve-year-old Jesus to his parents, when they found him in the temple: "Wist ye not that I must be about my Father's business?" (Luke, 2, 29). Ch'en Fan's reply too was cast in the form of a rhetorical question, expressing the same prophetic self-assurance. What jolted Sadanobu was the perception of a central political aim—the welfare of the realm—and the orientation of one's whole future to it.

This sense of election and political calling fit perfectly the politico-cultural heritage of the Tayasu house and the expectations placed upon Sadanobu. It is clear that Ch'en Fan's words had the effect of confirming his own self-image about his calling to solve the crisis of his age. Thus, at the age of twelve, Sadanobu forged a central perspective out of his childhood past, and projected it into his antici-pated adulthood.[75]

It is also important to observe that this vision of his future came in the year of his father's death, an event that must have taught Sa-danobu anew his own responsibility to shoulder Tayasu's destiny. Munetake's death at the age of fifty-six after a protracted illness was a reminder to Sadanobu of another facet of the Tayasu legacy com-pounding the cultural and political tensions—the family's debilitated physical heritage.[76]

Sickness and death seemed always present in the Tayasu house, and Sadanobu grew up believing that he too would die young. Munetake fathered fifteen children by four wives: three sons and four daughters by his main wife, a Konoe,[77] and four sons and four daughters by three secondary wives. Sadanobu was born thirteenth from Yama-mura, a secondary wife, when his father was forty-three. When Sadanobu was born, however, the family had already lost six children before they reached adulthood. Three had died in a single year.[78]

When Sadanobu was fifteen, Tayasu's heir, Haruaki, died at twenty-one. His death made Sadanobu—aside from Sadakuni (1757–1804), who was adopted by the Matsudaira of Matsuyama han—the only surviving male offspring of the family. Three years later, in 1777, a twenty-six year old sister died; Tanehime, another sister, died in 1793 at twenty-eight.

Sadanobu's preoccupation with death is woven into the auto-biographical part of his memoirs. Suggesting bare survival, he writes of his weak constitution from the moment of birth, and of a series of illnesses as a child. He feared that he would never reach twenty.[79] The precariousness of his health, combined with the high expectations put upon him, created in Sadanobu a tense orientation to his environment.

He drove himself relentlessly to work and study in order to achieve his ambitions within the short span of life he expected. He was much preoccupied with forming himself into an ethically responsible ruler. Systematic in his striving toward self-perfection, Sadanobu marshaled the aid of his close friends to correct the faults or imperfections they noticed.* His continuous effort at self-control was expressed in attempts to conquer his irrascibility and vain sensitivity to flattery, as well as in sexual abstinence. Sadanobu reports that he remained chaste until his marriage at seventeen, which apparently was unusual for a young man of his status.[80]

One can thus picture Sadanobu in his adolescence as an extremely ambitious and tense young man, stimulated by his family in his expectations but at the same time restricted by the hazards of bakufu politics and threatened by his physical heritage.

Sadanobu's single-minded political ambition can be explained superficially in terms of his personal hatred for Tanuma. As already noted, Tanuma was implicated strongly in Sadanobu's adoption out of the Tayasu house and in his replacement as shogunal heir by a Hitotsubashi. Sadanobu certainly had enough reason to hate Tanuma, and at one point admitted to planning his assassination. It is also true that Sadanobu finally became the principal actor in dissolving Tanuma's clique and reversing his policies. But Sadanobu's political career should not be construed as a personal vendetta against Tanuma. His political activities, including maneuverings against Tanuma, should be viewed in the wider context of his sense of election and mission, his moralistic approach to political reality, his commitment to self-discipline, and, above all, his obsession with death.

---

*One has the impression that in Sadanobu's friendships congeniality was secondary to moral high purpose. Such was, for instance the case with Mizuno Tamenaga, a retainer who was Sadanobu's elder by seven years and remained a close friend during his whole life: "I was being admonished by Mizuno Tamenaga, who told me every day about good and bad points. Any listener could fully feel what heights my irritation could reach. Each time anger welled up, I went and faced a scroll painting in the *tokonoma,* and stood there until my emotions had subsided" (*Uge,* pp. 28-29).

During his young adult years, the thought of death and of the fragility of his existence never left Sadanobu. Pressure of time undeniably stimulated him into performing at an exhausting pace and gave a sense of urgency to all his activities. Perhaps the most persuasive evidence is a note he wrote to himself, reminding him of the imminence of death. He kept this note in the drawer of his desk within easy reach for frequent perusal.[81]

Sadanobu's health continued to be frail. On his first month-long visit to Shirakawa in 1776/4, when he was seventeen, he fell sick shortly after his arrival and had to conduct most of his business from his bed.[82] Five years later, he developed severe pains in his back and shoulders, and his physician ordered him to stop his strenuous study routine. Sadanobu, however, circumvented his physician's order and dictated in eleven days his *Kokuhonron*, a two-scroll essay on government, followed by three supplementary scrolls.[83]

Misfortune continued to follow Sadanobu in his family life too. Of the four wives that Sadanobu had during his lifetime, he lost the first two before they bore him any children. His first wife, the daughter of his adopted father and lord, Matsudaira Sadakuni, died in 1781 at twenty-eight.

The next year the psychological strains grew to the breaking point. Still grieving over the loss of his wife, he again became ill. A severe mouth infection forced him to interrupt his studies for eight months. Further saddened by the deteriorating state of affairs in the domain, he despaired of ever accomplishing anything in life. In the twenty-third year of his life he thought there was no future. Thus, providing for a near end, he wrote his "legacy," the *Shūshin roku* and the now lost *Seiji roku*. Speaking about all his concerns, public and private, he wrote:[84]

> People [han officials] were content with makeshifts; there were no reserves for bad years; there were no provisions by customary law or by legislation; and they carried on, led by the problems of the moment. On top of that was the fact that since I had been weak since my childhood, I just would not live long enough to take over the house. Although I had thought since my childhood that I ought to make a name for myself in the realm, this too was about to vanish like dew or dust. Therefore, calling them my 'legacy,' I put down in the *Shūshin roku* among other things ... *Seiji roku* .... These two works, which I compiled and wrote down for the future, were for me the achievement of my life over as wide a field as my mind could reach.

In one passage of the *Shūshin roku*, where he addresses himself to the daimyo who continued to aggravate the conditions of their retainers, he clearly expresses his concern with death and his desire to rectify political wrongs. He warns that they will incur punishment from their ancestors, and, he adds, he himself will become a curse after death and join in chastising these unworthy rulers.[85]

Shimbu no michi (The Way of Psychic and Martial Power)

His twenty-third year marked a very important turning point in the development of Sadanobu's personality. At a time when the very meaning of his existence was profoundly threatened and when he feared for his physical survival, Sadanobu chanced upon a master whose intellectual and spiritual guidance became decisive for him. Under him, Sadanobu started a new type of physical and moral self-training which he was to pursue until the end of his days and whose significance he repeatedly acknowledged in his writings.[86]

The master was Suzuki Kunitaka (1722–90). A minor bakufu official, he was a *jūjutsu* master of the Kitō school and was famous throughout Edo.[87] The number of his disciples seems to have been as high as three thousand, mostly samurai, including thirty or forty daimyo.[88] For some time, Sadanobu had been urged by friends to join them in Suzuki's classes. What finally made him enter Suzuki's school in 1782/8 was the psychological tension in his personal life that year. Sadanobu himself relates his decision to his premonitions of an imminent death.[89]

From the start, Sadanobu's interest in Suzuki's teachings was quite different from his usual predilection for martial arts. It was part of his dual quest for mastery of his imperfect spiritual self and of his imperfect physical self. Suzuki offered him a way that integrated both— *Shimbu no michi*, "The Divine Martial Way" or, following R. L. Backus, "The Way of Psychic and Martial Power."[90]

One might expect that Sadanobu, in his spiritual pursuits, would have turned to Zen Buddhism, with its long association with the way of the warrior. There are two reasons why he rejected Buddhism. First, in good National Learning tradition, he shared his father's prejudices against Buddhism in general.* And second, Sadanobu was critical of Zen Buddhism in particular for its one-sided stress on mental exercise and its general neglect of the body.[91] In Shimbu no michi, purification of the mind and control of the body were the reward of a single effort.

---

*See e.g., *Kanjo*, RKI, I, 14; *Kagetsutei*, RKI, III, 28. Sadanobu accused Buddhist priests of being money-hungry, attacked expensive burials, and considered cremation, except in Edo, as being contrary to human feelings (*ninjō*). He said that in the past Buddhism had hurt Shinto and stolen its gods; he encouraged his retainers to give to the poor rather than to Buddhist priests. See: "Go-kerai e go-kyōjisho," Manuscript, 1783 (pp. 81-87).

Shimbu no michi was part of the Kitō tradition, itself one of several schools of jūjutsu, the ancestor of jūdō. [92] Like the other martial arts, jūjutsu was geared to a rational and economic use of one's mental and physical abilities. When the martial arts spread in Japan during the seventeenth century, they drew on the current philosophical traditions for intellectual underpinning. The genuine martial arts like swordsmanship, archery, or practice with the javelin borrowed Buddhistic terminology. Only the one called jūjutsu (–*jutsu*, "art," as opposed to –*dō*, "the way of") used Confucian terminology. [93]

The three short texts (three scrolls entitled: Heaven, Earth, Man) which today still form the philosophy of the Kitō school were written during Sadanobu's time, between 1797 and 1800. In this philosophy, man is conceived as a small universe (*shōtenchi*), filled with heavenly or divine ether (*shinki*). Where this heavenly substance or ether rises, there is yang, which equals *ki* (to rise); where it collects, there is yin, which equals *tō* (to fall). Hence the name *kitō*. The purpose of the training is to ease the flow of ether in one's body by means of bodily posture, because the ether is disturbed in movement and lost where strength is applied. The art, as a martial practice, consists in winning by both *ki* and *tō*. [94]

Shimbu no michi, being a branch of the Kitō school, held a similar physico-cosmological view of man. Soon after joining Suzuki, Sadanobu began to incorporate cosmological imagery in his writings about man and politics. [95] His lectures of 1784 (two years after Sadanobu joined Suzuki) to his retainers, are full of such ideas and images. And six weeks before his death he composed a set of three scrolls called "Shimbu no michi." Sadanobu's writings tell us that his view of Shimbu no michi was strongly ethical, perhaps more than other Kitō texts.

According to this philosophy, which owes its main tenets to Neo-Confucianism, man's nature is fundamentally good: [96] bestowed by Heaven (*tenchi*) with righteousness (*sei*) from birth, no man is originally different from the sages. [97] Heavenly virtue (*meitoku*) flows from Heaven to all, [98] so man's ethical task, after this original purity gets clouded, consists in returning to this pristine virtue. [99]

In the West, mystics like Ruysbroeck or Eckhart have sometimes described this godly essence in man as a divine spark in man's soul. In Neo-Confucian metaphysics, it is located in the physical principle of ether. It penetrates the whole creation, including man, who inhales it through respiration. [100] It is the principle of life. [101] Man lives in it, and it lives in him, like a fish in water. [102] Thus man is not only the child of Heaven; [103] man and Heaven are one (*tenjin ichiri*). [104] He is the soul of everything, [105] and, adds Sadanobu in an attempt to legitimize metaphysically his elitist views, the warrior class is the soul of mankind. [106]

This philosophy of man tied in perfectly with Sadanobu's political thought, where distinctions of private and public, ethics and politics were held to be only distinctions of the mind, not separate categories of life. Here also everything is everything: the universe is sincerity or righteousness,[107] which is no different from ether; the physical world and the value world of ethics are not distinguished; and nature's macrocosm and man's microcosm are identical.

In the way it accounted for evil, this philosophy established one more important equation: that between man and the divine. The flow of divine ether in man is hampered by his animal nature. The realm of beasts and birds is governed by drives,[108] and man too harbors seven desires.[109] Ether fills man only when he is not himself, when he has not the slightest desire of his own. In order to make ether circulate in the body, man has to apply himself to perfect patience and endurance. By cultivating the right attitudes, maintaining the proper personal appearance and bodily posture,[110] by breathing techniques and in general by mental techniques (*shinjutsu*), man controls at will the joining or separation of ether. In this way, he will nourish his five visceral centers.[111] Then no desire will be left,[112] and the universe will perfectly fill his body; which means that he will be a god-man.[113] The divine is thought of as within reach of human effort. Man in indefinitely perfectible through his own effort. All evil is ultimately conquerable.

Thus Shimbu no michi provided theoretical and practical solutions concerning the relationship between body and mind, good and evil, man and the divine. It was primarily a blueprint for action, offering Sadanobu a framework within which to continue his pursuit of moral self-perfection. It also enabled him to apply his efforts in an area in which he so far had been utterly powerless, namely his physical constitution. And it presented him with a program by which he could turn himself into a worthy instrument for his ethical and political mission, which he assumed a year after he first met Suzuki.

Shimbu no michi also provided Sadanobu with a philosophy of life. It brought him in contact with forces that regulated life and death. Through its teachings, Sadanobu, already a member of the aristocratic elite, developed a metaphysically grounded vision of himself as a human being with divine potential. In other words, Sadanobu had found his religion in Shimbu no michi's vision of the world and program for action.[114] It was the religion that best met Sadanobu's most personal concerns. It kept a place in his life for his obsession with death, enhanced his elitist sense of mission, and confirmed his belief that the solution of the ills of his time lay in a transformation of the human spirit.

SELF-DEIFICATION

In his late fifties, Sadanobu considered that he had achieved his principal life objectives: he had successfully completed his political mission, had conquered evil in himself, and had even held out against death. His belief in a divine state as a human possibility (which he mentioned for the first time in 1787, the year that he became chief councillor in the bakufu) inspired him to express that belief through a cult toward himself. In a shrine in the garden of his mansion where he had retired, before a curtain that hid other deities and spirits, he enshrined in a central position a wooden effigy of himself. There he performed daily a rite to his deified self.[115]

Katō Genchi, a scholar of religion, interprets this unusual practice as a kind of religious schizophrenia, whereby Sadanobu's imperfect self worships his perfect self.[116] This explanation, however, overlooks two important elements: Sadanobu's self-image in his later years and the aspect of himself to which he paid religious respect.

In the years after Sadanobu's retirement as daimyo in 1812 and after some three decades of earnest moral striving, he thought of himself as having attained a state of mind in which his desires had been overcome. In his account of self-training, the *Shugyō roku* (Record of self-training), he traces his spiritual development to a peaceful state of mind of near total self-possession and detachment.* The objectified image may thus have been a projection of his perfect self; the worshiper, however, was conscious not of his imperfection but of his quasi-divine state.[117]

Second, the name he had given himself, and which he had also decided upon as his posthumous name, was "Protector of the Country" (*Shukoku myōjin*), in homage to his achievements as a statesman.** The name shows Sadanobu's ideal image of himself and what he wanted to mean to posterity. Although during his unexpectedly

*Sadanobu gives even a quasi-statistical account of the gradual mastery of his sexual desire. See *Shugyō roku*, p. 192.

**In 1800/8 Sadanobu mentions in a poem for the first time his desire to become a protective spirit of the country (*Taikan*, NZZ, XIV, 408), but the history of this name can be traced back much earlier. On 1784/10/24, in the midst of a famine year, Sadanobu took the trouble to bring from Kuwana a wooden image of Sadatsuna (1592-1651), the founder of the family, and enshrined it inside Shirakawa castle. In 1792, he gave Sadatsuna the title of *Chinkoku* ("Pacifier of the Country") and in 1797, Sadatsuna was officially given by the Yoshida family in Kyoto the divine title of *Chinkoku daimyōjin*. Soon thereafter, however, Sadanobu added a wooden image of his own to the shrine (*Uge*, p. 60; *Go-gyōjō*, pp. 160-62), and between 1809 and 1819 started long life (he died at seventy) Sadanobu developed intellectual interests in many diverse fields of human activity,* he saw himself primarily as a successful statesman.

The practice of self-deification needs some further explanation. Usually a victorious confrontation with the ultimate challenge of death produces heroes;** and moral perfection is the path to sainthood. Sadanobu was not a hero, but he was more than a saint. The state he had reached was divine, but the halo he had given to himself was clearly political. This particular blend of the profane and the sacred must be understood within the context of Japan's indigenous religious mode of construing reality and human experience.

---

performing his daily rites in his Edo mansion, in front of yet another image (Katō, *Hompō seishi*, p. 90), calling himself *Shukoku*.

In his directions for the proper installation of this statue after his death (*Tōen-in no miya no tatekata sono hoka no sadamegaki*, in Fukaya, *Matsudaira Sadanobu-kō*, pp. 268-71), he ordered an official application for his divine title to be made in Kyoto. This was granted in three steps, in 1833, 1834 and 1855. Today Sadanobu is still worshiped as *Shukoku daimyōjin*, together with Sadatsuna, the famous Sugawara Michizane and two other celebrities, in the Chinkoku-Shukoku shrine in Kuwana, where Sadanobu's son was transferred in 1823. In 1918 a magnificent new shrine was built for his spirit in Shirakawa.

*Inamura Hiromoto divides the 130 works of Sadanobu in the following eleven categories: political writings; works on education and training; biographical writings; military science; writings on foreign policy; writings on tea ceremony and medicine; essays; travelogues and diaries; archeology; geography, history, customs and music; poetry; occasional poems; and selections from ancient poetry.

Sadanobu's collection of illustrated scrolls was very famous. For his accurate historical study on the Chinese origins of Japanese court music, see *Zokugaku mondō*, RKI, II. His most well known encyclopedia of historical paraphernalia is *Shūko jisshu* (4 vols.; Tokyo: Kokusho kankōkai, 1908). In his fifties and sixties, Sadanobu also developed a mania for copying famous works. He is said to have copied some 20,000 scrolls (Asano Genko, *Matsudaira Sadanobu, Ninomiya Sontoku-hen*, supplementary vol. to *Tōhoku sangyō keizai-shi* [Tokyo: Tōhoku shinkō-kai, 1943], p. 193). He wrote at a speed of ninety pages a day, and copied, among others (see list in Shibusawa, *Rakuōkō-den*, pp. 381-87) the *Genji monogatari* seven times. He took a special delight in miniature calligraphy; the Museum of Fine Arts in Kuwana possesses a sixty-three-volume copy of the *Tale of Genji*, with the volumes of the size of 1½ inches by 1½ inches.

**Robert Jay Lifton speaks of survivor formulations to render victorious encounters with death (which he calls "death immersions") significant. They face both ways, Lifton says: as justifications of the past and as contributions to the future. He speaks also of the survivor's sense of "reinforced invulner-

In Japan's religious tradition, which underlies institutional religions such as Buddhism, Confucianism, or Sectarian and State Shinto, the natural and supernatural are more continuous or overlapping categories than in the Judeo-Christian tradition.[118] It is not unusual for men to become gods and objects of ritual worship after their death. Ieyasu is an example, and Sano Masakoto,* the assassin of Tanuma's son, is another. More recently there is emperor Meiji, who has a magnificent shrine in Tokyo. What is even more relevant, though less known, is that the Tokugawa period saw the flourishing of personality cults of people during their lifetime, a practice that persisted until World War II. Katō Genchi collected some eighty-five such instances, half of them from modern times.[119] At least three people personally known to Sadanobu were the object of cults while still living[120]—Hosokawa Shigekata (1715–85), outside lord of the 540,000 koku domain of Kumamoto, who belonged to Sadanobu's early circle of friends;[121] Okada Kanzen (1740-1816), a follower of the Ansai school, who was called to Edo in connection with the ban on heterodox doctrines and later served as deputy (*daikan*) in a bakufu territory; and Hitotsubashi Narimasa, who in 1787, on Sadanobu's order, filled the latter's place as successor in the Tayasu house. Finally, Sadanobu himself was worshiped in some villages of his domain.[122]

In contrast to China, where the worship of "living gods" was also practiced but with a more mystical slant, in Japan the objects of cultic worship during their own lifetime were all exemplary or beneficent administrators.[123] These cultic expressions of religiosity were of a political mode.

One may argue that being worshiped by others is altogether another matter from worshiping oneself. But even the latter practice was not without precedents in Japan. The oldest mythological example is the deity O-ana-muchi (not unknown to Sadanobu), who enshrined his own spirit in a sanctuary after having pacified the country—the

---

ability," of "having met death and, by means of a special destiny, conquered it. It is this sense that permits the survivor to enter into the myth of the hero." Robert Jay Lifton, *Revolutionary Immortality: Mao Tse-Tung and the Chinese Cultural Revolution,* Vintage Books (New York: Random House, 1968), p. 14.

*Sano was called a *daimyōjin* (Hayashi, *Kyōhō,* pp. 364-65). Sadanobu takes note of several examples in the seventh scroll of his *Taikan zakki* (NZZ, XIV, 262, 263, 269), between the summer of 1796 and February 1797, just before Sadatsuna received the official title of *Chinkoku daimyōjin.* They concern a founder of a village, shrines dedicated to emperors, and the last will of his master Suzuki (who had died in 1790), expressing the wish to become a guardian spirit of the palace gate of which he had been in charge.

archetype of a work of statecraft.* Of more direct significance for
Sadanobu was Yamazaki Ansai. In agreement with his teacher Yoshikawa Koretaru (1616-94) Ansai bestowed upon himself the title of
Suika reisha, shrine of the Suika (Heavenly Blessing and Assistance)
spirit, and built a shrine for his cult.[124] There is evidence also that
Hoshina Masayuki (1611-72), Ansai's famous patron and disciple and
founder of the 230,000 koku domain of Aizu, had before his sudden
death taken the necessary steps for his own live canonization.[125]

It is difficult to trace precisely the relationship between these two
"autolatrists" or self-worshipers and Sadanobu, but they undoubtedly
influenced Sadanobu in other areas as well. First, there is a great
similarity between Sadanobu's world view and Ansai's teachings.
They both unconditionally rejected Buddhism; despised intellectual
sophistry; and held to the indistinguishable unity of Heaven and man
and to the essentially moral nature of the universe.[126] Sadanobu's
theory of the divine ether in man and the techniques to cultivate it
seem a further elaboration of Ansai's view of the divine within man,
the respect (*kei*) one has to pay to it in oneself, and the obligation (*gi*)
one has toward it in others.** For both Ansai and Sadanobu, the divine
character of man—a basic Shinto concept—was a dynamic force that
could always be activated, renewed, and perfected. In the service of
politics it could animate men in their commitment to the polity. The
influence of Ansai's teachings and disciples upon Sadanobu's ban on
heterodox doctrines will be analyzed in chapter 6.

Nihon shoki, I, part 1, Vol. I of *Kokushi taikei*, 48, or *Nihongi: Chronicles of Japan from the Earliest Times to* A.D. *697*, trans. William George Aston
(London: Allen & Unwin, 1956), p. 61. Sadanobu takes note of a shrine
dedicated to O-ana-muchi in Utsunomiya. He stopped there on 1794/5/13 on
his first return journey to Shirakawa, where he was going to rest after his
bakufu office (*Taikan*, NZZ, XIV, 329). This is also the only deity he
mentions in his diatribe against Buddhists, which is contained in his instructions of 1783/12 for his retainers. See "Go-kerai e go-kyōjisho," Manuscript,
1783 (p. 80).

**This philosophy was summarized in the formula *keigi naigai* (*naigai*
means "inward and outward"). See Abe Yoshio, "Yamazaki Ansai to sono
kyōiku," *Kinsei Nihon no Jugaku* (Tokyo: Iwanami shoten, 1939), pp. 343-
44. See also Ishikawa Ken, *Kinsei kyōiku ni okeru kindaikateki keikō:
Aizu-han kyōiku o rei to shite* (Tokyo: Kodansha, 1966), p. 56. Intrigued by
the possible genealogical relationship between Suzuki or Kitō teachings and
Ansai's philosophy I checked the philosophical affiliation of the thirty-four
Suzukis appearing in the 100-page genealogical charts (listing 2,900 names),
which appear as an appendix to Seki Giichirō and Seki Yoshinao, *Kinsei
kangakusha chojutsu mokuroku taisei* (Tokyo: Tōyōtosho kankokai, 1936).

Hoshina Masayuki's influence upon Sadanobu is more purely political. The younger brother of the third shogun Iemitsu, he had gained fame as the selfless regent of the fourth shogun Ietsuna and had become a legend of just government. Sadanobu presented Masayuki to his retainers as a model to follow.[127]

There were very specific aspects of Masayuki's career and government with which Sadanobu could identify in a personal way. Like himself, Masayuki was a collateral of the shogun but an outsider in Edo, where his advisory role was very limited and where he had no personal connections with bakufu officials.[128] Both were outsiders in their domains—Sadanobu as an adopted heir,[129] and Masayuki as the lord of an artificially established domain to be created by him from several bands of retainers who were not his own and whose cohesion had not been cemented through shared experience in the unification wars of Japan.[130] Although men of wide learning, they shared the same insights into the political use of ideology and applied it in the same rigorous and narrow way, branding dissenters as heretics— Masayuki, with Ansai's support, by persuading the bakufu to punish Yamaga Soko (1622–85) and Kumazawa Banzan (1619–91),[131] and Sadanobu by banning heterodox doctrines.

Let us take a final look at Sadanobu, in his mid-twenties, just before his succession to the house. Over the years he had prepared himself intensely for an office that he believed was still far away. He had drawn his own conclusions about the state of affairs in the country and the domain, but was so far denied the opportunity to test his solutions in concrete action. His mind was in a state of serious crisis. He lived in high tension concerning the future of politics and the course of his own life. The intensity of this sentiment, the urgency he felt to do something about it, together with his sense of election, had led him to mobilize all his energy for an ethico-political mission. The content of that mission was circumscribed by his own view of the source of political evil and of his own imperfections, which he had located in man and his desires.

One might expect one of two things to happen to a young man of such tendencies. If his sense of political reality is weak, the elitist self-perception of his role may prove powerless for the transformation of politics. If, however, he displays enough rationality to plan and

I then matched them with the genealogy of Kitō masters, as given in the *Dokushi sōran*, p. 1331 and with Suzuki's own genealogy as given in *Kansei jūshū shokafu* (Tokyo: Eishinsha, 1918), VIII, 452. The effort, however, yielded no results.

plot his way into politics, he may offer firm leadership. He may then be capable of remarkable achievements, but his power will be vulnerable and will continue only as long as the need for his exceptional views is acknowledged by others.

3   Savior and Politician

Saviors, political and religious alike, are myth builders. They may be a boon to students of religion, but pose intricate problems of analysis to historians of politics. In addition, if they are skillful as practical politicians, it becomes difficult to arrive at the truth behind the myth, a problem often compounded by the scarcity and unreliability of historical data. Still, myths are built on concrete situations. To realize their goals, political saviors work through structures that continually circumscribe and shape their actions. Within these structures, they meet, resist, or otherwise deal with the interests and aspirations of other men for the pursuit of their own goals.

The use of the word savior in the present context needs some explanation. In the Judeo-Christian and Buddhist traditions the term has an exclusively religious meaning. Here, however, "savior" best typifies the person to whom a work of *yonaoshi*, literally "rectification of the world," is ascribed, and who, therefore, often acquires divine status, being called *daimyōjin*, *"Great August Deity."* The general title *myōjin* (August Deity) is much older than the term *yonaoshi*. Tsuda Sōkichi, the famous Shinto scholar, traces it back to China, where it became part of the Buddhist tradition. In this way the title was first used in Japan during the early Heian period (first half of the eighth century). It was soon popularized and, in Japanese fashion, applied to deified human beings.[1] The term *yonaoshi* was used around the 1780s, becoming increasingly popular until the Meiji Restoration as a word to indicate recurrent popular movements to redress the social and political wrongs of society. Such movements were the positive and utopian counterpart of the destructive riots, *uchikowashi*. Yonaoshi movements were thus expressions of the reformist mood of the commoners. Sadanobu's administration was reputed among the general populace, even outside his domain, to be a work of yonaoshi. And, indeed, there was much in Sadanobu's government and political style that made him appear a "savior." Despite his aristocratic background, Sadanobu seems to have grasped the popular mood for reform, including its religious overtones, and perceived his achievements as a statesman as those of a daimyōjin.

Matsudaira Sadanobu viewed and styled himself a savior, but he was also a practitioner of politics. Although his sense for political strategy is less apparent in his capacity as daimyo of Shirakawa than in his efforts to gain political influence in the bakufu, Sadanobu relied, in Shirakawa and Edo alike, on charismatic appeal and practical political acumen. Personal charisma alone would not have saved his domain from famine; moreover, many of his measures were not his innovations but had precedents in the domain's past. Yet he succeeded in putting his personal stamp upon them so that they were accredited to his political genius. Without charisma he would not have succeeded in building a political clique in Edo; yet Sadanobu appears to have been considered more a savior in his domain than in Edo, where he plotted the rise of his own career and the downfall of Tanuma. Focusing on Sadanobu's two modes of political behavior—as a savior and as a strategist—we will discuss first his daimyo rule and then his role in the building of a reformist clique.

SAVIOR TO THE DOMAIN

On 1783/10/16, Sadanobu succeeded to the Matsudaira house in the middle of an economic and political crisis which Sadakuni, his fifty-five-year-old stepfather (sick for at least eight years), was unable to handle. Uninterrupted rains in the spring and summer of that year had spoiled the crop: 108,600 of the 110,000 koku of rice were reported lost.[2] The rice price went up from 4.3 *kammon* per koku in the first month to 7.5 on 8/23.[3] On 8/26 a riot broke out, a fact that is conspicuously missing in all traditional biographical material on Sadanobu.[4] For several days, the whole domain was in turmoil. In the castle town of Shirakawa, several dwellings were destroyed: three stores of wholesale rice dealers, the residence of a district deputy (*gundai*), and several wealthy houses. The rioters distributed rice to the poor and demanded that the rice price be fixed at 7.2 kammon. (The price, however, continued to rise to 11.4 in the eleventh month and to 19.1 in the spring of the following year.)

At the time of the riot, Sadakuni probably had just left the domain. In the sixth month he was scheduled to travel to Edo for his one-year residence duty, but his palsy ailment had held him up until the eighth month.[5] Soon after Sadakuni's return to Edo, however, Yoshimura Matazaeimon, the elder on duty rotation in Shirakawa (*tsukiban*, the highest official in charge during the lord's absence), arrived in person in Edo, with a request from the han officials that Sadanobu take over the administration.

Such requests are often the result of factional strife among han bureaucrats. Although the precise details of such developments in Shirakawa han are missing, it seems that a drive for new leadership started well before Sadanobu's accession to power, as indicated in Sadakuni's desire for an early retirement at least one year before his actual retirement.[6] In general, when a change in han leadership is anticipated, specific policy changes are expected or feared, and these expectations or fears are often rallying points for faction building. At first glance, one might think that in the case of Shirakawa the principal officials, who ruled quite independently from their incapacitated lord, would be opposed to a new lord out of fear of losing some of their power. It seems likely, however, that they were extremely concerned with the possibility of continued social unrest. Famine was imminent. The rice supply, even with rationing, would not last beyond the tenth month.[7] The drastic act of reducing the stipends of the retainers had been decided upon to meet the rapidly deteriorating economic condition of the han. Fresh leadership, therefore, gave new hope to peasants and retainers alike for redressing or "correcting" the tense situation that had developed.

When Sadanobu assumed power in the month in which the domain was almost at the end of its rice supply, his first task was to feed his vassals and the peasants. Through a massive relief program, he was able to save all his subjects; according to his own account no one fell victim to the famine in his domain.[8] All biographers, of course, give Sadanobu full credit for the program. Actually, as attested by a local history of Iwase district, one of the three districts in which the central parcel of the domain was located (the others being Shirakawa and Ishikawa), the program had started two months before Sadanobu came to power. According to this source, messengers had already been dispatched in the eighth month to the surrounding domains and to Osaka to buy rice.[9] If these steps were taken that early, there is a good possibility that Sadakuni had made the decision in Shirakawa before his return to Edo, and that Sadanobu in Edo had nothing to do with that decision. It was Sadanobu, however, who brought the relief program to a successful end and thus received the fame and credit for "saving" the domain.

We know of a total of 12,380 koku of rice that were sent to Shirakawa from the following places:[10]

4,000 koku from Kashiwasaki, a separate domain parcel in Echigo;
2,780 koku from Osaka;
2,400 koku from the Aizu domain (230,000 koku);
1,200 koku from the Taira domain (50,000 koku);
1,200 koku from the Asakawa encampment near Shirakawa (a separate parcel of the Takata domain);
400 koku from the Nihonmatsu domain (100,000 koku);
400 koku from the Moriyama domain (20,000 koku).

The rice was rationed and distributed daily to the retainers' families (5 gō for males, 3 gō for females) and every ten days to the peasants (30 gō per household).[11]

Although there are countless difficulties involved in trying to calculate how many months supply these purchases represented, a general estimate can be attempted. To compute the daily consumption of the entire domain, one must first calculate its population in terms of households for the peasants and in terms of male-female population for the warrior families. In 1659, when the domain was 10,000 koku larger than under Sadanobu, there were 15,444 peasant households;[12] taking into account the general increase of Japan's population until the Kyōhō era, 16,000 may be a fair number for Sadanobu's time. At the rate of 3 *gō* per day per household, the peasant population therefore consumed daily some 50 koku. Sadanobu's office-holding retainers numbered 1,503;[13] but the total male population of his retainers was higher than that number. If one accepts the figure 2,000, the daily rice consumption of the male retainer population would have been ten koku. One now has to add to these figures an estimated five koku for female members of the retainer families and for the commoners in the towns. The total amount of rice consumed daily under Sadanobu's ration regime amounts then to some sixty-five koku. The purchased rice plus the small amount that was harvested amounts to about 14,000 koku: at the rate of sixty-five koku a day, this constituted a supply for some 200 days. Later, in 1784/1, great amounts of vegetables from Edo (34,000 dried white radishes, 10,000 carrots, etc.)[14] were added to the purchased rice.

Let us now estimate the cost of this massive relief. First one can assume that the 4,000 koku from Kashiwasaki were not purchased, since they came from a separate domain parcel. Without taking into account transportation fees, the remaining 8,380 koku, at the rate of twenty-five kammon per koku (in Nihonmatsu the rate was thirty kammon),[15] should have cost 210,000 kammon.[16] It is difficult to evaluate this cost in terms of the domain's income. But one can estimate how much of a burden it was for the domain by analyzing two other kinds of data: the payroll of the han officials and the size of the previous loans contracted by the domain.

The yearly total of stipends handed out to officials and retainers was about 60,000 koku, which corresponds to about 320,000 kammon.[17] Thus, an amount equivalent to two-thirds of the yearly stipend expenditures was needed for the rice purchases. Since there was a crop failure that year, the amount was impossible to raise. Moreover, if one looks at previous loans and at the measures needed to liquidate them, one can understand the extreme penury of the domain. In 1705, when the size of the domain was 150,000 koku, a 20 percent stipend cut was declared in order to pay back a loan equivalent to 26,000 kammon. Again during the years 1708–13 the domain contracted debts with moneylenders, equivalent to 237,000 kammon, which gave rise to years of factional strife over financial policies for liquidating these debts.[18]

Where did the funds come from this time? Certainly not from the domain, because according to Sadanobu its coffers were as empty as its storehouses.[19] Probably not from the bakufu either, because in the twelfth month of that same year it declared a seven-year suspension of all loans. Chances are that the funds came from Tayasu. Sadanobu's stepmother had always had a high interest in political affairs and especially in Sadanobu's career. She was the leading figure in Tayasu's refusal to adopt an heir other than of her own choice (see Appendix B). She is also given credit for obtaining on 1783/12/18 the fourth honorary rank for Sadanobu, an honor usually preserved for people over forty;[20] and for having succeeded on 1785/12/1 in seating Sadanobu in the Antechamber.[21] Tayasu's income (tax returns from 100,000 koku from bakufu house land) was almost as great as that of the Shirakawa domain; Tayasu, however, did not have to provide for the upkeep of a castle and for the livelihood of 1,500 retainers.[22] It is therefore quite plausible that Sadanobu was able to meet this economic crisis through the support from his native house. Maybe also the han bureaucrats had urged his succession in order to open these resources for the rescue of the domain.

There seems, then, to be more than a grain of truth in Sadanobu's assertion that he was able to save all of his subjects. There can be no doubt that he gained quick fame within and outside his domain for having prevented famine. Even while the supplies were being transported to Shirakawa, Sadanobu's fame had already spread throughout the land. It is reputed that Shirakawa-bound supplies were handled with special care at the way stations.[23]

A NEW KIND OF LEADERSHIP

From the outset, Sadanobu firmly established his personal control over the situation. He made it very clear that he was determined either to survive with his subjects or to bear with them the hardships of a famine.[24] During the first weeks of his rule, at the height of the crisis, there was feverish activity at the Edo mansion of the Shirakawa domain, where Sadanobu directed the relief program and organized his policies. In order to speed up operations and the flow of information, he eliminated various steps for transmitting messages. Considerations of rank and precedence were bypassed; the Interior was opened to most officials, who were often kept at work until late at night. Sadanobu also made it a point to meet twice a month with his Edo officials, even if there was no immediate business to discuss.[25]

Sadanobu first sent Yoshimura back to Shirakawa with detailed instructions for the district deputies (*gundai*), the superintendant of finances (*kanjōgashira*), the inspectors general (*ōmetsuke*), inspectors (*yokome*) and all other officials.[26] On 10/18, two days after his succession, Sadanobu called the officials together and exhorted them to adopt frugal ways, pointing to himself as a model and pledging that nobody was bound to keep the regulations if he himself were to break them. He also stressed the need to frankly report all available information.[27] In the eleventh month he issued instructions to the peasants through the district deputies;[28] in the twelfth month further exhortative instructions (some 200 pages in manuscript) were delivered to his retainers; and in 1784/1 and 4, detailed advice on agricultural technicalities was sent to the peasants.

Sadanobu's directives were an assertion of firm leadership on all levels of the domain. He tried to guide his subjects on all aspects of their life—in their official duties as devoted administrators or industrious producers and in their private life style, where everybody was urged to practice frugality. This new sense of control and direction was achieved in three ways.

First, with a scrupulous eye for practical detail, Sadanobu saw to it that no sector in the political, social, or economic life of the domain would impede his goal of making optimal use of the limited resources. All the minutiae concerning meals, garments, festivals, or luxurious habits had this as their purpose.

Second, he tried to elicit the maximum response and loyalty from his subjects by upholding his own commitment as an example. Over and over again, he points in his instructions to his own frugal life style.[29] Sadanobu made sure never to miss an occasion to set an example. For instance, when in 1784/6 he journeyed for his first year of residence to Shirakawa, he reduced the expenses of his procession, postponed unnecessary repairs at the castle such as the replacement of tatami mats, and reduced the number of personal servants he brought along from Edo to two middle-aged women.[30]

Third, his continual stress on the need for clear information was as much, if not more, to prevent corruption and faction building among his officials, as to obtain warnings about possible peasant unrest. In his instructions to inspectors (*yokome*, an office with 68 incumbents and also 36 *shita yokome* or lower inspectors),[31] Sadanobu urges them to know the feelings of the people (*ninjō*) and the movement of the times (*jisei*). But he stresses that their first duty is to watch over the retainers.[32] In another set of instructions, dated 1795, Sadanobu was more specific. Elders on duty rotation, he warned then, should care about the quality of the different offices but not discuss the direction of politics (*seijimuki no gi*) with stewards, district deputies, and the like.[33] Superintendents (*bugyō*; 29 incumbents) should foster no familiar relationships with inspectors general (*ōmetsuke*; 9 incumbents) or elders on duty rotation.[34] Stewards (*yōnin*; 10 incumbents) should confer directly with the elder on duty rotation and the superintendents, without cultivating relationships in the Interior through chamberlains (*toritsugu*). They are not officials of the Exterior (*omote yaku*) or policy makers (*seijikata*), Sadanobu reminds the stewards.[35]

From these instructions, it appears that Sadanobu was seriously concerned with the problem of preventing executive bureaucrats from building alliances or cliques within the bureaucracy which could eventually bring undue pressure upon the policy makers. The number of inspectors at all levels (totaling 107) seems also extraordinarily large if Shirakawa is compared, for instance, with the Taira domain, half the size of Shirakawa, where only twenty-four were employed (eight inspectors general and sixteen *kachi metsuke* or itinerant inspectors).[36] Another indication that administrative discipline was a problem is that Sadanobu modified the house rules, making loyalty and filial obedience (*chū-kō*), rather than loyalty and trust (*chū-shin*), the cardinal virtues he expected from his retainers.[37] Obedience indeed, more than trust, is a dynamic quality that assures political integration. And in the first eighty pages of his 1784/12 instructions, where he addresses himself to the main officials (elders, stewards, masters of ceremonies, officers, inspectors, and superintendents), the theme of sincerity (*jitsugi*) arises again and again.[38]

BENEFACTOR TO THE PEASANTS

After the efficient relief measures of 1783–84, the agricultural economy of the domain was still beset with serious problems in three areas. Programs of assistance to the peasants were still needed because the three crops of 1784–86 never reached the normal quota (in these three years, the partial crop failures increased from 20,000 to 38,000 to 70,000 *koku*);[39] a population policy to safeguard the stability of the peasant labor force was essential for the economic and financial health of the domain; and a system of checks and controls at the local level was necessary to assure the proper tax returns.

Sadanobu rationalized his land policy as *jinsei* or benevolent government. This benevolence, however, was determined by the needs of the administration rather than by those of the peasants. For instance, Sadanobu stated in his twenty-two directives of 1783/11 addressed to the peasants that only those peasants who apply themselves wholeheartedly to farming will receive blessings from the gods; that they ought not to engage in trade or covet wealth; and also that peasants over twelve should not engage in reading or writing.[40] Neither were taxes necessarily lighter under a government that called itself "jinsei" (see Appendix A). Benevolent government was inspired by a limited enlightenment which understood that the ruling class depended on the stability and general obedience of the peasant class, a theme that was very prominent in Sadanobu's *Kokuhonron*.

Benevolent government is also the style of government that fits perfectly the purpose of a ruler who wants to portray himself as a father or benefactor of the people. It is therefore not surprising that Sadanobu tried, wherever he could, to give his rule a benevolent character. It was more difficult in the third sector of the land policy (the system of controls), because there the purpose of exploitation was more apparent. The first two sectors, however (Sadanobu's program of assistance and his population policy), lent themselves more easily to practical applications of jinsei.

Sadanobu took the following measures to assist the peasants in the famine year: he canceled land taxes;[41] annulled half of the debts, the other half to be repaid in five yearly installments; and started repair works at the embankment of the Abukuma river in Shirakawa, thus providing a livelihood for some.[42] He sent out a call inviting the wealthier peasants or townspeople to assist their neighbors, and awarded those who responded with a tablet to be hung at their entrance gates as official recognition of their selfless deeds. In 1784 Sadanobu brought also medicines to the domain as a preventive measure against the possible outbreak of epidemics, which often follow famines.

Sadanobu understood how to become personally involved in assisting his people. The reward tablets were one way of expressing his concern with their welfare. In 1784 he also ordered the planting of seedlings within the castle precincts which were later distributed to villages that were particularly short of them. He also expressed a special compassion for elderly peasants and townspeople by ordering the distribution of a supplementary rice ration to homes with persons over ninety.[43] On two occasions when a fire broke out in Shirakawa, Sadanobu, in unprecedented fashion, personally led firefighting operations and supervised the distribution of food and clothing to the victims.[44] Sometimes he also toured his domain, giving special donations to particularly poor villages.[45]

This direct involvement of a daimyo in the administrative affairs of his domain was undoubtedly an unusual phenomenon in the domain's history. Even in Japan's overall political tradition, delegation of power, rather than direct government by the highest authority, was the rule. Powerful ministers or councils of elders were likely to be the

policy makers, not the emperors or shoguns whom they were expected
to serve. With Sadanobu, however, the charismatic awe that was
vested in the highest authority holder was brought to bear upon
concrete policies that were intimately identified with his person.

The second policy that greatly benefited the peasants had the long-
range purpose of solidifying the peasant base of the economy. In
order to increase the peasant population, Sadanobu resorted to three
different methods: population transfers, prohibition of abortion and
infanticide, and issuance of birth allowances. It should be noted
that, contrary to the impression official biographies convey, none of
these methods were original creations of Sadanobu. They all had
precedents in the domain's history, although it is difficult to determine
from existing information whether they were more successful before Sadanobu.

Population transfers from a separate domain parcel in Echigo had
already occurred in the 1720s and '30s.[46] Sadanobu repeated the
policy. Because of infanticide practices, women were scarce in the
region: the Aizu and Sōma domains, for instance, prohibited the
exportation of its women to other domains.[47] Therefore Sadanobu
invited prospective brides from a separate domain parcel in Echigo—
an invitation which apparently came to be issued on a yearly basis.[48]
To young men in the domain he provided marriage allowances of
three *ryō* (to be paid back in monthly installments), an amount
equivalent to a wage laborer's one-year or one-and-a-half-year
earnings.[49] Sadanobu also moved whole peasant families and settled
them in the central section of the domain. In seven years, 1785–92,
the population is thus said to have increased by 3,500.[50] This increase
was largely the result of Sadanobu's population policies.

In order to stop the practice of abortion and infanticide, Sadanobu resorted first to religious indoctrination. Buddhist priests were
ordered to visit the villages and, displaying a picture of the horrors of
hell, to warn the peasants against the consequences of their sins.
Women necromancers were also sent into the countryside to evoke the
spirits of dead children;[51] and a Shingaku teacher was engaged to
encourage the peasants in the ways of frugality and child rearing.[52]
The moralistic approach, however, seems to have failed, and Sadanobu was forced to appeal to the less noble instincts of his subjects
through a system of birth allowances.

Allowances had been granted in previous decades, apparently with
some success. At least for the northern part of the domain—the
territory of the daikan Naitō Heizaemon, who resided in the town of
Sukagawa—the birth allowance records for the years 1751–95 have
been preserved.[53] From 1751, two bu were distributed at the birth of

each child after the first child, and two more bu at the end of the following year, the total amount being thus one ryō per child. The numbers of allowances granted per decade were: 128 in 1751–59; 55 in 1760–69; 11 in 1770–79. Four were granted in the first four years of the 1780s, and 34 between 1784 and 1794, the first decade of Sadanobu's rule. Sadanobu's policy seems not to have reached the same scope as Heizaemon's initiative of the 1750s and 1760s.

Sadanobu's birth allowances were also less generous at first than Heizaemon's. In 1784 he ordered an allowance of one bale of rice (worth approximately two bu) to families with more than five children.[54] In the years 1790–94 he raised the stipend to one ryō for every child beyond the first; in 1798–1802 he doubled the amount.[55] The sum of two ryō, the equivalent to a whole year's wage of a hired laborer, led to abuses, as indicated in the warnings of 1811 issued to village headmen to prevent misappropriations of funds.

The attractive wages of hired labor posed another threat to agriculture: poor peasants were enticed into wage labor to obtain ready cash for paying off debts, or simply because wage labor was more rewarding than working one's own plot of land. They abandoned their land (reducing the land tax income of the domain), and signed labor contracts, usually for a one-year period. Wages were paid in advance so that their labor had the character of the liquidation of a debt. In his instructions to the peasants of 1783/11, Sadanobu mentions the problem, and in later years, when the finances of the domain were restored, he made loans available at a minimal interest or at no interest at all for these indebted laborers to free themselves.[56]

The third aspect of Sadanobu's land policy had to do with checks and controls in the countryside. We have already seen how he himself occasionally toured his domain. In his instructions of 1783/12, he urged the gundai (five incumbents) to delegate as few of their duties as possible and to get acquainted with the local situation;[57] in 1806 he further implemented this policy by ordering daikan (probably four incumbents)[58] to take up residence in the countryside and take over the responsibilities of the collective village heads (ōjōya).[59] In order to prevent abuses at the lowest administrative level, Sadanobu introduced a system of double bookkeeping, whereby one copy of the tax register was kept by the village representative (osa-hyakushō) and handed over to an inspector (yokome), while the copy of the village head (shōya) went to a county messenger (kōrizukai).[60]

Complaints about possible abuses could be dropped in complaint boxes (meyasubako), originally a Chinese system which Sadanobu reintroduced, imitating Yoshimune and an earlier daimyo, Yūki Matsudaira Yoshinori. In 1737 Yoshinori had placed a complaint box in Shirakawa, but he withdrew it after twelve days since the box was immediately filled with petitions for deferments of tax payments.[61] In 1784/8, Sadanobu placed several such boxes: one in Edo at the office of the lower inspectors, three in Shirakawa and one at the encampment of the Kashiwasaki separate parcel. Each document had to be signed; complaints had to be about administrative matters and not personal grievances about particular officials. Once a month the boxes were picked up by an inspector, handed over to an attendant, and opened personally by Sadanobu.[62]

Sadanobu's land policy was effective. By 1790, the domain's finances were restored. There were even 10,000 *ryō* in savings, which made economic expansion a possibility.[63] All through the 1790s, Sadanobu invested capital in industrial and agricultural as well as in commercial ventures. Before 1790, two new industries had been established in Shirakawa under Sadanobu's encouragement (porcelain and metal industry), but in the '90s a new enterprise was started almost every year: a lacquer industry, paper manufacturing, dyeing, mining (copper, lead, and iron), a flourishing horse market, the cultivation of tobacco and medicinal herbs; sake brewing was improved and sericulture expanded. Often experts were called from outside to establish a particular industry: masters from Aizu taught the techniques of lacquer fabrication and improved sake brewing methods; an artisan from Edo introduced violet dyeing.

Domain capital backed all these enterprises, and most of them were supervised by the superintendent of finances; many of the products were exported to other domains. Some industries (the horse market in particular) by means of fee levies were very rewarding to the domain. The proceeds were never integrated into the domain's budget but were thought of as something extra; they went into a special fund for the relief of the poor, thus adding to Sadanobu's reputation that he had the welfare of his people at heart.[64]

After the turn of the century, Sadanobu seems to have turned his major attention back to agriculture: loans were made available for the building of new farms (in 1800) and for the opening of new land (in 1805).[65] Throughout his rule Sadanobu also worked at his favorite program of building storehouses to provide for disaster years: when he retired in 1812, he left the domain thirty storehouses.[66]

OYAKATA (PATRON) TO THE RETAINERS

Although agriculture and the peasants were Sadanobu's main concern, he could not have implemented his reforms without the help of his warrior-administrators. He displayed toward his retainers the same caring paternalism that typified his agricultural policies and built his fame as a model ruler.

Before Sadanobu's administration, Shirakawa han politics had always faced a dilemma: whether to reestablish financial solvency by squeezing out more taxes (mostly miscellaneous taxes) from the peasants, or by demanding frugality from the retainers and eventually cutting their stipends. The magnitude of the 1783 emergency and the subsequent lean years lasting until 1789, however, made any one-sided solution impracticable. The whole domain had to make sacrifices. Sadanobu, therefore, prescribed a four-year period of frugality starting in 1783; it ended in 1787, the year after a massive crop failure, so that the period was extended for another four years. Stipends were cut by half in 1783 and were restored only in 1790.[67]

The retainers, however, enjoyed preferential treatment, in the food rationing. Their ration in 1783–84 was higher than that of the peasants, and arrangements were made to let them buy rice at less than the official market price.[68] In general, through a loosening of certain regulations (for example, by allowing sick officials in Edo to receive visits from their wives and children), Sadanobu showed a concern for his retainers' problems.[69]

These differences aside, Sadanobu's treatment of his retainers displayed the same characteristics as his land policy. Close identification with his subjects was both an invitation to follow his example and a means of direct control. Sadanobu made an effort to maximize their function in the polity. He also relied heavily upon moralistic indoctrination, seasoned occasionally with material rewards for good performance.

Sadanobu's effort to keep close to his subjects may have been encouraged by his status as adopted heir, although this fact cannot explain all of his policies. In his first instructions of 1783/12, he asked his retainers to disregard the circumstance of his adoption, to be loyal and open, and to come directly to the Exterior or the Interior if they had anything to discuss.[70] This was obviously a measure to prevent faction building, against which he warned explicitly.[71] When he entered the domain for the first time as daimyo in 1784/6, he devised further means to assure the integration of the domain. Twice a month he assembled his retainers for a lecture which he himself delivered; once a month he held poetry-reading meetings, followed by a frugal meal— which furnished an occasion to display his ascetic life-style.[72] Sadanobu also organized a club for retainers over seventy.[73]

Sadanobu found symbolic and religious means further to express his will to be one with his subjects. In the autumn of 1784, while the domain was still struggling with the effects of food shortage, he dispatched a team of fourteen men to Kuwana near Nagoya to bring back a wooden image and some paraphernalia of Sadatsuna, the founder of the house.[74] The relics were deposed in a humble shrine in the precincts of the castle, together with a scroll of the house rules and Sadanobu's personal pledge to fulfill his duties as adopted heir and young lord.[75] In 1792 Sadatsuna was awarded the official divine title of *Chinkoku daimyōjin* (Great Deity of the Pacification of the Land). A couple of years later Sadanobu's own image joined that of the founder.[76]

This shrine became the center of a double festival in spring and autumn, which was meant to revive the military spirit of the retainers. These festivals were called *Bubisai* (Festival of Military Preparedness) and were contests in the martial arts. The contests were held on what had once been a flower bed, converted by Sadanobu into a practice ground. The winners of these contests had their names written on tags, which were then deposited in the shrine.[77]

The avowed purpose of this revival of military preparedness was to prepare men to intervene in peasant uprisings.[78] The military force is not known to have been used against Shirakawa peasants, but its effectiveness was proved on 1798/1/24 in suppressing a riot in the neighboring domain of Asakawa. Asakawa was a separate parcel of the Takata domain of Echigo, adjacent to Shirakawa and until 1741 an integral part of the Shirakawa domain. Almost all 117 villages of Asakawa participated in the three-day riot, which resulted in the destruction of some temples as well as eighty dwellings of collective village heads, village headmen, horsekeepers, heads of five household groups, and farmers. The mob even assaulted the Asakawa encampment, leaving twenty-six dead and numerous wounded. Neighboring domains rushed to crush the revolt. The largest contingent (480 men) was sent by Sadanobu on the twenty-sixth and was directly responsible for the quelling of the riot in a day.[79]

Sadanobu also organized "military maneuvers" for his warriors. Even high officials were made to participate in these maneuvers, which included fifty-mile hikes. The hikes served not only to provide military training but also to integrate Sadanobu's retainers and to bring them into contact with the actual conditions of the peasants in the countryside. They were, moreover, a direct way of demonstrating to the countryside the strength of Sadanobu's retainers, ensconced in the castle town of Shirakawa.

Sadanobu also put his warriors to use in nonmilitary ways. In order to alleviate the burden of supporting large warrior families, he made provisions for second and third sons to serve some function, or else to contribute to their livelihood in an independent way. They were employed, for instance, in Sadanobu's forestation program. In a span of ten years (1783–93), more than 715,000 trees were planted in the domain, mainly along the roads, in order to protect the crops against

the cold northern winds that often caused crop damage on the
Shirakawa plateau. The program, which included patrolling and
checking the woodlands of the hinterland, was organized from six
centers. The warrior-foresters were instructed to keep an eye open for
the social and economic conditions of the countryside.[80] Sadanobu
further allowed, like the reformer Hayakawa Mozaeimon in the
Kyōhō era, second and third sons of warriors to return to the land
without changing their warrior status. In 1792 he provided them
with ten *ryō* to help them in building their houses; they were also
granted a five- to seven-year tax break. In times of crisis they could
be called upon to provide military service. In peacetime their only
aristocratic obligation was a ceremonial visit to the castle at the
beginning of each new year. Moreover, they were not allowed to
mingle with peasants or marry peasants' daughters, and were therefore settled in locations separate from the peasants. In 1797, more
retainers were allowed to take up farming, although only on a
temporary basis. As soon as they had become financially solvent, they
were expected to return to the castle town.[81] Others were allowed to
take up part-time occupations such as the manufacturing of wicker
trunks; their wives and daughters were encouraged to start spinning
and weaving as a supplementary source of income.[82]

Sadanobu's moralizing tendencies, already manifest in his writings,
were translated into action as soon as he was in charge of the domain.
Because of his belief that the smooth functioning of his administration
depended upon the spiritual improvement of his subjects, he provided
his retainers with a plethora of exhortative instructions in the first
months of his rule. He delivered biweekly lectures to them during his
first year of residence in Shirakawa, and filled his subsequent directives with edificatory messages. Later Sadanobu came to understand
that he needed further institutional means to make his retainers
internalize the moral truths he taught them. Around 1800, he therefore established societies among his retainers for the mutual encouragement of moral thought and behavior. They met once or twice
a month and were invited to criticize their own and each other's
conduct, using as a guideline Sadanobu's moralistic treatise, the
Sekizen shū, written for the purpose of group discussion.[83]

Sadanobu's practical sense, however, guarded him from exclusive
reliance upon indoctrination and moral incentive. He occasionally
rewarded good performance in a very tangible way. In 1787, at the
end of his first five-year frugality period and before inaugurating the
next one, he distributed five ryō per 100 koku throughout the domain.
This amount was worth one koku of rice or the equivalent of a 3
percent tax refund.[84] Sadanobu also rewarded villages that paid their

taxes in time with the equivalent of 4.8 gallons of sake and ten slices of dried cuttlefish.[85] Retainers and peasants that distinguished themselves were rewarded with honorary citations in a logbook of civil deeds.

In 1788/5, when Sadanobu journeyed to Kyoto, he was greeted as a savior along the roadside by the populace with the words, "Gratitude for having redressed the world" (*yo no naka o naoshi kudasaru katajikenasa yo*).[86] His fame as savior had spread quickly. In Shirakawa, Sadanobu had managed in only a few years to build an image of a selfless ruler, sincerely concerned with the welfare of his subjects. This, he accomplished first through the tangible success of his administration and, second, through a personal political style, whereby he portrayed himself as the protective *oyakata* (patron) of his subjects. His rule was thus marked by two qualities that complemented each other. He showed an almost condescending, yet genuine, concern for his people. This personal quality of the true leader animated in him an acute sense for practical government that gave political soundness to his agriculturalism. It also made him cautious in his paternalism toward his retainers. His sense of the pragmatic thus prevented both his agriculturalism and his paternalism from becoming liabilities for administrative efficiency.

Sadanobu's rule in Shirakawa turned out to be a useful apprenticeship for his bakufu office—and not merely by chance. He had never given up his youthful ambition to "rectify the realm." During his four years in Shirakawa, he quietly concentrated on his bakufu ambitions and made his rule as daimyo the testing period for the reform that he intended to bring to Edo. Through his fame as an efficient daimyo, he made himself the obvious candidate for renovating bakufu administration, and he went far in actively seeking that candidacy by putting his personal and practical gifts of leadership to work among a group of political discontents in Edo.

POLITICAL COTERIE IN EDO

When Sadanobu was appointed chief councillor on 1787/6/19, his ability and accomplishments as daimyo of a poor regional domain were well known. He was not, however, an innocent country lord, ignorant of the politics of the big city. He moved with dignity and ease in high political circles in Edo. He had a sharp sense of political intrigue, and had formed a group of like-minded daimyo to discuss renovating the bakufu bureaucracy. As already seen, he was well acquainted with the political writings of his day, and had proved himself an able administrator in exceptionally difficult times in his domain. With this experience, and driven by his ambition, he was confident that he could manage the bakufu. Thus, he set about building a clique of political discontents and exploring possible avenues for gaining power and bringing about political change in the bakufu.

Two documents throw light upon the composition of Sadanbou's circle of political friends. They relate to two different groups of people with whom he had contact. The first of these documents is his autobiography, in which Sadanobu gives us detailed information about a group of daimyo friends. The second is an unpublished collection of 124 letters (*Sōrishū*), addressed to Sadanobu by a wider circle of acquaintances between the time he was fifteen, when he was adopted in the Matsudaira family, and his twenty-ninth year, when he became chief councillor in the bakufu. Of the two documents, the autobiography is the more informative because it provides a personal view of his closest associates.

In his autobiography, *Uge no hito koto* (Words of a man under the eaves), Sadanobu often comments on eighteen daimyo, many of whom he calls his friends (see table 2). His closest and oldest ally was a fudai daimyo, Honda Tadakazu (1739–1812), lord of the tiny Izumi domain (15,000 koku) in Mutsu. Between 1778, when Sadanobu at age nineteen on his own initiative befriended Tadakazu, and 1784, when he left Edo for his first year of residence in Shirakawa, Sadanobu's group of friends consisted of nine daimyo. After his return in 1785 from his first-year residence in Shirakawa, nine more joined his circle.

Sadanobu's associates were overwhelmingly fudai daimyo. Only two were tozama, and one was, like Sadanobu himself, a relative of the Tokugawa house (kamon). Of the fudai daimyo, ten were medium vassal daimyo (holding fiefs of 30,000 to 100,000 koku), while five belonged to the category of minor vassal daimyo (10,000 to 30,000 koku). Except for two who were masters of shogunal ceremonies (*sōshaban*; an office with some thirty incumbents), and one who was one of the twelve captains of the great guard (*ōbangashira*), none of them held bakufu offices. None of them was thus connected with, or deeply indebted to, Tanuma's clique.

As far as their seats in the honorary chambers of the shogun were concerned, one tozama daimyo was member of the Great Hall (*ōbiroma*), where the kamon also was seated; two fudai daimyo held seats in the Hall of Geese (*gannoma*), and one was member of the Antechamber (*tamarinoma*). All others were members of the Hall of Emperors (*teikannoma*). Among these chambers, only the last two were politically important: the Antechamber was an advisory body to the shogun and thus offered a possibility to maneuver against the ruling clique; the Hall of Emperors, to which Sadanobu belonged before he was appointed to the Antechamber on 1785/12/1, was the chamber from which highest-ranking bakufu officials were chosen.[87] Most of Sadanobu's friends were colleagues from this chamber.

From the *Sōrishū* we know that Sadanobu was in contact with six court nobles and seventy-seven daimyo, of whom twenty-two held fiefs of over 100,000 koku (out of a total of forty-seven). His correspondents, again, were overwhelmingly fudai daimyo (some fifty-five). They included five members of the Antechamber and thirty-five members of the Hall of Emperors. This means that Sadanobu was sometimes in contact with half the members of both chambers.

Many of the letters are of a perfunctory nature (new year's greetings,etc.), but they testify to the widespread prestige Sadanobu enjoyed among the daimyo even before his bakufu tenure. Sadanobu is frequently asked for his opinion on political problems; other letters are inquiries about the rules he had set up for his han officials, about his writings (the *Kyūgen roku* and the *Koshi-itsu* are mentioned), or about books in his private library. These books are not limited to the Neo-Confucian school and give no indication of Sadanobu's view of certain schools as heterodox, as did his ban on heterodoxy of 1790. Neo-Confucian classics such as the *Daigakuengi*, a Sung commentary on The Great Learning, are mentioned together with Muro Kyūsō's *Shundai zatsuwa* (Sundry talks at Suruga dai), strictly Neo-Confucian, and Nakae Tōju's *Okina mondō* (Discussions with a venerable old man) or Kumazawa Banzan's *Usa mondō* (Discussions of Usa), both belonging to the "heterodox" Wang Yang-ming school.

Many of Sadanobu's acquaintances were never to hold office. Some were celebrities in their day, like Hosokawa Shigekata, outer lord of Kumamoto (540,000 koku) and Uesugi Harunori (Yōzan), outer lord of Yonezawa (150,000 koku). A substantial core of them, however, were to occupy key bakufu offices during and after Sadanobu's tenure. Among them were five future senior councillors, six junior councillors, ten superintendents of temples and shrines, and three grand chamberlains. Of these, thirteen are commented upon in *Uge no hito koto*.[88] Together they constituted Sadanobu's political coterie. They were a group of well over a dozen middle range fudai daimyo; they belonged to the same honorary chamber as Sadanobu; they held no offices and were thus outsiders to Tanuma's bureaucracy;

TABLE 2 Careers of Sadanobu's Associates

Name	Matsudaira Nobuaki	Honda Tadakazu	Toda Ujinori	Makino Tadakiyo	Arima Shigesumi	Matsudaira Nobumichi	Kanō Hisachika	Matsudaira Norisada
Han (koku)	Yoshida (70,000)	Izumi (15,000)	Ōgaki (100,000)	Nagaoka (74,000)	Maruoka (50,000)	Kameyama (50,000)	Hatta (10,000)	Nishio (60,000)
Fud./Toz.	Fudai	Fudai	Fudai	Fudai	Tozama	Fudai	?	Fudai
Chamber	Antech.	Hall Emp.	Hall Emp.	Hall Emp.	Hall Emp.	Hall Emp.	?	Hall Emp.
Dates	1760–1817	1739–1812	1754–1806	1760–?	1766–1819	?–1791	1753–1811	1752–1793
Entrance into circle of friends	1785	1778	1782	1784	1785	1785	1785	?
Office before 1787/6	'84 Master sh. cer.			'81 Master sh. cer.			'84 Capt. gr. guard	'81 Master '87/3 Temples
1787/6		4/17 Jun. c.		12/13 Temples			6/26 Chamb.	12/23 Kyoto dep.
1788	2/2 Gr. ch. 4/4 Sen. c. till 1803	5/15 Gr. ch.				6/26 Temples		
1789			6/18 Master 11/24 Temples			4/15 Master		4/11 Sen. c. till 1793
1790	4/16 Sen. c. till 1798 Financ. till 1793		4/16 Gr. ch. 10/16 Sen. c. till 1806					
1791	8/30 Fin. till 1795				8/28 Mast.	(died)		
1792				8/27 Osaka				
1793/7	1806–1817 Chief c.		'93/10 Fin. till 1796				1/27 Jun. c. 1800–1810 Fushimi	(died)
After 1793/7				'98 Kyoto 1801–16 Sen. c. '06–16 Fin.	d. '10 Templ. '12 Jun. c.			

Abbreviations and Total Number of Incumbents per Office

Sen. c.:	Senior councillors, 4 or 5
Jun. c.:	Junior councillors, 4 or 5
Templ.:	Superintendent of temples and shrines, 4
Kyoto dep.:	Kyoto deputy, 1
Osaka:	Keeper of Osaka castle, 1
Gr. ch.:	Grand chamberlain, 1
Chamb.:	Chamberlains, 14
Mast.:	Masters of shogunal ceremonies, 20 to 40
Capt. gr. guard:	Captains of the great guard, 12
Fushimi:	Fushimi magistrate, 1
Fin.:	Overseer of shogunal finances (office concomitant with that of senior councillor), 1 or 2

Number of Members in the Honorary Chambers

Antechamber, 10
Great Hall, 25
Hall of Emperors, 66
Hall of Geese, 44

Other Associates Mentioned in the Autobiography:

Honda Tadayoshi (Yamazaki: 10,000 koku); fudai, Hall of Emperors (1741–94): friend since '82; captain of the great guard (1788); ("faithful; a leader of men; loves what is good; rejoices in good things as if they were done by his own children").

Hosokawa Shigekata (Kumamoto: 540,000 koku); tozama, Great Hall (1718–?): friend since '84.

Hotta Masayoshi (Miyagawa: 13,000 koku); fudai, Hall of Emperors (1762–?): friend since '82; captain of the great guard (1788–97); master of shogunal ceremonies (1797–1800); superintendent of temples and shrines (1800–1806).

Makino Fusashige (Tanabe: 35,000 koku); fudai, Hall of Geese (1764–?): friend since '85 ("a very warm gentleman, but almost a fool; illiterate but very trustworthy.")

Matsudaira Nobuyuki (Kaminoyama: 30,000 koku); fudai, Hall of Emperors: friend since '82; broke off friendship later.

Matsudaira Sadafumi (Imaji: 35,000 koku); fudai, Hall of Emperors: friend since '85.

Matsudaira Tadatsugu (Amagasaki: 40,000 koku); fudai, Hall of Emperors: friend since '85.

Matsudaira Yasuji (Tsuyama: 50,000 koku); kamon, Great Hall: friend since '84 ("unparalleled erudition and eloquence").

Okudaira Masatoki (Nakatsu: 10,000 koku); fudai, Hall of Emperors (1763–?): friend since '82.

Ōoka Chūyō (Iwatsuki: 20,000 koku); fudai, Hall of Geese (?–1786).

they were roughly of the same age as Sadanobu (half of them were of
Sadanobu's age group or younger), and shared the same political ideals.

This group of friends gathered regularly for poetry readings and for
mutual moral encouragement.[89] Gradually the moral purpose prevailed, and discussions increasingly dealt with government, economics, and administration—especially after Sadanobu's triumphant
return from Shirakawa in 1786/6. To judge from the early available
copies of the *Kokuhonron* and of his lengthy instructions of 1784/12
to his han officials, Sadanobu's writings were eagerly studied by his
friends. Sadanobu was undoubtedly the leader.

One of his friends, however, was more a master to Sadanobu than a
disciple. Honda Tadakazu was twenty years Sadanobu's elder. In
1778, Sadanobu had taken the initiative of gaining his friendship
because he had heard that Tadakazu was a famous man.[90] Tadakazu
remained Sadanobu's best friend throughout his life. Sadanobu speaks
of him as a model ruler and true hero, a man of utter sincerity and
justice who assisted his subjects in time of distress. Sadanobu also
acknowledged his indebtedness to Tadakazu, even for his own success
in Shirakawa.[91] The two men must have worked closely together.
Measures taken by Tadakazu in his domain are strikingly similar
to Sadanobu's.

Like Sadanobu, Tadakazu introduced to his domain of Izumi in
1792 a system of birth allowances of one ryō and two bu, and three
bales of unhulled rice to every child beyond the firstborn. In 1797,
Tadakazu reduced the cash amount to one ryō, perhaps because the
policy was only partially successful. At best it stabilized but did not
increase Izumi's population, which in 1792 stood at 10,353 and in
1798 at 10,341.[92] In a further effort to increase the population,
Tadakazu also transferred peasants from Echigo to Izumi. In
order to elevate his subjects to a higher sense of morality, he invited
Hokujō Genyō, the same Shingaku teacher who was brought to
Shirakawa and whose lectures in Edo had deeply impressed Tadakazu
and Sadanobu in the 1780s, to visit his domain in 1794.[93] Under
Sadanobu, Tadakazu became junior councillor (1787/7/17), grand
chamberlain (1788/5/15), and senior councillor (1790/4/16 until
1798), a post which he also combined with that of overseer of
shogunal finances until 1793/10.[94]

In view of Sadanobu's recognized reputation as an earnest student
of politics, and later as an able administrator, it was no small honor to
be counted among his friends. Sadanobu's friendship was very
demanding. It was because he recognized in certain people an
unusual strength of character and leadership talents that Sadanobu

admitted them to his circle of friends. In his autobiography he left some very personal and not always flattering evaluations of his fellow daimyo.[95]

Matsudaira Nobuaki (1760–1817; lord of Yoshida, 70,000 koku; master of shogunal ceremonies; member of the Antechamber since 1784) was praised for his sharp intellect, his ability to deal with people and the true-heartedness with which he asked advice from Sadanobu. His talent, however, was greater than his character, and Sadanobu warned him not to be too idealistic. Nobuaki also became grand chamberlain (1788/2/2), senior councillor (1788/4/4 until 1803), chief councillor (1806–1817), and overseer of shogunal finances (1792/8/30 until 1795). It was mostly he who was responsible for the continuation of Sadanobu's policies beyond 1793, especially concerning the ban on heterodox doctrines.

Toda Ujinori (1754–1806), lord of the 100,000 koku domain of Ōgaki, was a man of great eloquence and patience who applied himself earnestly to his task of government. While Sadanobu was in Shirakawa, Toda consulted with him, by letter, about problems of government. After a short term as master of shogunal ceremonies (1789/6/18) and superintendent of temples and shrines (1789/11/24), Toda filled the same key positions as Tadakazu and Nobuaki: chamberlain (1790/4/16), senior councillor (1790/10/16 until 1806), and overseer of shogunal finances (1793/10 until 1796).

Kanō Hisachika (1753–1811) was lord of Hatta, a 10,000 koku domain, and a captain of the great guard since 1784. He was judged to be a person of integrity with a good judgment of people, sturdy and upright. Sadanobu said that he trusted him from the very first but that Hisachika's inclination to revere him as a god made him uncomfortable. Seven days after Sadanobu's nomination as chief councillor, Hisachika was promoted to chamberlain, and later he became junior councillor.

Some of Sadanobu's friends failed to obtain offices because they did not live up to his standards. Sadanobu judged Makino Tadakiyo (born in 1760; lord of the Nagaoka han of 74,000 koku, and master of shogunal ceremonies since 1781) to be too impetuous, although sincere and devoted to the task of government. He doubted that Tadakiyo was fit for important appointments. During Sadanobu's tenure, Tadakiyo held only the posts of superintendent of temples and shrines, and keeper of the Osaka castle. Only long after Sadanobu's retirement did he become Kyoto deputy and senior councillor.

Matsudaira Nobumichi (died in 1791; lord of Kameyama, 50,000 koku; superintendent of temples and shrines, and master of shogunal ceremonies under Sadanobu) was gentle but narrow-minded, asking for Sadanobu's advice even in private matters. Others, like Arima Shigesumi, Matsudaira Sadafumi, and Matsudaira Tadatsugu, "had no special talent but the talent of youth." Of these, only Shigesumi held the minor office of master of shogunal ceremonies under Sadanobu. Twenty years later, however, he rose to superintendent of temples and shrines, and junior councillor.

Sadanobu was tolerant of friends not outstandingly gifted, but he did not hesitate to break off his friendship with someone who showed no virtue or effort at moral improvement. Such was the case with Matsudaira Nobuyuki (lord of Kaminoyama, 30,000 koku), who was a passionate bird lover and squandered his resources on this luxurious hobby.

It is thus quite clear that Sadanobu was earnestly interested in talent, and that he had a keen eye in selecting capable collaborators. He proved that he could maintain the allegiance of his followers without resorting to extravagant material rewards. If the latter had been the case, there would have been justification for a purge of his clique after his resignation in 1793. When Sadanobu resigned, however, all his friends stayed in office.

REFORMIST INTRIGUE AND PLOT

Sadanobu's circle was, of course, not merely a group of uninvolved students of politics. Their concern with the state of bakufu affairs was prompted by the general discontent (referred to in chapter 1) that the bakufu had aroused among its vassal daimyo by its inability to assist them in coping with their problems and by its expansionist mercantilist policy. It is hard to say at which point their talk of discontent changed into a discussion of tactics to bring about political change; or to what extent they were aware of Sadanobu's plans in this respect. It is, nevertheless, certain that Sadanobu harbored such plans, as we know from an undated memorandum he allegedly sent to the shogun some months after Tanuma's fall toward the end of 1786 or early in 1787.

This document, discovered by Tsuji Zennosuke and first published in 1936 in his famous study on the Tanuma regime,[96] is a lengthy discussion of several administrative improvements that had to be made. Bribery and corruption, sumptuary laws, prostitution, reform of the mores of the shogun's retainers, the reclamation of land, and fire prevention zones in Edo (1786 had witnessed another conflagration in Edo) are all treated in great detail. It is the information in this document about Sadanobu's plot against Tanuma that is of interest in the present context.

Sadanobu describes how he had resolved in a patriotic spirit (*shishirashii*) to die for his ideal of rectifying the realm by assassinating Tanuma. He had been driven since the age of six, he observed, by a desire to serve the shogun. With assassination in mind, he went several times to the shogun's palace with a dagger hidden in his belt. He knew that fame would await him. But then he had had second thoughts. He realized that he was plotting an act of disloyalty toward the shogun, and that as a result of his action several senior councillors might lose their post (*tachiba o ushinau*). He therefore dismissed the assassination plan. Instead, in consort with Tayasu (which meant his stepmother), and with some faithful councillors, he decided to obtain an important office in the bakufu and to work from there toward Tanuma's downfall. Sadanobu admits rather candidly that, in buying his way into Tanuma's bureaucracy, he might have blemished his good reputation. He finally succeeded (on 1785/12/1) in securing for himself a seat in the Antechamber.[97]

In order to reconstruct the development of Sadanobu's shift in tactics, one has to take a close look at the major events between his succession to the house in 1783 and his official appointment as chief councillor in 1787:

1783/10/19	Sadanobu's succession;
11/	Tanuma Okitomo becomes junior councillor; opposition of the daimyo in Osaka; seven-year frugality plan declared by the bakufu;
1784/3/24	Okitomo assassinated;
6/24	Sadanobu leaves for Shirakawa;
1785/6/	Sadanobu returns from Shirakawa;
12/1	Sadanobu enters the Antechamber;
1786/6/	Sadanobu leaves for Shirakawa;
8/27	Tanuma Okitsugu resigns;
12/15	The Three Houses propose Sadanobu as a candidate to the bakufu;
1787/2/1	Sadanobu's candidacy is rejected;
5/20–24	Riot in Edo;
6/1	Sadanobu rushes back from Shirakawa;
6/7	Withdrawal of some objections against Sadanobu;
6/19	Official appointment as chief councillor.

The memorandum discussed above was written between Tanuma Okitsugu's resignation and Sadanobu's appointment—possibly at the end of 1786—when the Three Houses and the house of Hitotsubashi (the native house of the shogun) recommended Sadanobu as the new head of government.

It was also about this time that some high official wrote the recently discovered *Tenmei kōsetsu*, revealing the existence of a rather widely known plot in the Interior to assassinate Tanuma a few days prior to the shogun's death. The possibility exists, one may argue, that Sadanobu never seriously intended to assassinate Tanuma Okitsugu; that he merely tried, after the revelation of a plot, to enhance his own position in the power vacuum after Tanuma's fall. The element of well-timed pressure was undeniably present in Sadanobu's disclosure of his own assassination plan and, as such, is revealing of his political sense. But within the context of the events and of his own psychology, Sadanobu's words gain considerable credibility.

Hayashi Motoi conjectures that Sadanobu started his drive to enter the Antechamber after he came back to Edo in 1785/6.[98] There exists, however, another undated document, listing swords, cash, embroidered gossamer, etc., given to different officials and ladies of the Interior as gifts in connection with the Antechamber (*tamarinoma onrei*). (I discovered the document at the house of a former deputy in the town of Sukagawa in Shirakawa; for a translation, see Appendix C.) The document appears to be a notification that such gifts were sent to the appropriate persons. But if Sadanobu had started his drive after his return to Edo, there would have been no need for such a note to be sent to Shirakawa. Its existence is an indication that Sadanobu, in agreement with his stepmother, had switched his plans from assassination to politics, probably before leaving for Shirakawa in 1784/6. There are therefore good reasons to believe that he changed tactics after he had realized that the assassination of Tanuma Okitomo on 1784/3/24 had no political consequences (Sano Masakoto, the assassin, actually became very famous, but he was ordered to commit suicide on 1784/4/3). Sadanobu's own plans to assassinate Tanuma Okitsugu and his visits to the castle with a hidden dagger should therefore antedate Okitomo's slaying.

This brings us very close to the end of 1783 when anti-Tanuma feeling among the daimyo had reached a climax, and when the Three Houses had already been highly displeased by Tanuma's appointment (in 1781) of a shogunal heir without consulting them. Sadanobu's determination to bring about political change, if necessary through a coup d'état, thus goes back at least as far as 1783 and possibly farther.

It should be remembered that in the years 1781–82 his despair about the political situation was particularly acute, and that at that time also he started his training in Shimbu no michi, which heightened his self-perception as a man with divine potential and with a mission to accomplish. Sadanobu's political friends may for some time have been ignorant of his strategy to reform politics, but they certainly were well informed about his ultimate purpose.

Sadanobu's decision to bring about political change by bureaucratic maneuvering rather than by a bloody coup d'état had far-reaching consequences. Usually the intensification process of the will to alter the political system takes the other direction, namely, resort to violence when bureaucratic means fail. With Sadanobu, the same intense concern with political improvement that had nearly led him to become an assassin was now directed into his determination to become a bureaucrat. The deep trust in his own willpower was turned inward and given an institutional orientation. The conviction of his divine mission was redirected to animate a bureaucratic task.

Sano, Okitomo's assassin, had in no time been acclaimed as *yonaoshi daimyōjin* (Great August Deity of the Rectification of the World) and had become the object of a cult that caused great embarrassment to the bakufu.[99] Sadanobu too viewed himself as rectifier of the world. His entry into the Antechamber, however, did not automatically bring about the desired change. Two months before Tanuma's resignation, Sadanobu returned to Shirakawa, but the drive for new leadership continued, led by the Three Houses, which were instrumental in Tanuma's downfall. They had to reckon with massive bureaucratic opposition; and had it not been for the added pressure of a vicious riot that erupted in Edo at the end of 1787/5, they might never have succeeded in breaking the deadlock over Sadanobu's appointment.

Hitotsubashi Harusada, father of the shogun Ienari, was worried about the lack of leadership shown by the senior councillors. In 1786/10 he wrote a letter to the lord of Mito, expressing his concern about finding someone who could restore the affairs of the bakufu to a situation similar to the Kyōhō era of Yoshimune's reforms. He thought it wise first to get the consent of the Three Houses on some candidates before presenting them to the senior councillors. He also advised Mito to keep these consultations secret from the Mito elder, lest the news reach the bakufu too early.[100] Mito, together with Owari, won Kii over to their plan. Next, Hitotsubashi proposed to Owari and Mito three candidates for the post of senior councillor (Matsudaira Sadanobu, Sakai Tadamitsu, and Toda Ujinori, a friend of Sadanobu), especially recommending Sadanobu, and two for the post of junior councillor (Inagaki Sadagazu and Sadanobu's closest friend, Honda Tadakazu).[101]

On 1786/12/15, the Three Houses proposed Sadanobu to the senior council. One month later, the lord of Mito inquired about the reaction to their proposals but received the elusive answer that the matter was under consideration. Obviously the Tanuma faction was still firmly in power. On new year's day, Tanuma, with a rank equivalent to that of senior councillor, even paid a visit to the shogun.[102] And there was talk about bringing Tanuma back. On 1787/2/1, Lady Ōzaki, leader of Tanuma's associates in the Great Interior, notified the lord of Owari in his Ichigaya mansion that the senior councillor Mizuno Tadatomo, one of Tanuma's most powerful protégés,* was opposed to the nomination of Matsudaira Sadanobu. Moreover, she argued, a rule laid down by Ieshige, the ninth shogun, forbade close relatives of the shogun to hold an important office.[103]

Shogunal precedent was a weighty argument to use against the collaterals. Nevertheless, Hitotsubashi Harusada argued that the rule applied only to in-laws of the shogun so that the objection did not apply to Sadanobu. On 2/13 Lady Ōzaki communicated to the lord of Owari that the case would be reconsidered, but on 2/21 she announced that Lady Tanehime, Sadanobu's sister and adopted daughter of the former shogun Ieharu, was opposed to the appointment. On 2/28 the official answer from the senior council to the Three Houses stated that Sadanobu could not be appointed because of Ieshige's rule, and because Sadanobu through his sister (adopted by Ieharu and thus stepsister to the present shogun Ienari) had become brother to the shogun.[104] It was around this time that Sadanobu wrote the memorandum on administrative reform. According to Hayashi Motoi, its content and style make it unlikely that it was intended for the shogun. Motoi is inclined to think that it was meant for the elder Mizuno Tadatomo, who opposed Sadanobu's nomination but who was also informed about the plot in the Interior to assassinate Tanuma. Mention of the plan to assassinate Tanuma may well have been a threat to Mizuno in order to win him over to the reformist camp.[105] In any case, the tactic seems to have failed. Two new senior councillors were appointed (Torii Tadaoki in 1786/11 and Abe Masatomo in 1787/3) without regard for the reformists' wishes.

*Mizuno Tadatomo and Tanuma rose together in the bakufu hierarchy. He started out as chamberlain with 7,000 *koku*; by 1781, he had been put in charge of shogunal finances, and when in 1785 he became regular senior councillor his holdings amounted to 30,000 *koku*. (Hall, *Tanuma Okitsugu*, pp. 51-52.)

In 1787/5 the situation suddenly changed. This time again, as in 1783, it was a riot that finally brought Sadanobu to power. The Edo riot was the culmination of over a hundred disturbances caused by another exceedingly disastrous year for agriculture (there was a nationwide crop failure of over 30 percent) which had erupted all over Japan between 1786/10 and 1787/6. In the fifth month alone there were nineteen disturbances in major cities and towns throughout the country.[106] In addition, Edo had been ravaged by fires in the spring of 1786 and by a flood in the summer of the same year, strengthening the popular belief that 1786, an unfortunate hino-e uma zodiac year (a combination of the first fire sign with the horse) that comes around once every sixty years, was bound to be a year of disaster.* By the end of 1786, elderly men and women from the surrounding countryside swarmed into Edo, beggars who sang and danced in an eerie, trancelike fashion. The phenomenon was a forerunner of the *eeja-naika* frenzy ("anything goes"—a chant to which thousands of elated commoners danced in the city streets) of the fall of 1867. In 1787, prices soared higher than they had even in 1784; one koku of white rice cost 167.9 momme as compared to 111.2 three years earlier (the price had never been higher than 100 momme since 1716 and would not return to that level until the 1830s. Sake reached an all-time high for the same period: 153 momme per koku in 1784 and 162 in 1787.[107]

The riot that broke out on 1787/5/20 was the worst Edo had ever known. In a few days, 980 rice shops and hundreds of licensed merchant stores, pawnshops and sake shops were destroyed.[108] It was also the first riot that was clearly of the yonaoshi type, which was to spread throughout Japan in the bakumatsu period; the destruction was carried out by people who, in their desperation, hoped in a semireligious way for a new, more egalitarian world order. Low-class Shugendō exorcists and magico-religious reciters seem to have been the spiritual leaders of the movement,[109] which obviously had political overtones. As we have seen, Tanuma Okitomo's assassin had three years earlier been acclaimed as a deity. In the Edo riot also, two different documents report that the rioters believed they were being led by a sturdy and fierce-looking samurai (possibly suggesting Sano) and by a handsome young man who rode in front of them in the

---

*Tamura Eitarō, *Yonaoshi* (Tokyo: Yūzankaku, 1960), p. 50. The belief in an unlucky zodiac year undoubtedly exerts some influence upon the "mood" of a time. This was still evident in 1966, also a *hino-e uma* year. Girls born in such years are said to be prone to devouring their husbands, and thus their parents find it somewhat difficult to make a match. In the first six months of 1966, a 25 percent drop in births was reported in Japan (*Japan Times*, Sept. 12, 1966, Editorial).

skies—a symbol of their hopes represented by the twenty-eight-year-old lord of Shirakawa?[110] From the bakufu's viewpoint the situation looked frightening. After two days of turmoil a militia totaling three thousand men was sent into the city to restore order, a force equivalent to the one that was to meet Commodore Perry in Shinagawa sixty years later. The dismissal of three chamberlains (*sobayō-toritsugi*) in the wake of the riot, allegedly because they misinformed the shogun about the seriousness of the situation, cleared the way for Sadanobu. On the twenty-fourth, Hongō Yasuyuki was dismissed, followed on the twenty-eighth by Tanuma Okimune, and on the twenty-ninth by the most senior chamberlain, Yokota Noritoshi.[111]

The day before Sadanobu's scheduled return to Edo for his yearly residence duty, a messenger arrived in Shirakawa (two days travel away from Edo), with the news of the Edo riot, which made Sadanobu hasten his departure by a few hours.[112] On 6/7 Lady Ōzaki appeared again at the Ichigaya mansion with the good news that Lady Tanehime had withdrawn her objection. Two days later she let it be known informally that Sadanobu would be appointed. His appointment as chief councillor was made official on 6/9.[113] Sugita Gempaku, a contemporary observer, points out that, without the riot, there probably would not have been a change in the bakufu at all.[114]

In making himself the obvious and almost indispensable candidate to reform bakufu leadership, Sadanobu, like most statesmen, skillfully matched his ambitions, personality, and leadership image to the needs of his time. To assume his role of reformer, he used a variety of political levers: the prestige and wealth of his family, the political flair of his stepmother, the discontent of a politically relevant sector of the elite, the image of a selfless ruler in a time of corruption— even bribery and intrigue, including a plan for assassination, when these seemed the only access to power. His mode of operation was a mixture of personal leadership and strategic planning. This political style continued to characterize Sadanobu during his rule as chief councillor.

4 Bureaucratic Reformer

The establishment of efficient government was Sadanobu's central aim and his greatest achievement. Although historians have tended to characterize him as a "traditionalist" and a "conservative," Sadanobu reveals in his bureaucratic reform of the bakufu administration a statesmanlike vision of great realism. He seems to have developed a growing awareness of the need to broaden the scope of government in the management of certain key areas of society.

First, Sadanobu improved bakufu bureaucracy. He purged corrupt officials and promoted new talent. He then went beyond the immediate bureaucracy, seeking to establish administrative regularity in the financial and economic world, which was in the hands of a small group of independent merchants. Through his decree on the cancelations of debts (*kien-ryō*), Sadanobu brought the credit system under state regulations. Second, in a long dispute with the imperial court (the *songo jiken*, or Title Incident), Sadanobu unambiguously reasserted the bakufu as the primary political authority. Finally, for the first time in Japanese history, he made systematic use of ideology as an instrument for the mobilization of talent for governmental service. This was the implication of the ban on heterodox doctrines (*igaku no kin*) and the revitalization of the Bakufu College.

In the short span of six years, Sadanobu not only corrected the mismanagement of his predecessor but laid solid foundations for a wider government role in regulating society.

Sadanobu dealt with the bakufu bureaucracy in terms of its composition and its policies. He renewed its personnel and reversed its policies. In both regards, he proceeded in strict bureaucratic manner, always properly submitting his policies for shogunal and councillor approval. In purging the bureaucracy, he never issued punitive measures singlehandedly. And he gave shape to his policies through an exchange of drafts, proposals, and amendments between himself and his cabinet (the Senior Council) or ad hoc committees. Despite this propriety in bureaucratic performance, Sadanobu's regime continued to bear the imprint of his personality. He relied heavily on his persuasive powers to make others accept or implement his policies. He continued to see himself as a chosen figure, pursuing a sacred mission. The personal character of Sadanobu's political style can be perceived most clearly in his dealings with bureaucratic personnel. His rational

administrative gifts are most prominent in his economic and financial reform.

RENOVATION OF THE BUREAUCRACY
Compared with the great political purges of the twentieth century,
Sadanobu's purge seems mild. It was, however, one of the major events
in the political history of the Tokugawa period.

Sadanobu purged the bureaucracy at all levels, including the high
councillor level and the administration of local bakufu territories. It
was a delicate task, requiring political refinement. Sadanobu came as a
solitary reformer to a bureaucracy packed with Tanuma protégés,
whose cooperation he needed to cultivate, though he knew that some
would inevitably fall victim to his reform. Moreover, Tanuma's cabinet
was an entire generation older than Sadanobu: four of his five
colleagues were twice his age (see table 3). At age twenty-eight, he was
the youngest senior councillor ever to hold the position, except for
Hotta Masamori, who in the early bakufu in 1633 became senior
councillor at age twenty-five (until Sadanobu's time, the average age of
senior councillors at the time of their appointment was forty-six).[1]
Sadanobu, it is true, had a clear shogunal mandate, but the shogun was
still young and manipulatable and thus open to eventual maneuvering
by Sadanobu's opponents.

About three months after he took office, Sadanobu started his reform
with a purge of the central bureaucracy below the councillors. He
dismissed thirty functionaries of the finance office (*kanjōkata*), twenty
in the office of public works (*fushinkata*), and one of the two Kyoto
magistrates. Punishments followed the dismissals. He further reduced
Tanuma's domain to 10,000 koku and had Tanuma himself placed
under house arrest.[2] At the end of 1786, he also placed two superintendents of finance, Matsumoto Hidemochi and Akai Tadaakira, under
house arrest and deprived them of half of their stipends. He sentenced
to death a former section head in the finance department, Tsuchiyama
Sōjūrō, for falsification of census registers and involvement in a rice
scandal. Numerous functionaries under Tsuchiyama were punished,
receiving sentences ranging from fines to death penalties.[3] As late as
1789, Sadanobu reports dismissing over fifty officials in a single year.[4]

Sadanobu had to conduct the purge of 1787 with all of Tanuma's
cabinet members still in power. Since all cases were well documented
public offenses, it was impossible for the councillors to refuse their
approval. Neither could they charge Sadanobu with conducting the
dismissals in an indiscriminate way. Here, as in all serious matters,
Sadanobu never acted alone. From the beginning, his regime was a
cabinet government. Abandoning the system of monthly rotation by

TABLE 3 Turnover of Seats in Senior and Junior Councils under Sadanobu

(a) Senior Council

Age[a]	Name	'87	'88	'89	'90	'91	'92	'93	
	TANUMA OKITSUGU ('72–86/9)								
68	Matsudaira Yasutomi ('63)		4/3(d)						
56	Makino Sadanaga ('84)				2/2(r)				
56	Mizuno Tadatomo ('85)		3/28(d)						
70	Torii Tadaoki ('86/i10)							2/29(r)	
42	Abe Masatomo	3/7							
28	MATSUDAIRA SADANOBU	6/19	2/29(r)					7/23	
28	Matsudaira Nobuaki		4/4					8/15(†)	1803(†)
37	Matsudaira Norisada			4/11					1798(ds)
41	Honda Tadakazu				4/16				1806(†)
36	Toda Ujinori				10/16				
54	Ōta Sukeyoshi							3/1	1801(r)

Junior Council

Name	'87	'88	'89	'90	'91	'92	'93	
(Tanuma Okitomo, '83/11–'84/4/2†)								
Ōta Sukeyoshi ('81)			4/11 (Kyoto deputy)				8/24 (Sen. c.)	1812(ds)
Andō Nobunari ('84)								
Matsudaira Tadatomi ('86/i10)		4/11 (r)						
Ii Naoakira ('86/i10)								
Honda Tadakazu	7/17		4/4 (Grand Chamberlain)					
Aoyama Yoshisada	3/22						9/18(r)	1808(†)
Kyōgoku Takahisa	6/16							
Hotta Masaatsu				6/10				1832(r)

Symbols

a Age of Tanuma's senior councillors when Sadanobu became chief councillor, and of Sadanobu's appointees at the time they joined the Senior Council.

i Intercalary.

d Dismissed.

r Retired.

† Died.

ds Dismissed for reason of sickness.

Compiled from the *Ryūei bunin* and Watanabe, *Denki dai Nihon-shi: Daimyo-hen.*

which one senior councillor was periodically responsible for routine affairs, he involved all senior councillors in political consultations. Often junior councillors, inspectors, superintendents of temples and shrines, superintendents of finance, and the Edo city magistrates (the so-called three *bugyō*) were all involved in deliberations. Matters on which no agreement could be reached were shelved. In the purges too, Sadanobu examined each case separately and brought it to the attention of the shogun before issuing sentence.[5]

In order to give a solid basis to his reform, Sadanobu had to have control of both councils. The Senior Council functioned as a cabinet and had wide authority over the formation of government policy and the administration of bakufu affairs on a nationwide scale. The junior councillors were important for their management of the shogun's vassals, attendants, and guards.[6] Above the councillors was the office of great councillor (*tairō*), a post without political importance. During the entire Tokugawa period only ten incumbents filled this office for short periods of time; it amounted to little more than a symbolic title. In 1784, Ii Naohide obtained the honor from Tanuma through bribery.[7] On 1787/9/11, he preferred to resign his superfluous post on his own accord, rather than wait for his dismissal from a bureaucracy that was being streamlined toward greater efficiency.

Toward the end of 1787, six months after Sadanobu took office, all senior and junior councillors from Tanuma's time were still in power. Since they were his colleagues, it was virtually impossible for Sadanobu to have them removed. On 1787/11/4, he sent a memorandum to the Three Houses, expressing his desire to change certain appointments "when the opportunity would arise, perhaps in the coming spring." Three months later, in a memorandum of 1788/2/19, he was more emphatic. He stated that he needed more power, and suggested for himself either the post of great councillor, vacated by Ii Naohide, or the rank of major general (*shōshō*). On 2/28, the Three Houses and the lord of Hitotsubashi, the shogun's father, proposed to nominate Sadanobu the shogun's regent.[8] They reasoned that great councillor was a fudai office, but there was a precedent for nominating a *shimpan*, or related daimyo, to the office of regent (Hoshina Masayuki, lord of Aizu and regent to the fourth shogun, Ietsuna). As regent, Sadanobu's decisions were virtually identical with shogunal will.

This additional power in Sadanobu's hands had its desired effect. Four days before Sadanobu was officially nominated the shogun's regent on 3/4, the first senior councillor, Abe Masatomo, left his post; and within one month one junior councillor (Matsudaira Tadatomi) retired, and two senior councillors (Mizuno Tadatomo and Matsudaira Yasutomi) were dismissed without any explanation. The vacant places were filled by Sadanobu's associates, who were considerably younger than their predecessors. By the beginning of 1790, only one of the five senior councillors and two of the four junior councillors who had been in office at the time of Sadanobu's appointment remained on the two councils.

In 1789, after he had secured his base among the bureaucrats in Edo, Sadanobu focused his attention upon local administration. Here bribery and corruption at the daikan level and below had taken the form of embezzlement of taxes, peculations with grain deliveries, and profitable arrangements with the merchants. It is not known how many of the more than fifty officials deposed in 1789 were local officials, but at least eight or nine deputies out of an approximate total of forty were replaced.[9]

The problem was not limited to corrupt officials. Licensed merchants, for example, abused their position as intermediaries between the tax-paying villagers and the bakufu storehouses. In the 1750s, the government had licensed several guilds of *osameyado*, collectors, in Edo, Osaka, and Kyoto. They were responsible for the transport of the tax grains, and in that capacity had ample opportunity to make deals with the peasants, engage in moneylending, or press for commissions under a variety of pretexts. In 1789/9, Sadanobu dissolved the Osaka and Kyoto collector guilds;[10] one year later, he also abolished the twelve Edo guilds. This first step in expanding bureaucratic control to tax collection not only prevented merchants from enriching themselves on a service to the state, at the expense of the peasants; it also brought down the cost of this service (which was shouldered by the peasants) from forty silver momme per hundred bales (equals thirty-five koku) to seventeen momme. From 1790/9 the villages in the Kanto area were directly responsible for the storing of the grain, and Sadanobu entrusted the control of the operation to a private rice merchant, Ōmiya Kizaeimon, who was joined two months later by three other merchants. They still functioned as private entrepreneurs, but in 1794, with the establishment of an agency for rice collection (*mawari kome osamekata kaisho*), under the jurisdiction of the superintendents of finance, they became four official purveyors (*goyōtachi*) in the service of the government. In Osaka, the bakufu bypassed altogether the technical skills of merchants and entrusted the checking and storage of incoming rice to two deputies.[11]

Sadanobu profited greatly from his experience in Shirakawa to redress the morale of the bureaucracy. In order to stress the public character of the officials, he had, for instance, added in Shirakawa a record keeper to every office.[12] Sadanobu took similar steps for his bakufu functionaries. He prohibited them from bringing official records to their private residences, and held them responsible for classifying and shelving the records of their offices so that they would be available to their successors.[13]

Renewal of personnel and morale and refinement of bureaucratic procedures would not have had lasting effects had Sadanobu not tackled the problem of bureaucratic decay at its root. The problem lay in the distorted power relationships between the Exterior (public functionaries) and the Interior or the shogun's court. Tanuma had completed the shift of power from the Exterior to the Interior—a trend already started by Yoshimune. In the Interior the chamberlains (*go-yōtoritsugi*) had developed their role as intermediaries between the shogun and the senior councillors into a key political position: the grand chamberlain (*sobayōnin*) especially had become the central figure in all policy making, and many officials sought to influence him to their own advantage. Sadanobu saw to it that legitimate power returned to the Senior Council, and that this cabinet had direct access to the shogun.

He appointed his trusted friends to the office of grand chamberlain (Matsudaira Nobuaki on 1788/2/2, Honda Tadakazu on 5/15, and Toda Ujinori on 1790/4/16). After Toda became senior councillor on 1790/10/16, Sadanobu left the office vacant (the next appointment as grand chamberlain was made in 1812). In a policy statement issued shortly after he became regent (*Yōkun hōshi kokoroe*, Directives for service of the young shogun), Sadanobu urged the severance of all political ties between the Interior and the Exterior. The intermediary role of the *go-yōtoritsugi* was abolished. Clerks (*yūhitsu*) and section heads (*kumigashira*) no longer shared decision-making power and state secrets. These prerogatives were returned to the Senior Council. His regime, Sadanobu declared, rested on two supports: The Three Houses and the Senior Council. These two institutions had to check each other, and both had to ensure that political authority did not pass again to the Interior.[14]

This reallocation of political power had far-reaching consequences. It made a clean break with Tanuma's practice and gave a new base to political power for the coming decades. The cabinet of the Senior Council regained its authority, and the collaterals received unprecedented although ill-defined political prestige.

Reversal of Tanuma's Policies

It is fashionable for historians to criticize Sadanobu's retrenchment policies, which, after Tanuma's mercantile expansionism, "turned back the development of Japanese society" or "restrengthened the feudal aspects of society."[15] This view, however, rests upon the dubious conception that liberal mercantilism, if unhampered, will lead to unqualified liberation, welfare, and progress, regardless of temporal or social conditions. Recent historical developments in the developing countries have prompted economists and sociologists to discount that view. Two things should be borne in mind in evaluating Sadanobu's reaction to Tanuma's legacy.

First, the socio-political bakuhan system was still vital and flexible enough to reinvigorate and adapt itself and to gain enough new momentum to survive for another two generations. If there had been no resources of institutional vitality, Sadanobu's reform would have been a failure from the outset. Second—and more speculatively—no matter how innovating or "modern" Tanuma's policies, there is no indication that they would have salvaged the government without greater cost to the whole of society. Those of his policies that were adopted were unable to meet the social and economic problems of a particularly difficult period. Other projects were rejected as too radical by an opposition that had grown strong enough to weigh seriously the extreme possibility of political assassination.

With Sadanobu, it is generally admitted, politics again took precedence over economics. From the political point of view, Sadanobu's bureaucraticism and his use of ideology precurse cardinal features of the modern Meiji state. But even in the economic field, where Tanuma is said to have been ahead of his time, Sadanobu was not simply setting the clock back. His agriculturalism did not blind him to the potential of merchant capital for the well functioning of the government. On the contrary, he found means for subjecting it to bureaucratic control and initiative.

On the basis of statistics alone, Sadanobu's economic record is a good one. When, in 1787, Sadanobu inquired about the following year's budget, he was told that the bakufu was running into a deficit of 1,000,000 ryō.[16] (The average yearly cash income of the bakufu in the eighteenth century was around 800,000 ryō.)[17] After three years, Sadanobu had drastically changed that situation: in 1789 the deficit was down to 39,000 ryō; the next two years each saw a surplus of 75,000 ryō; 1792 recorded a small deficit of 12,000 ryō; but in 1793, the surplus was again substantial—62,000 ryō, and 36,000 koku. After Sadanobu's tenure the treasury maintained a balance for some years but then slipped back into the red; in 1815, the accumulated deficit had reached 4,409,000 ryō.[18]

Financial solvency was in Sadanobu's words a question of "returning (*kisuru*) the hold on capital and rice, now in the hands of merchants, back to the government."[19] In order to do so, Sadanobu had to break the autonomous power of the merchants, cut expenses, strengthen the peasant base of the bakufu's revenues, reestablish control over the market, and bring money circulation under government regulation. This vast program was nothing less than a reversal of Tanuma's liberal mercantilist and expansionist policies.

The most salient aspects of this reversal are well known and need not be elaborated upon here. Sadanobu abolished a number of guilds and monopolies established under, or prior to, Tanuma: the monopolies on iron, brass, and ginseng; the guilds of firewood wholesalers and brokers, of charcoal wholesalers, and of blacksmith charcoal brokers in Osaka; the rapeseed wholesalers guild; and the cottonseed wholesale and brokers guild in Edo.[20] Furthermore, in a move of economic retrenchment, Sadanobu curtailed foreign trade in Nagasaki and scrapped the plans for the economic development of Ezo (Hokkaido).

Perhaps the most famous—and most disliked—feature of Sadanobu's regime was the straightjacket of his sumptuary laws. Government regulation of consumption was not his innovation. Even Tanuma had issued frugality laws. What was new was that under Sadanobu such laws were seriously enforced and were effective. Inevitably, however, they interfered in the daily life of the people; prostitutes, hairdressers, gamblers, writers of popular literature, and expensive fashions fell victim to Sadanobu's moralistic zeal for austerity.

Sadanobu asked from his subjects the same discipline that he practiced in his own life. He implemented his frugality program partly by government imposition and partly by an appeal to the people for self-restraint. Details of the restrictions were spelled out in the regulations issued during the first two-year frugality period, which started in 1789/9. These regulations certainly contributed to the bakufu's financial recovery, but they did not complete it. It will be seen that other bureaucratic measures were perhaps more decisive.

RELIGIOUS ZEAL IN BUREAUCRATIC SERVICE

Whatever the merits and demerits of Tanuma and Sadanobu in terms of the results of their respective policies, it is clear that their achievements were the outcome of two totally different political styles. Tanuma, who gained power through intrigue and politicking in the Interior, continued to rely on bribery and favoritism, both for ruling the bakufu and for aggrandizing himself. Sadanobu's reliance on political intrigue was only an additional means of obtaining an important political post to which he had made himself the natural claimant through his administrative achievements in Shirakawa. The political zeal, stemming from his sense of mission, that animated his rule in Shirakawa and brought into play his personal qualities as a leader characterized also his bakufu rule. Sadanobu ensured the loyalty of his followers as he had done in Shirakawa and in his political coterie in Edo, not through bribery or the promise of rewards, but through moral persuasion.

After the spring of 1788, when his associates were seated in key positions, Sadanobu continued to command their respect as he had done during his Shirakawa years. But even earlier in his rule he made full use of his personal qualities as a committed and persuasive leader.

For instance, as he had done in Shirakawa, Sadanobu inaugurated his regime with a general meeting of his main officials. On 1787/7/1, he summoned one representative of each office to an assembly where they were first addressed by the shogun. He subsequently exhorted them to close cooperation in bringing about administrative reforms patterned on Yoshimune's Kyōhō Reform. Sadanobu saw to it that these officials returned to their offices with a copy of his statement.[21] And again in 1788/1, after having fixed the budgets for the various offices at their lowest level, he called all major officials individually and inculcated in them the need to curtail expenses and not to exceed the new budget ceilings. He thus communicated his personal concern to the city magistrates; the superintendents of works, finance, public works, construction, and repair; the magistrate of Nagasaki; the attendant heads, and the food purveyors of the shogunal kitchen (*makanaikata*).[22]

Sadanobu maintained a religious devotion to his work as statesman, and his zeal permeated his exercise of authority through persuasion. It should be noted that religion in this context is not conditioned by the acceptance of a religious doctrine, as is a common assumption in the West. Dogma is not necessary for convictions and behavior to acquire a religious quality. Sadanobu's subjective sense of the absolute character of his mental, emotional, and behavioral orientation gave deep religious quality to his personality. Neither should modern scholars deny the possibility of a genuine religious quality to the political behavior of a statesman of the past. Sadanobu looked upon himself as a yonaoshi daimyōjin, a god who rectifies the wrongs of society. His commitment to that calling was total. In the same month that Sadanobu exhorted his major officials to cooperate with his reform (1788/1), he paid a private visit to the Kitsushō cloister in Reiganjima (Edo). There he pledged to the Kangiten deity*

---

*The Kangiten deity is a god of Buddhist origin, whose function it is to eradicate evil and bring happiness. In Japan, this god is usually represented by the statue of an embracing man and woman; the male representing the angry god, ready to unleash calamities over the world; the female, an incarnation of Kanon, through her compassionate embrace inviting him to bring happiness that he would bring his reform to a successful end. More specifically, Sadanobu vowed to make rice again available at a normal price and to bring about financial solvency; to this purpose he offered his own life and that of his wife and children.[23]

Sadanobu made two other vows of a similar nature. One is recorded toward the end of his autobiography; here also he puts his life and that of his family at stake for the restoration of peace in the country, and he adds that he directed these requests to Ieyasu, seven, eight, ten times a day.[24] The second document, deposited in the shrine of the Hisamatsu Matsudaira family's founder in Shirakawa, was written shortly after Sadanobu became regent to the shogun in 1788/3; it adds some detail to his program of return to the Kyōhō era: government control of money and rice, and the building of reserves as a preservative measure against natural disaster.[25]

These documents are genuine reflections of Sadanobu's persistent religious perception of his task. Not meant to be seen by outsiders (the first vow of 1788/1 was discovered in 1838, eleven years after Sadanobu's death), the vows were made at a crucial moment of his reform. After the purges, he was seeking means to establish his own cabinet in order to start his own program. Since he saw his task essentially as one of rectifying the empire during the shogun's minority, he had only a few years left and therefore could not simply wait until Tanuma's councillors retired. Moreover the thought of a premature death never left Sadanobu. At this juncture, the zeal of the near-assassin-turned-bureaucrat expressed itself with new sharpness in his vow to offer his own life and that of his family for the successful completion of his mission.

RESTORATION OF TAX FARMING

The economic health of the country depended upon the stability of the peasant class. Both the bakufu and the domains had taken sporadic measures, with different degrees of success, to preserve that stability. Sadanobu's Kansei Reform was the first national attempt to restore the peasant tax base of the country.

According to Sadanobu, the national census figures for 1786, compared to those of 1780, showed a drop of 1,400,000. Obviously, he adds, all these people did not die: having become vagrants or mountain priests (*yamabushi,* "lower-class ascetics of questionable religious quality"),[26] or having flocked to Edo, they disappeared from

instead. Inobe mentions that during one of Sadanobu's youthful sicknesses, a lady-in-waiting (*rōjo*) had made a pilgrimage here. In a diary of his later years (*Kagetsu nikki*) Sadanobu relates that he often visited the temple (Inobe, "Hosa shūnin," pp. 9-10).

the records because of the instability of the economic conditions.[27]
This state of flux in the agricultural sector created social problems in
the cities and no doubt contributed to the violence of the 1787/5 Edo
riot. Through his efforts to tie the peasants to the land, Sadanobu
tried to solve both rural and city problems at the same time.

His policy was not limited to bakufu territories. Sadanobu repeatedly issued edicts (in 1788, 1790, 1791 and 1793) for the repatriation of
Edo vagrants to their home provinces or to other locations; in
addition to cash for the return trip, loans were made available at
lenient terms for the purchase of farm equipment and seeds, or for
house construction.[28] Peasants throughout the land were prohibited
from seeking employment outside their native provinces. In addition,
Sadanobu established in 1790/3 a workshop (*yoseba*) on Ishikawa
Island for the homeless and jobless of Edo. It accommodated some
two hundred persons, and its purpose was to rehabilitate vagrants and
criminals who had no employment or families to return to. They
worked there at simple crafts for a salary until an opportunity for
their return to society was found. The project was the realization of a
plan that had twice been suggested prior to Sadanobu's time (in the
1720s and the 1770s) but had never been acted upon. Sadanobu took
particular pride in this expression of "benevolent government."[29]

In the countryside, Sadanobu alleviated the burdens of overtaxed
peasants. In his *Kokuhonron* he points to the particular stress of
sukegō corvée levies. *Sukegō* were levied at the waystations for the
transportation of persons and goods. In 1789, Sadanobu forbade any
excess of the fixed amount of loads, numbers of persons, and horses
for each station.[30] His major project for the countryside was, however,
the building of reserves for bad years. In 1788, he ordered the
construction of storehouses in bakufu territories; in 1789/9 he set a
nationwide storage quota of 50 out of 10,000 koku over a five-year
period; the next year he ordered the building of storehouses in all
daimyo domains. Up until then, bakufu regulations as to rice storage
in daimyo domains had pertained only to castle rice, which was the
name for rice supplies for military purposes. This time, the implications were social and economic. The new local supplies played a role
in Sadanobu's efforts at stabilizing the rice price: they functioned as a
stabilizer at the local level through the commercial manipulation of
the stored grain at appropriate times. The peasants, by having their
savings managed at the district (daikan and gundai) level, were shown
the tangible results of Sadanobu's benevolent government and of their
own frugality.[31]

The problems of the bakufu, however real they may have been in
the countryside, were most serious in Edo. Here Sadanobu could not

rely upon his previous experience in Shirakawa han. He nevertheless produced new solutions that marked a clear departure from Tanuma's policies.

Edo Centrism

Tanuma's bakufu-first policy had developed at the expense of the daimyo domains and contributed in no small way to his downfall. Sadanobu's concern with the welfare of the bakufu was not less than Tanuma's, but his policy took the form of Edo centrism: he boosted the financial and economic strength of the bakufu's main territories around Edo; he did this mainly at the expense, not of the daimyo, but of the Osaka region and its merchants.

This attention to Edo's problems was no doubt inspired by the threat the government had experienced during the riots of 1787/5. Politically it was certainly a wise course of action. Sadanobu also displayed a shrewd economic skill, somewhat surprising in a man who so relentlessly stressed ethics in all his writings, even in his economic treatise of prices (*Bukkaron*), written in 1789/10. After a clear analysis of the three main items in inflation—the distorted equilibrium between the three currencies, the imbalance between dwindling production and overspending, and the inflationary mood of the people who grow accustomed to rising prices—he concludes conventionally that all three items are really symptoms of the craving for luxury.[32] But in Sadanobu's economic writings, as in his political ones, the moral rhetoric often concealed a sophisticated pragmatic view on financial and economic policy. His formalistic ethical characterization of social problems reflects an intellectual fashion of his time.[33] His program, however, was not a simple return to the moral purity of "Kyōhō times," as his own rhetoric made subsequent historians believe.[34]

Sadanobu's Edo centrism was manifested in three different ways: his monetary reform, the development of Edo's hinterland, and the new credit system that was set up after the cancelation of debts.

The Tokugawa currency system suffered chronic difficulties because it was (like the political system) only partly unified: it was a tri-metal system with fluctuating exchange rates, and with each metal limited, by custom and preference rather than by law, to a certain region or social class. The exchange ratio was based upon gold, the currency that prevailed in Edo. Silver, which circulated by weight, was Osaka's favored currency, and copper coins were used mainly by retail merchants for small financial transactions. Periodically, the government issued new denominations, sometimes debasing their value to its own profit, sometimes increasing the volume of a currency to respond to the growing commercial demands.[35]

In 1772, Tanuma had issued a new two-*shu* silver coin; its quality was 98 percent pure silver, and its official Edo exchange rate with gold was set at eight pieces for one ryō (or sixty momme per ryō). The new coin, however, became so much in demand that in Osaka it brought the price of gold down to fifty-three momme per ryō.[36] Copper coins met with an even greater devaluation. Around 1740, the scarcity of copper cash had pushed its value up to around 2,800 *mon* per gold ryō (the official rate was 4,000 mon to the ryō). In 1768, however, four-mon brass pieces were minted in great quantity, resulting in a surplus; five years later its market value fell to 5,780 mon to the ryō and continued to drop afterwards, causing commodity prices to rise steadily.[37]

Sadanobu's understanding of the monetary situation was in accord with Arai Hakuseki's theory, which ascribed the rise of commodity prices to the low quality of the denominations and to their overdistribution.[38] Sadanobu accordingly proceeded to revalue the gold and copper currencies by improving the quality of the former and reducing the quantity of the latter. In 1788 he stopped the minting of copper coins altogether, and at the same time recoined the two-shu silver coins. By 1791, the exchange rate of silver was back to sixty momme per ryō.[39]

Sadanobu's monetary reform was in fact a measure to strengthen Edo's financial and economic position. The previous more advantageous exchange rate of silver in Osaka had resulted in a constant 10 percent profit for Osaka merchants dealing with Edo: goods worth fifty-three momme in Osaka were sold in Edo for one ryō, which converted into silver in Edo yielded sixty momme. The monetary imbalance also had a negative effect on the flow of goods from the western part of Japan to Edo: Osaka merchants convinced western daimyo to sell their rice and goods in Osaka rather than ship them directly to Edo, which added to the inflationary trend of prices in Edo. On 1787/6/17, two weeks after the Edo riots, Getaya Jimbei had already drawn attention to this situation in his memorandum to the Kanto district delegate Ina Hanzaeimon.[40]

Great quantities of copper coins were shipped into Edo, where the official exchange rate was kept artificially high. Sadanobu prohibited their further importation and bought up great quantities of the coins.[41] This revaluation of the gold and copper metals functioned simultaneously as a device to restore the economic balance between Edo and Osaka, reduce the upward pressure on commodity prices, and weaken the economic position of Osaka merchants.

The development of Edo's hinterland had the same purpose. The commercial relations between Osaka and Edo were those of seller and

buyer: Osaka provided Edo with goods, and Edo's capital accumulated in Osaka. The importation of sake from Osaka, for example,
unnecessarily drained capital from the Kanto to the Kansai area. A
limitation on the importation of Osaka sake, together with a promotion of breweries around Edo, was directed at making the bakufu
economically more self-sufficient.[42] Sadanobu sought to reduce the
price of lamp oil in 1791 when he ordered the direct shipment of oil to
Edo from the producing areas Nagame, Nishinomiya, and Hyōgō in
the Kansai area, bypassing the Osaka market.[43] The rural cotton
production of the Kanto area was also organized and directly linked
up with the wholesale merchants of Edo without any intermediaries;
merchants that bypassed the wholesale merchants could not market
their goods at a cheaper price and threaten the wholesale merchants'
prices. The local rural merchants were thus directly involved in
strengthening the competitive position of the Edo market against
imported cotton. The same happened with the paper industry of
the nearby Mito domain: the ten paper guilds of Edo established direct
links with the rural merchants, bypassing the licensed wholesale
merchants of the castle town.[44]

The economic strengthening of the Kanto area was accompanied by
tighter administrative control, which explains the dismissal of the
Kanto district gundai, Ina Hanzaeimon Tadataka. His family had held
the office since its establishment in 1733. During the Tenmei famines,
Tadataka had become famous by distributing rice to the population of
Edo on a number of occasions.[45] Immediately after the Edo riot of
1787/5, his power and prestige increased even further. As Kanto
district deputy, Tadataka was under the jurisdiction of the office of
finance, but on 6/8 the office of the city magistrates put him in charge
of solving the problem of Edo's food supplies in the aftermath of the
riot. It will be remembered that Getaya Jimbei's memorandum was
addressed to him nine days later.[46]

The appeal to a local administrator for solving Edo's problems was
highly irregular, as Uezaki Kyūhachirō, a minor official, pointed out
in his memorandum to the newly appointed Sadanobu one month
later in 1787/7.[47] It had been prompted by the unresponsiveness of
one of the city magistrates, Magabuchi Kagetsugu, to the people's
needs. On 6/1, immediately after the riot, Kagetsugu had been
replaced by Ishikawa Tadatomi, but he in turn, on 9/27, was
succeeded by Yagyū Shuzennokami Hisamichi, who contributed
much to Sadanobu's financial policies. Tadataka wielded undue
power not only in Edo; he ruled his Kanto territories almost as an
independent lord.[48] In 1792, Sadanobu dismissed him from his deputy
post, and no new appointment was made: the responsibilities of his

office were now joined to that of the superintendents of finances. In the beginning of the nineteenth century, the office was abolished altogether.

CANCELATION OF DEBTS

Sadanobu's monetary reform of 1787 was only the first and least complicated step toward the financial and economic recovery of the bakufu. The circulation of capital and the stabilization of prices, especially the rice price, were necessary conditions for a return to economic normalcy. Any measures in this area, however, would clash with the economic interest of a well-established group of merchants. Over the last decades, a limited number of merchants had amassed great amounts of capital, kept it under control, and thus commanded its availability to the warriors. They also controlled the rice market and were often able to manipulate rice prices to their own advantage. Manipulation of the rice market not only affected the financial situation of the retainers, who were dependent on the cash value of their rice allowances, but it also interfered with the lives of the commoners by its effect on all commodity prices.

In handling this problem of the circulation of capital and goods, Sadanobu showed himself as an ingenious innovator. The solutions he adopted were not the product of his mind alone but were the result of a lengthy bureaucratic process of decision making. Sadanobu profited greatly from the expertise of men whose talents he skillfully coopted for the construction of his policies. Far from relying exclusively upon appeals to frugality and cutbacks in expenditures, Sadanobu's program succeeded by means of three new agencies (*kaisho*), which assured the bakufu of a permanent control of the economy—at least for some decades. The administration of the kaisho was entrusted to a new group of merchants called government purveyors (*goyōtachi*). Sadanobu secured their permanent and multifaceted assistance by establishing the agencies as joint ventures between the merchants and the government, structured so that the initial capital investment of the government was minimal and the profits of the merchant-administrators were limited. Not only were the kaisho financially self-sufficient, but they were also productive of new capital. The three agencies were the Loan Agency (*Saruya-machi kashikin kaisho*), the Edo Township Agency (*Shichibu kintsumitate Edo chōkaisho*), and the Collectors Agency (*Osamekata kaisho*).[49] All three were essential to the implementation of Sadanobu's reform, and the latter two were central for the execution of his decree on the cancelation of debts.

By the cancelation decree of 1789/9/16, Sadanobu succeeded in breaking the grip of the official rice brokers (*fudasashi*) on Edo's economy. The fudasashi were the most powerful segment of Edo's merchant class, and amassed their wealth by handling for the bakufu retainers their rice allowances and converting these allowances into cash. It should be noted that not all retainers depended on the services of the rice brokers, but the great majority did. Landed vassals (*jikatatori*), numbering some 2,600, lived from basic rank stipends, but some 19,800 minor vassals, accounting for about 545,000 koku, were provisioned from the bakufu's basic house land tax income (they were called *kuramaitori* because they received rice allowances from the bakufu's storehouses, *kura*). Since 1675, their yearly allowance was distributed in three portions: one-fourth in the second month; another fourth in the fifth month; and the remaining half in the tenth month. Very early in the Tokugawa period, the kuramaitori fell to the mercy of rice dealers for the conversion of their rice allowances into cash. Beginning in 1652, the bakufu tried to limit abuses by posting, on the pay days, an official exchange rate (*harigami nedan*) at which from one to two thirds of the received rice had to be exchanged; the rest could be sold through the rice merchants on the wholesale rice market in front of the bakufu's storehouses at the going market rates.[50]

Since 1724/7, the rice merchants were officially organized in a licensed rice brokers guild (*fudasashi kabunakama*), and over the years they became the financial elite of Edo.[51] They built their capital in three ways: from the handling fee for converting part of the allowance rice into cash (2 bu or half a ryō per 100 bales)[52]; from the 18 percent interest rate on loans made to needy retainers, who advanced their future rice allowances as securities; and from manipulating the rice market with the portion of the allowance rice that was not immediately converted into cash at the bakufu established rate.

In the decade preceding Sadanobu's regime, the bakufu had made an attempt to suppress the abuses of the rice brokers and to alleviate the debts of its retainers. In 1776, the bakufu ordered the rice brokers to lower their interest rates and to desist from manipulating the rice market; the brokers, however, retaliated with a general strike and forced the government to back down.[53] In 1786/11, loans (to be paid back in five yearly installments) were granted to *jikatatori* vassals with territories under 10,000 koku who had lost more than half of their crops through natural disasters; and in 1787/6, two-year loans were written for *kuramaitori* vassals with allowances under 100 bales of rice and five man rations. As stated in the decree's preamble, the cancelation of debts was the rescue measure for the *kuramaitori*, the bulk of whom had not benefited from the 1787 loans.[54]

The first initiative against the rice brokers under Sadanobu's administration was taken in 1788/3 by the northern city magistrate, Yagyū Shuzennokami Hisamichi, when he ordered the interest rate reduced from 18 to 15 percent.[55] From around that time, there was talk in administrative circles of taking serious action concerning the credit system of the rice brokers. Planning was started early in the following year on two fronts: the cancelation of debts and the establishment of a new credit system. The deliberations involved different levels of the administration and continued for several months. I will outline these deliberations in some detail, because they throw light on Sadanobu's style of collegiate rule and on the process of decision making in his regime.

Around 1789/2, Sadanobu proposed (a) that all debts older than twenty years be canceled; (b) that all debts contracted between ten and nineteen years previously be amortized over a twenty-year period without interest; (c) that debts contracted between five and nine years previously be amortized over a fifteen-year period; (d) that debts of the past five years be amortized with the usual interest (see table 4). The proposal was made to two superintendents of finance (Kuze Hirotami and Kubota Masakuni) and two city magistrates (Yamamura Yoshio and Hatsugano Nobutomo). The four officials immediately started an investigation of the financial situation of the rice brokers and found that, out of a total of ninety-seven rice brokers, only seven operated with their own capital, twenty-two showed fair financial health, and sixty-eight worked with loaned capital.[56] They concluded that, if Sadanobu's plan were executed, it would produce financial chaos. The situation was discussed by the comptrollers, one or two of the newly appointed financial purveyors, and the city elder Taruya Yozaeimon. On 3/13, the superintendent of finance, Kuze Hirotami, submitted the following amendments: (b') that the amortization period be adjusted within a range from thirty to fifty years, commensurate to the various amounts involved; (c') that the amortization periods in proposals (c) and (d) be changed to ten years at the reduced rate of 10 percent. Moreover, in their concern about the availability of capital after the cancelation, a factor which had been completely overlooked by Sadanobu, the committee proposed (1) to grant the rice brokers a 50,000 ryō loan, to be amortized over twenty years at no interest; and (2) to establish a loan agency.

The role of the city elder Taruya in this counterproposal was very important. The historian Matsuyoshi Sadao thinks that it was Taruya who proposed to make the bakufu share part of the burden of the cancelation through the investment of public money, and that he also

TABLE 4 Planning Stages of the Decree on the Cancelation of Debts

Sadanobu's proposal, 1789/2	Kuze Hirotami's counterproposal 3/13	Taruya Yozaemon's amendments, 7/	Cancelation decree, 9/16
Old debts			
(a) debts older than 20 years; cancel	(a') unchanged	debts before '84/12, to be amortized in adjusted repayments	→ cancelation
(b) 10-19 years old: pay back at no interest in 20 years	(b') at no interest, in 30-50 yearly installm. depend. upon amount		
(c) 5-9 years: in 15 yearly installments;	(c') at 10% in 10 years	debts between '85/1 and '89/5: at 6% in 5 yearl. installm.; after '89/5, at 12% from the fall rice;	→ idem
(d) 1-4 years: as usual.			
New credit system			
Public money	50,000 ryō at no interest, in 20 yearly installments;		2 x 10,000 ryō at 20 yearly installments
Agency	Loan Agency		
		new interest rate of 12% after '89/5	→ idem

Adapted from Kitahara, "Kien-ryō," pt. I, p. 72.

was behind the idea of the agency—an idea that would later successfully be applied in other areas as well.[57] City elders did not usually
participate in policy making at this high level. After the initial
deliberations, however, a proposal was made to make Taruya a full
member of the drafting committee, and Sadanobu, after due investigation, gave his consent. The three hereditary city elders (the two other
names are Naraya and Kitamura) usually served as go-betweens
between the city magistrates and the local township organizations;
they also controlled the township unions and were general managers
of the townsmen. They enjoyed the privilege of sword bearing, and
were granted shogunal audiences.[58] Neither Naraya nor Kitamura was
consulted in the secret deliberations that preceded Kuze's counterproposal. In Taruya, Sadanobu again had picked the right person. In the
later stages of the deliberations, his influence was decisive for the final
shape of the decree.

In the seventh month, Taruya improved the draft in two ways. He
more clearly defined canceled debts versus repayable debts; and he
suggested new interest rates. Reasoning that, at the old interest rate of
18 percent, all borrowed capital was redeemed after six years, he
rephrased the (a) proposal and (b') amendment so as to liquidate the
borrowed capital before 1784/12 in adjusted repayments, which, he
said, in fact constituted a cancelation without using the term (in the
final decree this was changed into a simple cancelation). He proposed
the amortization of debts contracted in the past five years (1785/1 to
1789/5) at the further reduced rate of 6 percent, and the liquidation, at
12 percent, of loans contracted in 1789/5 through the rice allowances
of the next pay day in the tenth month. Twelve percent was also to be
the future interest rate on loans contracted from the loan agency (all of
this was accepted for the final form of the decree). The final
amendment was made by Sadanobu, who succeeded in persuading his
colleagues to reduce the amount of public money from 50,000 to twice
10,000 ryō to found the new credit system. The draft went to
Sadanobu on 9/12. After changing some minor details, he resubmitted
it the next day to the committee; on the fourteenth, the draft returned
to Sadanobu; shogunal approval was secured, and the decree was
promulgated on the sixteenth.

The preceding description tells us some important things about
Sadanobu. First, Sadanobu did not fully appreciate, from the start,
either the extreme penury of the retainers (the age range of the
canceled debts was modified from more than twenty years old to more
than six years old), or the disturbance that the new measure would
cause in the financial world. Second, he did not have a constructive
plan of his own to modify the credit system; nor did he see the
necessity of government support to assure the continued service of the

rice brokers. To Sadanobu's credit, it is clear that he was able to select talented officials and was flexible enough to allow these men to state their views and to contribute decisively in the formulation of his policies.

The new credit system that was created together with the cancelation of debts was centered on the idea of the loan agency. In Kuze's counterproposal of 3/13, the argument ran as follows. The circulation of money after the cancelation of debts should be assured through a composite capital, consisting of the holdings of the rice brokers, levies from rich merchants from Edo, Kyoto, and Osaka, and a government loan of 50,000 ryō (to be redeemed in twenty years at no interest). This capital would be controlled by an agency and operated by the rice brokers for their loaning operations, at 10 percent interest (1 percent would be kept by the rice brokers; 9 percent would return to the agency). The advantage of such an arrangement was not only that cash would thus continue to be available to the retainers at more reasonable rates, but also that the rice brokers would be kept in check; moreover, the amassed wealth of the merchants would be distributed. It was suggested that Yagyū, who meanwhile had become superintendent of finance and was in Kyoto at that time, investigate the possibilities of levies from the merchants in the Kansai area.[59]

The final shape of the Loan Agency came very close to this blueprint. The agency was run by Taruya, first at his residence, but since 1790/2 at the new office in Saruya-machi. During the first two or three months after the cancelation, Taruya was very busy checking the dates at which the loans to be canceled or amortized had been contracted. The starting capital was provided by the bakufu and the merchants. On 10/7, 10,000 ryō were distributed by the superintendent of finance to the rice brokers (during the first ten years it was to stay unredeemed, but after that period it had to be paid back at no interest in twenty yearly installments). Another 10,000 ryō were distributed through the Loan Agency on 12/14 and were to be paid back at the interest rate of 6 percent the first five years, and at 9 percent for another fifteen years (1 percent of the interest would stay with the agency). And 10,000 ryō were distributed to ten financial purveyors (kanjōsho goyōtachi). They each received 1,000 ryō, which they were allowed to store at home but had to keep available together with their own private capital as a reserve fund (this solution probably replaced the proposed levies from merchants).[60]

The interest rate at which the rice brokers could write out loans to borrowing retainers was fixed at 12 percent, but this amount was broken down in different ways, depending upon whether the capital was bakufu money or purveyors' money. The interest on bakufu

capital was distributed as follows: 1 percent to cover the expenses of
the agency; 3 percent as a commission to the brokers; 5 percent to pay
back the capital invested by the bakufu over a twenty-year period; 3
percent to be added to the agency's fund. Of the 12 percent interest on
purveyors' capital, 4 percent was allocated to the brokers as a
commission fee, and the other 8 percent returned as a profit to the
purveyors (later these ratios were corrected in favor of the brokers,
whose share fluctuated between 4 and 6 percent).[61]

Sadanobu had personally fixed borrowing procedures very rigidly.
The Loan Agency would advance money to the brokers only upon a
request that was approved by all three broker unions; the money had
to be distributed throughout the union, which was responsible for the
amortization of the loan; the name, rank and office of the retainers for
whom the loan was made had to be duly recorded.[62]

The cancelation of debts had some remarkable results. With an
investment of a mere 30,000 ryō, Sadanobu relieved the bakufu of
1,180, 000 ryō in debts contracted by its servant-warriors. Tokutomi
Sohō, without giving his sources, claims that the government invested
80,000 ryō;[63] Shibusawa Eiichi speaks of 120,000 ryō, probably
relying on Sadanobu's autobiography.[64] There is, however, no evidence that the bakufu's contribution to the new credit system sur-
passed 30,000 ryō. The higher amounts given by the above scholars,
and by Sadanobu himself, probably include the total amount of the
capital out of which the Loan Agency operated, which consisted
mainly of the private wealth of the ten financial purveyors.

Moreover, Sadanobu had guaranteed the continuation of the credit
system. In contrast to the Tempō purge of rice brokers half a century
later, none of the brokers went out of business as a result of the
cancelation (only one had his license suspended temporarily).[65]
Sadanobu had succeeded in turning the wealthy rice brokers into
bureaucratic functionaries who worked for a commission. The new
system was also established without exacting loans from other rich
merchants. Instead, by means of the joint venture with the ten
financial purveyors, Sadanobu had not only permanently enlisted the
financial skill of the merchants but, through a sharing of the profit,
had made their capital available as a fund that assured the circulation
of money on a more equitable basis.

THE TEN FINANCIAL PURVEYORS

The ten financial purveyors played a key role in the implementation of
Sadanobu's financial policies. A year before the cancelation decree
they were already part of Sadanobu's plan to reestablish bakufu
control over prices. The government had made use of merchant

capital on previous occasions; in 1744, for instance, in order to raise the rice price, the bakufu had ordered merchants to buy rice.[66] Reliance of the bakufu upon the merchants had in the past been limited to extreme situations, and the merchants had never been called upon as a group. In 1788/10, however, as part of an overall plan to lower all commodity prices, the superintendent of finance (after consultation with the senior councillors in the seventh and ninth month) nominated seven merchants as permanent *kanjōsho goyō-tachi*, or purveyors of the office of finance.

The first task of these seven financial purveyors was to provide the government with 338,000 ryō in the form of a forced loan. This money was not only welcome additional revenue to the bakufu; it also enabled the bakufu to proceed with its reminting of the two-shu coins in 1788/12. But the purveyors had more to do than pay forced loans, as was customary in the past; from the beginning, their alliance with the bakufu took the form of a joint venture.

In 1789/3 and 6, the bakufu granted the seven purveyors a loan of 33,500 ryō against the low interest of 6 percent,[67] but bakufu returns from this investment were not restricted to the yearly interest of 2,000 ryō. The loan changed the private capital of the seven purveyors into semipublic capital and therefore bound eventual borrowers to a much stricter observance of amortization dates on loans contracted with these purveyors. In other words, the purveyors could lend bakufu capital at rates higher than 6 percent, make a handsome profit and at the same time enjoy the backing of bakufu authority on loans granted from their own private capital. Four of the seven purveyors were money changers (among the other three were two sake merchants and one oil merchant), who counted among their clients daimyo from the most powerful fiefs, such as Yonezawa, Akita, Aizu, Kuwana, Takamatsu, Fukui, and even two lords: Hitotsubashi and Tayasu.[68] Sadanobu, with bakufu authority (and with a minimal capital investment), solidified the financial sources of the most important daimyo houses at a time when he was unable to grant loans from the bakufu treasury. This formula, no doubt, was a new and successful version of Tanuma's abortive attempt to create a reserve fund for the daimyo by levies from Osaka merchants, with the promise that the bakufu's authority would guarantee prompt repayments from the borrowers (see chapter 1).

The next function the purveyors performed was in connection with the cancelation decree and the new credit system. As noted above, they had participated in some of the deliberations that preceded the decree. On 1789/9/30, two weeks after the issuance of the decree, three new purveyors were appointed, bringing their number to ten. (Significantly, all three new members were also bankers for important daimyo houses.) The ten purveyors each received 1,000 ryō from the bakufu, by which they and their private capital were drawn into the operation of the Loan Agency. The agency was headed by the city elder Taruya, but the technical operation of the capital was in the hands of the financial purveyors on a rotation basis.[69]

The financial purveyors' original function, as we have seen, was to control the price of rice. Control of the rice price was thought to be important for stabilizing the prices of other articles; it also reflected upon merchant wealth and the income of the retainers. In times of high prices, the rice wholesale dealers made outrageous profits, but a low market price considerably reduced the income of the retainers, who received less money for the portion of their rice allowances that they converted into cash. Sadanobu intended to normalize the rice price by massive buying when the market was low and by releasing reserve rice when it was scarce and expensive.

Massive buying required capital. In Osaka, the bakufu acted on its own strength: in the first two months of 1789, it purchased at four intervals 30,300 koku (and severely disciplined dishonest rice dealers). In Edo, Sadanobu normalized the market without financial self-sacrifice by working through the purveyors. In the same year, and again in 1791 and 1794, the financial purveyors were ordered to buy rice in great quantities (in 1791, they bought 30,000 ryō worth of rice). This purchase did not necessarily result in financial loss for the purveyors, for they could sell the rice later at a more favorable price.[70] In this way, the rice market, formerly manipulated by rice brokers who had speculated upon the difference in price between the bakufu's officially listed price (*harugami nedan*) and the market price, passed into the hands of the financial purveyors. The connection between the rice brokers' official *fudasashi* function of converting part of the allotted rice allowances of the retainers into cash, and their private dealings as rice brokers, *komeurikata*, was definitely broken when their licensed guild that protected this double function, the *fudasashi komeurikata nakama*, was dissolved in 1791/5.[71]

The release of rice at times of high speculation required considerable rice reserves, which as yet were nonexistent. The purveyors' capital was probably insufficient to shoulder the burden of building these reserves, and Sadanobu was unable or unwilling to use bakufu funds for the purpose. At this point another agency, the Edo Township Agency, came to the rescue of the bakufu. Its principal function was analogous to that performed by the cancelation of debts: to ensure the circulation of money and to lower the cost of living for the townspeople; its capital, however, was controlled by the ten financial purveyors.

THE EDO TOWNSHIP AGENCY

The theory that a low rice price produces corresponding low prices for other commodities proved false in 1789, when the rice price was stabilized at a low level, while all other prices remained high. Sadanobu, obliged to resort to other means to fight inflationary prices, adopted three measures.

The first was a nationwide decree to lower the prices of goods, based on a detailed, seven-year investigation (1783–90) of the prices of twenty-four goods. The investigation took into account the different aspects that determined the various prices: transportation routes, the price of stockpiles in the production areas, etc. The new prices, of course, were set not with the producers' price in mind but according to the consumers' needs in Edo.[72] Second, Sadanobu revalued the copper coins by reducing the amount in circulation. Third, he ordered a 10 to 20 percent reduction in land and house rents in Edo.[73] In order to offset the loss to the land- and houseowners occasioned by the third measure, Sadanobu made it possible for them to enjoy a public refund, thanks to the savings in the townships' expenditures. The savings were administered by the Edo Township Agency, which was established on 1791/12/31.[74]

On 1790/2/13, Sadanobu appointed a price committee to investigate the ways in which a revision in the township laws could bring about a lowering of commodity prices. The committee consisted of the two city magistrates (Hatsugano Nobutomo and Ikeda Osae) and two superintendents of finance (Kuze and Yagyū); it will be remembered that Hatsugano and the two superintendents had also participated in the planning of the cancelation decree. Sadanobu suggested that funds should be established in each township union with the help of an initial 20,000 ryō from the bakufu; from these township funds, loans could be made, and with the interest, grain storehouses were to be built (an idea prompted, no doubt, by the 1787/5 riot); the rest of the money would be saved for extraordinary expenses. Expenditures were to be curtailed, and the purchase of copper coins would revaluate copper currency; this would help compensate for the loss land- and houseowners suffered from the lower rents.

The committee launched a thorough investigation into the rents and the township expenditures of the twenty-three township unions (representing over 1,600 townships), and on 1791/3/20 drew up a report based upon the average figures of the past five years (1785–89). On the basis of this information, three extremely detailed, drafts for cutting down expenditures were submitted to Sadanobu. One of the plans, calling for a 10 percent cutback, was approved and submitted to the representatives of the unions on 4/15. On the last day of the year, the revised township law was promulgated and the Edo Township Agency established. It was the agency's task to manage the 10 percent savings, which were allocated as follows: 1 percent was set aside for extraordinary expenses, which, if not spent, would be refunded to the house owners;[75] 2 percent was refunded to the land owners; and 7 percent was added to the capital of the agency as a fund for disaster relief. About half of the capital was used for purchasing rice.[76]

The Edo Township Agency fulfilled its purpose beyond expectation. Meant as a reserve fund for times of economic distress, so that the city could rely upon its own resources rather than await bakufu assistance, the agency accumulated substantial capital over the years. Thirty years after its establishment, in 1828, its assets consisted of 462,400 ryō in savings, 280,000 ryō in loans, and rice reserves of 467,178 koku.[77] In 1872, when the agency was abolished, its capital of 1,430,000 yen, which was property of the townships and not of the bakufu or of the Meiji state, was spent on social welfare projects under the supervision of Shibusawa Eiichi, the great advisor of the Meiji government in matters of industrialization, and author of the standard biography of Sadanobu.[78] Originally these funds were managed by rich townsmen (who had also contributed to the funds) and five representatives of the landowners of each township.[79] But their role was soon reduced to verification of the records, while management passed into the hands of the two groups of government purveyors: the ten financial purveyors, and the five rice purveyors. The financial skills of the former were used for managing capital, while the technical knowledge of the latter was used for buying and selling rice.

Of the five rice purveyors, four had been nominated in 1790/11, and one more was added in 1794/7 when they started managing the newly established Collectors Agency (see table 5). They performed thus a double function: as *mawari kome osamekata goyōtachi* (collector-purveyors) they ran the Collectors Agency and supervised the incoming rice revenues of the bakufu; as *komekata goyōtachi* (rice purveyors) they managed the rice of the Edo Township Agency.[80]

The Edo Township Agency was modeled on the Loan Agency: a minimal investment of the bakufu justified government control over the new fund; the agency was self-sustaining and capital-producing; and its well functioning was guaranteed by the administrators' self-interest (the refunds to land- and houseowners) and the managers' technical knowledge of finances and the rice market.

It is intriguing to speculate on the origin of this type of agency. Earlier, the name of the city elder Taruya was mentioned in connection with the Loan Agency, but another official who certainly

TABLE 5 The Government Purveyors and Their Agencies

Year	Loan Agency (Canc. decree)	Ten Financial Purveyors	Edo Township Agency	Collectors Agency (Five rice purveyors)
1788	3/ Interest down to 15% (order of Yagyū)	10/16 Nomination of 7 purveyors; enforced loan of 338,000 ryō		
1789	2/–9/ Planning of cancelation & agency 9/16 Loan Agency established	3/ Loan of 33,350 i6/ ryō from bakufu to 7 purveyors 9/30 Nomination of 3 more purveyors		1/2/ Bakufu buys 33,300 koku in Osaka; disciplines rice dealers 9/ Osaka & Kyoto's *osameyado* abolished
1790			2/13 Sadanobu proposes revision of township laws	9/ Edo's *osameyado* abolished; Ōmiya in charge 11/ Nomination of 3 more purveyors.
1791			3/20 Report of the committee on financial situation of townships 4/15 Adoption of one plan of action 12/31 Edo Township Agency created	
1794				7/ Nomination of one more purveyor; establishment of Collectors Agency

i = intercalary

contributed greatly to the agency idea was Yagyū Hisamichi. When still city magistrate, he took the first measure against the rice brokers in 1788/3 and suggested a restructuring of the whole credit system. On 9/10 of the same year he became superintendent of finance, and a month later, on 10/16, the seven financial purveyors were established by a superintendent of finance. Later, in 1790–91, he was member of the committee on commodity prices that finally set up the Edo Township Agency. Whatever Yagyū's contribution may have been, it is clear that these new institutions were the product of a small group of imaginative officials and merchants who, in a consular fashion, assisted Sadanobu in the formulation of his economic and financial reform. As usual, credit for the reform went, not undeservedly, to Sadanobu as head of the government.

Sadanobu had severed the ties of the government with the old, well-established merchants, who had already lost much of their vitality and under Tanuma had become more of a burden to the government than an asset. Tanuma, for instance, supported the gold monopoly by exactions from the money exchangers and by government money.[81] Instead, Sadanobu assured the permanent and multifunctional service of two new and separate groups of merchants, by making their joint venture with the government a profitable enterprise to them. He skillfully interlocked their skills, interests, and capital in such a way that these three ingredients of capital building would not come under the exclusive control of one group. An analysis of the composition of the two merchant groups will clarify this point.

The ten financial purveyors were all wealthy businessmen but did not belong to the upper strata of Edo's merchant class. All (except their leader, Mitani Sankurō) had started their businesses in the Shōtoku-Kyōhō era (1711–35), and had developed their commercial activities during the Tanuma era without becoming entangled with the Tanuma regime. Their business was marked by small profits and large sales; three of them dealt in consumer goods and seven were money changers, who counted many daimyo among their clients.[82] Moreover, they were all Edo merchants, with no ties to Osaka merchants; none was a rice broker or rice wholesale dealer.[83] Their skills and interests were exclusively financial.

The five rice purveyors (headed by Ōmiya Kizaeimon) were all experts in rice transactions: four were private rice brokers (*kome nakagaishō*), and one was a wholesale dealer in rice and vegetables in Edo's hinterland. They also were wealthy businessmen without belonging to that class of very rich rice brokers who had met the ire of the populace in the Edo riot of 1787/5; neither were they connected with the official rice brokers (*fudasashi*); none was nominated financial purveyor to the government.[84]

The two groups consulted with each other for the management of the Edo Township Agency and for stabilizing the rice price through government ordered purchases. The financial purveyors provided the capital, and the rice purveyors suggested the time, nature, and amount of the transactions. For example, the 1791 government order to the financial purveyors to purchase 30,000 ryō worth of rice was executed only after Mitani, the head to the financial purveyors, had consulted with the four rice purveyors.[85] What Sadanobu had thus achieved, by the creation of these two separate purveyor bodies, was a disjunction of the double control function over capital and rice that had formerly been in the hands of one group, the *fudasashi* or brokers.

Sadanobu's success was remarkable: in his first year in office, the bakufu had a deficit of 1,000,000 ryō; ten years later, in 1798, the treasury had a surplus of 338,000 ryō.[86] Restoration of the bakufu's finances was only partly the result of the traditional short-term remedies of enforced loans. Sadanobu had found more durable solutions by bringing under bureaucratic control the free entrepreneurs whose activities had been harmful to bakufu interests. He achieved this through the creation of new institutions (the agencies), run by a new managerial class (the purveyors), which, however, still employed the old entrepreneurs (the rice brokers) as new bureaucratic servants.

Sadanobu thus fully realized his pledge to establish government control over the circulation of capital and rice. Undoubtedly his rigid sense of propriety and fixed status (*taigi meibun*) had inspired him to outline more sharply than had been done in the past the place of the merchants in Japanese society as servants of the government. This functional redefinition of the merchants' role amounted to no less than a complete turnabout of their past role under Tanuma. Then, profit seeking had dictated the behavior of even the warrior-administrators. Sadanobu, in denying the most influential sector of the merchant class unchecked development of maximum profits, imposed upon them the warrior ethic of public service. His practical political sense and his judicious use of collaborators enabled him to translate this new view of the merchants' role into a durable institutional reality.

5　In Defense of the Bakufu

In the past, scholars viewing history as a succession of regimes, upheavals, and wars have looked upon the Tokugawa period as a particularly uneventful period in Japanese history. At most, they found a dozen "incidents" that brought some relief to the flat landscape of its 250-year political history. In contrast, a new generation of historians has discovered great wealth of interesting data in the economic, institutional, and intellectual development of the period. Through their analyses, these political "incidents" have lost much of their significance, and have dropped almost entirely out of sight.[1]

These incidents, however, deserve new attention because, like the large-scale reforms, they reveal at different points in the period the strains that developed within the sociopolitical system. An examination, within the general political framework of the Tokugawa order, of the actors involved in these incidents, of their political ideology, and of the issues at stake will be instructive. The incident that traditionally has occupied a central place in the history of Sadanobu's rule is the so-called Title Incident (*songo jiken*). This incident came to a final solution in 1793/3, four months before Sadanobu's retirement, but it virtually spans his entire career, beginning in 1789/2 when he was first confronted with it.

Starting as an apparent innocent divergence of views between the bakufu and the imperial court on a question of propriety and titles (*taigi meibun*), the incident developed into a near collision between imperial and bakufu authority. It thus took on the semblance of open defiance of bakufu authority by the court.

A second, lesser incident, the Laxman affair, confronted Sadanobu with Russia's desire for commerce with Japan. With the protection of the bakufu's political autonomy in mind, Sadanobu showed great reluctance to open trade relations with Russia.

An astute politician, Sadanobu quickly perceived the political implications in both of these incidents although the issues seemed unrelated to politics. The incidents reveal the clarity with which Sadanobu understood how a political system functioned as well as the manner in which he exercised bureaucratic authority.

Sadanobu viewed the conflict with the court and the Laxman affair as a threat to the bakufu from without, much as he saw heterodox systems of thought as a threat from within, a subject we shall look at in detail in the next chapter. Sadanobu's actions stem from the consistent assumption that the organizing principles of the political system ought not be tampered with in matters of political authority and of economic underpinning. He could agree neither to a symbolic expression of imperial autonomy nor to fundamental trade concessions to Laxman and Russia.

The Title Incident especially allows additional insights into the bureaucratic activity of Sadanobu in the context of high-level bakufu politics. It set in motion a protracted and subtle political interplay between men in the bakufu, the court, and Sadanobu. The political interaction was highly convoluted, with confusing information exchanged between Kyoto and Edo, constant deliberations of the Senior Council, appeals to the shogun and the collateral houses, calculated procrastinations, indirect and intricate personal pressures, and timely retirements by key officials.

A QUESTION OF PROPRIETY

The Title Incident had its origin in a succession anomaly at the imperial court in Kyoto. Emperor Go-Momozono (reigned 1770–79) had died, leaving only a daughter, and Kōkaku (1771–1840; reigned 1779–1817) was selected as successor from among the Kan'in no miya family, one of the cadet branches of the imperial house. The situation in the imperial family was thus similar to that at the shogun's court. Ienari, it will be remembered, had not succeeded to the shogunal office by right of primogeniture; he also had been brought in from a collateral line. Emperor Kōkaku's father, prince Sukehito (1733–94), like the shogun's father, Hitotsubashi Harusada, had never held the office that fell to his son.

It is not clear why prince Sukehito, forty-four when Go-Momozono died, was passed over in favor of his son, who was only eight at that time. Herschel Webb thinks that the court officials may have had precedents in mind where, during the titular rule of an infant or adolescent emperor, the emperor's father functioned as the real head of the dynasty.[2] On the other hand, since the middle of the ninth century, regents (sesshō) had taken care of imperial affairs during the minority years of an emperor, and in 1779 there was no delay in the appointment of a regent. The same month in which Go-Momozono died (1779/11), Kujō Naozane was appointed regent, a post which he held until Kōkaku reached adulthood in 1785 at the age of fifteen.[3] It would seem then that the court did not attempt to give Kōkaku's father the title as well as the duties of a former emperor during the reign of his infant son, especially since the real drive for the title started after Kōkaku had come of age.

The Title Incident originated with the expressed desire of the young emperor to change the status of his father from prince to former emperor by conferring upon him the title *Dajō-tennō* (Great August Emperor), a title reserved for retired emperors. The reason given by Kōkaku for this anomalous, but not unprecedented, elevation to former emperor of someone who had never been emperor, was "filial piety." If prince Sukehito were to hold the rank of an abdicated emperor, he would rise to the level of his son, Emperor Kōkaku, which would solve embarrassing problems of ceremonial precedence at the court, where the prince ranked below some ministers. This new position would no doubt also increase prince Sukehito's power at the court, but imperial privileges were conspicuously devoid of political meaning. The whole "national" business of the emperor consisted of conducting the cycle of court ceremonies, conferring rank and title appointments, and annually issuing the calendar.[4]

When the court wished to take some action that was unprecedented, it had to confer with the bakufu through the bakufu's Kyoto deputy (*Kyoto shoshidai*). Contact with the deputy was maintained through two court officials (*buke densō*, messengers to the military) who were in charge of transmitting memorials to and from the Kyoto deputy. The deputy relayed important matters to the Senior Council in Edo by couriers, who traveled the distance between Kyoto and Edo in about six days. Bakufu decisions followed the same route back to the court messengers, but these latter had no direct access to the emperor. They contacted the *kampaku* or imperial advisor who then conferred with the emperor. The *kampaku* was the counterpart of the *sesshō* or advisor for adult emperors, an office that, unlike the *sesshō*, was rarely without incumbent.[5]

Emperor Kōkaku informed the Kyoto deputy of his desire in 1782. He was eleven at the time. Probably the father (or some other), was behind this filial plan, which may have been an attempt at obtaining some of the power and prestige that would have been the father's if he had been elected emperor. Kōkaku expressed his intention to bestow the title after reaching adulthood, and he therefore requested the deputy to readjust prince Sukehito's rank. This was communicated to the bakufu, and in 1784, a thousand koku were added to the prince's original fief of a thousand koku. Five more years passed before a formal request to confer the title was submitted to the Kyoto deputy.

There were reasons for this delay besides the number of years that separated the emperor from his coming of age, but the slow approach and the opportune timing of the request indicate that the court was aware of the seriousness of the matter and that more than "filial piety" was at stake. In 1787, the project of conferring the title had again become the object of discussions at the court, but because of the *Daijō-e* (the Great Thanksgiving Festival, which takes place after the

enthronement of a new emperor), the request had been postponed.
The burning of the palace in 1788/1 had caused a new delay. In 1788/4,
however, the emperor ordered Nakayama Yoshichika, a court official
in charge of imperial memorials (*gisō*), to look up precedents;
Yoshichika discovered that emperors Go-Horikawa (1222–32) and
Go-Hanazono (1429–64) had done for their fathers what emperor
Kōkaku was contemplating for prince Sukehito. Almost a year later,
in 1789/2, the two court messengers handed over the formal request
to the Kyoto deputy.

At this time, the court anticipated no fundamental objections from
the bakufu, since the relationship between Kyoto and Edo had been
very satisfactory during Sadanobu's new regime. The bakufu,
although in financial straits, had spared no expense in rebuilding the
imperial palace. In 1788/5, Sadanobu had even come down to
Kyoto—an extraordinary visit for a senior councillor—to supervise
the start of the reconstruction. The court was impressed with his
reverence for the imperial family.

Six months passed before the court's petition was sent to Edo on
1789/8/25. There is no clear explanation for this unusually long
delay. The deputy may have taken time to investigate the matter
before transmitting the petition to Edo. He did, in fact, append a short
note to the document, tracing the history of the request from 1782,[6]
but it is very unlikely that the investigation would have taken six
months. Nor can the delay be attributed to a change in deputy (on
4/18, Ōta Sukechika replaced Matsudaira Norisada, who joined
Sadanobu's cabinet as senior councillor). Considering Sadanobu's
attempt, in the later development of the affair, to avoid an open
refusal of the request, it is very likely that he had been deliberately
procrastinating from the very outset. Sadanobu had heard about
Kōkaku's plan, and may have given oral instructions to Norisada, one
of his own appointees who had become deputy on 1787/12/16.

Indeed, in 1788/5, one month after Nakayama had received the
imperial request concerning the historical investigation into the title,
Sadanobu was in Kyoto in connection with the rebuilding of the
palace. While there, he conferred with the kampaku Takatsukasa
Sukehira, the man closest to the emperor, and, as he notes in his
autobiography, the subject of the title came up during their conversa-
tions.[7] Since Sukehira was to play a central role in the further
development of the affair, Sadanobu probably tacitly agreed with
Sukehira on what course to follow. Sukehira's position, however, was
very delicate. In his role of kampaku, he was advisor to the emperor;
but he was also the brother of prince Sukehito and thus uncle to the
emperor. To complicate matters still further, he was related to
Sadanobu by marriage.[8] It was thus through Sukehira that Sadanobu

first heard about the emperor's plans, and it was through him that he
kept himself informed about inside developments at the court.[9]

On 1789/11/19, Sadanobu sent an answer to the Kyoto deputy,
arguing that the two historical precedents were invalid because they
had both occurred in times of social upheaval (the Jōkyū disturbance
of 1221, and the Ōnin war of 1467–77), when customs and laws were
not being properly observed. He also drew attention to the seriousness
of the request (*fuyōigi*) because it was a matter of propriety and status
(*taigi meibun*). With the approval of the shogun and the consent of the
senior councillors, Sadanobu requested the court in gentle but
unequivocal language to reconsider the matter. He clearly wanted
there to be no doubt in the court about his feelings. He therefore
informed the kampaku of his plan to further investigate Japanese and
Chinese precedents.[10]

Phase I: A Question of Propriety

1788/4	Kyoto: Nakayama is ordered to study precedents.
1789/2	Two messengers address request to Kyoto deputy (Matsudaira Norisada).
8/25	Kyoto deputy (Ōta Sukechika) transmits request to Edo (arrives 9/2).
11/13	Sadanobu writes to the kampaku, Takatsukasa Sukehira, about the historical precedents.
19	After consulting with the shogun and the Senior Council, Sadanobu writes the deputy to ask the court to reconsider the matter.
1790/3/7	The kampaku asks for Sadanobu's own study of historical precedents, which Sadanobu sends him on the 16th.
1791/1/11	The kampaku asks Sadanobu for a reconsideration of the case (letter arrives the 26th).
2/21	The two messengers ask the deputy to rebuild the Sentō Hall; Sadanobu answers the kampaku that the title would be a breach of taigi meibun.
4/12	The kampaku writes to Sadanobu that the building of the hall would solve ceremonial problems of precedence; Sadanobu consults with the Senior Council, Shibano Ritsuzan, and two superintendents of finance; Sadanobu also shows his correspondence to the lords of Owari and Mito.
6/3	Prince Sukehito is given a stipend increase of 1,000 koku.
8/20	The kampaku Takatsukasa retires; Ichijō Terunaga succeeds him.

Sadanobu's oblique approach seemed to bear fruit. An open confrontation between Sadanobu and the court was unlikely. During the next year, the only communication from Kyoto was from the kampaku, requesting (on 1790/3/7) that Sadanobu produce the findings from his historical investigation. Compiled chiefly by Shibano Ritsuzan, a Neo-Confucian scholar brought to Edo by Sadanobu in 1788, Sadanobu sent these results to the kampaku, emphasizing again his objections against the title.

Although Sadanobu believed that the matter had been settled, the debate had only just begun. Sadanobu received a note from the kampaku on 1791/1/16, suggesting this time that Sadanobu reconsider the issue. One month later in Kyoto, on 2/21, the two court messengers appeared again before the deputy with a new plan. They avoided altogether mention of the title, but they requested the rebuilding of Sentō Hall (the palace for retired emperors), for the benefit of the prince, which would result in another way in elevating the status of prince Sukehito. That same day, in Edo, Sadanobu reiterated his position in a letter to the kampaku, saying that the title would be a breach of the principle of taigi meibun.[11]

On 4/12, the kampaku explained that the building of the Sentō Hall would resolve knotty problems of ceremonial precedence. Sadanobu consulted with the Senior Council, two superintendents of finance (Yagyū and Kuze), and Shibano Ritsuzan, and on 6/3 they agreed to grant the prince another raise of 1,000 koku. Sadanobu may again have believed that the affair was closed, and he submitted his correspondence with the imperial advisor to the two collaterals of Owari and Mito.[12]

A CONFLICT OF AUTHORITY

In Kyoto, however, the imperial advisor Takatsukasa Sukehira sensed the uneasiness this settlement had produced at the court. He undoubtedly felt that the affair would flare up again, and saw himself being caught in the web of conflicting loyalties to the court, to the bakufu, and to his relatives on both sides. He therefore resigned on 8/20 and was replaced by Ichijō Terunaga, an advocate of the court in this matter. Without the moderating influence of Sukehira and with a new supporter close to the emperor, it was only a matter of time before new attempts were made to further the cause of the title.

Indeed, in the twelfth month, the question was raised again. This time, many more court nobles were involved, no doubt to apply greater pressure on Sadanobu. On 12/25, at a council where forty-one courtiers were present, a vote was taken on the issuance of an imperial proclamation to grant the title to prince Sukehito. The vote was overwhelmingly in favor of taking immediate action: thirty-six courtiers, among whom was the new kampaku, backed immediate proclamation; three were in favor of a proclamation some time in the future; and only two, the former kampaku Sukehira and his son, opposed it.[13]

Sukehira immediately informed Sadanobu about the latest turn of events. Receiving the letter on 1792/1/15, Sadanobu presented it to the Senior Council, calling attention to the fact that the affair had become a grave national problem (*go-kokutai ni tori fuyōigi*).[14] The court and the bakufu thus silently geared themselves for a confrontation that was, essentially, a conflict between two authorities. Protracted diplomatic skirmishes delayed resolution for another year.

On 1/20, the two imperial messengers presented to the bakufu's deputy in Kyoto a request that the title be granted at once in the light of the advanced age of the prince.[15] Meanwhile, the Senior Council in Edo worked out an appropriate course of action. Receiving the new request in Edo on 1/27, Sadanobu presented to the Senior Council ten days later a plan for dilatory action and indirect refusal. He would again raise the matter of historical precedents. If the court persisted in its requests, he would then start negotiations to increase the prince's personal income. The increase would take place gradually, but the title would be refused. If the court went ahead and proclaimed the title, then he would take punitive measures against the imperial advisor, the memorializing officers, and other court nobles. He would also demand that the prince renounce the title.[16] The Senior Council adopted this plan, and on 2/28 the bakufu's deputy in Kyoto was ordered to refuse the title in the manner outlined.

The affair developed as Sadanobu had foreseen. The tone of the correspondence between Edo and Kyoto in the following months grew increasingly impatient. Prince Sukehito, meanwhile, had fallen ill.[17] On 8/3, the two court messengers informed the bakufu that the imperial proclamation of the title would take place in the eleventh month, just before the Harvest Festival (*Niiname-sai*). Such disregard of bakufu authority was unprecedented. On the following day the bakufu deputy, who had been unable to prevent this turn for the worst, feigned illness and resigned.

Sadanobu received news of the aggravated situation on the eighth, and forthwith instructed the Senior Council to draft a letter demanding that the imperial proclamation be stopped. Seeking shogunal support, Sadanobu sent an explicit order to the new deputy in Kyoto (Hotta Masaari), to reject the title. Assuming responsibility for the

strong language used against the court, and attempting to elicit
additional support for his policy with a display of sincerity, Sadanobu
handed in his resignation—which was refused.[18]

Phase II: A Conflict of Authority

1791/12/25	Title question erupts again in Kyoto; ex-kampaku informs Sadanobu immediately (letter arrives 1792/1/9).
1792/1/11	Senior Council meets to find a solution.
20	Kyoto: two messengers present new request to the deputy (letter arrives in Edo the twenty-seventh).
2/7	Sadanobu expresses to the Senior Council his intention of refusing the title through dilatory tactics.
28	Order from Edo to deputy to that effect.
i.2/7	Letter arrives in Kyoto and is shown to the kampaku.
6/	Two messengers press again for the title with the deputy.
8/3	Two messengers announce proclamation of title begin eleventh month (news arrives in Edo the eighth).
8/4	The deputy resigns. Hotta Masaari takes his place the twenty-seventh.
14	Senior council drafts letter for the two messengers.
20	Sadanobu requests the shogun's support.
28	Order to deny the title is sent to the new deputy.
31	Similar letter to the Kyoto City magistrate; request to resign by Sadanobu.
9/18	The two messengers reject the deputy's letter, enjoining them not to proceed with the proclamation (news arrives in Edo the twenty-fourth; the shogun is informed the next day).
29	Sadanobu proposes to summon three court nobles to Edo.
10/1	Plan approved by the shogun.

2	The messengers decide to go ahead; the deputy returns the decision, and informs Edo (news arrives on the sixth).
4	Messengers informed of Sadanobu's decision to summon three courtiers to Edo.
5	Reply of the messengers: the title and the *Niinamesai* are postponed until the bakufu grants permission; refusal to send three courtiers to Edo (news arrives in Edo the ninth).
6	Edo: Sadanobu receives approval for his decision from Hitotsubashi (approval from Owari and Mito had arrived the fourth).
11	Edo to Kyoto: only two courtiers are summoned, and the title should be abandoned (news arrives in Kyoto the fourteenth).
21	The ex-kampaku answers inquiry by Sadanobu written the seventh.
22	Two messengers promise to postpone the title, and deny the need for the two courtiers to go to Edo (news arrives the twenty-eighth, and is shown to the shogun).
11/4	Absolute and clear refusal by the bakufu to grant the title.
13	Messengers to deputy: the title is dropped.
1793/1/9	The bakufu forces the two courtiers to come to Edo.
2/11, 16, 22	Three interrogations by the Senior Council.
3/1	Shogun, Owari, Mito, Hitotsubashi approve of punishments adopted by the Senior Council.

Despite strong warnings and stern injunctions by Sadanobu on behalf of the bakufu, the court proceeded on the course it had decided upon. On 9/18, the messengers from the court flatly rejected Sadanobu's plea. As he had previously planned, Sadanobu then embarked upon some disciplinary action. He proposed at first that one or two senior councillors be sent to Kyoto to punish some courtiers. This proposal was reversed as too extreme, and it was decided instead to summon three courtiers from Kyoto to Edo.[19]

Sadanobu's decision reached the court at the moment when the proclamation was about to be made, and it produced a severe shock. Sadanobu's stern stance had its effect. The court was forced to retreat or face rude punitive treatment, which evoked memories of a previous incident.[20] The court, however, retreated in such a way as to cause embarrassment to Sadanobu and the bakufu. On 10/5, the court messengers agreed to postpone the proclamation of the title, but they also postponed the Harvest Festival, which was a festival of national importance, until the bakufu should grant permission for the proclamation. This left the bakufu vulnerable to a charge of irreverence. The court, moreover, refused to send the three courtiers to Edo as requested by Sadanobu.

Sadanobu meanwhile had not been inactive. He received approval from the lords of Hitotsubashi, Owari, and Mito for his general plan vis-à-vis the court. To gain clearer insight into developments at the court, he had requested information from the former kampaku, Takatsukasa Sukehira. In his answer of the twenty-first, Sukehira singled out Nakayama Yoshichika as the main instigator. When the court on the twenty-second argued again that it would not send courtiers to Edo because the proclamation had been postponed, Sadanobu took a decisive stand. On 11/4 he abandoned the circumlocutory formulations of his earlier tactics and ordered that the title not be bestowed under any pretext. Faced with Sadanobu's clear dictate, the court surrendered its prerogatives in the entire affair.[21]

The final act of the incident took place in 1793/2 in Edo. On 1793/1/9, Sadanobu compelled two courtiers (the memorializing officer Nakayama Yoshichika and the messenger Ōgimachi Kin'aki) to come to Edo.[22] Interrogations were then conducted by the senior councillors, who recommended punishment.[23] On 3/1, the shogun and the lords of Owari, Mito, and Hitotsubashi approved the actions of the Senior Council, and six days later the two courtiers were summoned to the residence of senior councillor Toda Ujinori, where— in the presence of all the senior councillors, the three magistrates (*bugyō*), the inspectors general, and the inspectors—the courtiers Nakayama and Ōgimachi were sentenced to 100 and 50 days house arrest respectively.[24] The court was forced to dismiss both of them from their office. In addition, scores of other courtiers were disciplined to domiciliary confinement or were reprimanded.[25]

Having established a firm victory for the bakufu, Sadanobu was now in a position to be conciliatory. He granted a raise of 2,000 bales to prince Sukehito. The prince, the ostensible cause of so much confusion over proper jurisdiction of authority, died in the following year. It may be noted in passing that the title of *Dajō-tennō* was granted posthumously to the unlucky prince a hundred years later, in 1884, when the Meiji government conveniently made a hero out of a "victim" of the bakufu's repressive policy toward the imperial court.

SIGNIFICANCE OF THE TITLE INCIDENT

Sadanobu may appear to have overreacted in a trivial affair, and it is easy to ascribe his intransigeance to his personal dogmatism. But what is impressive about the incident is the tenacious manner in which the court asserted itself against the bakufu. The friction that the incident caused between court and bakufu in their power relationship within the Tokugawa political order is open to varying interpretations.

Western historians have hardly taken notice of the incident.[26] Japanese historians have concentrated on explaining Sadanobu's stance and have paid little attention to the court's show of strength. They have referred both to Sadanobu's intransigeant character and to a movement within the bakufu's Chiyoda castle that paralleled the court's drive for the title.

It will be recalled that emperor Kōkaku and the shogun Ienari were in the same position toward their fathers. There is some scant evidence that, while the emperor was endeavoring to bestow upon his father the title of *Dajō-tennō* and move him into the Sentō Hall, the shogun was planning to move his own father into the Western Citadel of Chiyoda castle by giving him the title of *Ōgosho* (the title reserved for an abdicated shogun).[27] If Hitotsubashi Harusada was thus elevated to the status of former shogun, he inevitably would have a much greater voice in bakufu politics. The political influence of a collateral, however, would run counter to the real, but limited and independent, role of the collaterals that Sadanobu had envisioned in his statement of aims when he first took office. Thus, in a convoluted manner, Sadanobu's policy toward the court can be seen as being aimed in part against the shogun Ienari and Harusada.

There is very little existing evidence to document Harusada's drive, and it is perhaps going too far to suggest that the new privileges granted him by the shogun were steps toward his elevation to the status of former shogun. It is certain that his ambition never took the shape of a formal request.[28] Nor is there much evidence to support the view that Harusada was behind the court's movement for the title.

The origins of the Title Incident go back to 1782, one year after Harusada's son became heir to the shogun Ieharu. It is unlikely that at that point Harusada would have instigated emperor Kōkaku's desires concerning the promotion of prince Sukehito. Not only was it much too early for such a plan to take shape, but Harusada seems to have had no court connections whereby to realize his aims. Moreover, the

court was certainly not inclined to be used for warrior ambitions. The
possibility that Harusada instigated the unexpected flare-up of the
affair in 1790/12 must be ruled out for the same reasons, although he
may have harbored secret hopes for his own promotion if the court
were able to bring the affair to a successful end.

It is possible that Sadanobu understood Harusada's secret hopes
and that he therefore involved him in the crucial decisions against the
title so as to block any political ambitions that he might have. On the
surface at least, Harusada was involved in the decisions, but he seems
never to have been a decisive influence. Looked at from this stance, it
is clear that Sadanobu made it impossible for Harusada to gain a
favored position within the bakufu. Given the broad base of authority
within the bakufu which Sadanobu had secured for his decision,
Harusada could not raise the question of his own promotion, even
after Sadanobu's retirement.

Historians admit that Sadanobu's respect for propriety, titles, and
the fixed and predictable nature of political structure was strong, and
that he personally would have refused the title in Kyoto, even if the
possible implication of Harusada's promotion in Edo had not
existed.[29] Tokutomi Sohō reached the same conclusion, but he
underlined the changing nature of the conflict from a matter of
"propriety" into a question of "authority." One could go even further,
it would seem, and say that Sadanobu's strict adherence to taigi
meibun standards was from the outset motivated by his political
perception of the conflict, because he had seen the court's petition as
part of a diffuse loyalist movement that had caused treasonous events
such as the Hōreki Incident of 1758 (the year Sadanobu was born).[30]

The Hōreki incident was not aimed directly at the bakufu. It had its
origins in a struggle between two factions at the court, and, as
Tokutomi clearly indicates, it resulted in the banishment of Takenouchi Shikibu (1712–67) and the punishment of certain court nobles
by the Kyoto deputy, only after one faction had asked the bakufu
to intervene.[31]

In the 1750s, a faction of court nobles sought to gain influence with
Emperor Momozono (reigned 1747–62). The emperor had become a
fervent disciple of Shikibu's Suika Shinto, which had been founded by
Yamazaki Ansai and stressed the importance of the imperial dynasty
in the life of the nation. The loyalist content of Shikibu's teachings
was certainly a cause of concern to the bakufu, but no immediate
action was taken. What stirred opposition at the court, however, was
the use of Shikibu's teachings by his followers in their attempt to oust
the kampaku, and thus to gain greater control over the emperor. The
kampaku, seeing his position threatened, rallied to his cause the

go-sekke ("five regency houses")[32], the mother of the emperor, and also the officially orthodox Shinto of the Yoshida house. The kampaku decreed that Shikibu's Suika Shinto was too controversial and that Shinto teachings should follow the orthodoxy of the Yoshida school. And finally it was he who asked the bakufu's deputy in Kyoto for punishments.

It is interesting to note that these struggles for a shift of the power structure or for its maintenance had their ideological counterparts. Takenouchi had also advocated a unification of teachings focused on the emperor—an indication that the ideal of ideological uniformity was very much alive in the latter half of the eighteenth century.[33] Takenouchi wanted to center this unity on the emperor, while Sadanobu, with his ban on heterodoxy, sought to center it on the bureaucratic needs of the bakufu.

If one examines closely the main actors of the Hōreki and the Title incidents, Sadanobu's intransigeance in the latter becomes more understandable. In both incidents the kampaku played a major role: in the Hōreki Incident it was he who organized the resistance, and in the Title Incident, it was again the kampaku that was Sadanobu's best ally and informer at the court. The kampaku during the Hōreki Incident was Konoe Uchisaki, the brother of Sadanobu's Tayasu stepmother. It will be recalled that she proved herself a politically astute woman by the role she played in Sadanobu's acquisition of court rank and in his appointment to the Antechamber, and by her views on the Tayasu succession problem. The kampaku during the Title Incident, Takatsukasa Sukehira, also related by marriage to Sadanobu, was in 1758, though only eighteen, Minister of the Interior (*Naidaijin*) and actively involved in the deliberations of the *go-sekke* in the Hōreki Incident.[34]

Sadanobu was thus quite familiar with the Hōreki Incident. He understood that its ideological aspect was closely linked to a power conflict that might upset the institutional status of the imperial house. This must have been a lesson to him on the disruptive potentialities of skillfully used counterideologies in general; and, when the Title Incident occurred, he was forewarned about the political dimension of apparently innocent questions of propriety or "filial piety." The same unwavering conviction that made Sadanobu, in his revitalization of the bakufu bureaucracy, unambiguously support the fixed character of institutional structures made him oppose any change in the authority relationship between the bakufu and the court.

Two more details show that Sadanobu did not overestimate the issue of the Title Incident, by interpreting it from the outset as part of a larger drive to reassert imperial power. First, there is a further continuity between the Hōreki and the Title incidents on the side of the anti-bakufu camp. Among those who were most severely punished in both incidents were father and son of the Hirobashi house: Katsutane, messenger in 1758, and Koremitsu, who was put under house arrest in 1793.[35]

Second, Nakayama Yoshichika, the main culprit of the Title Incident, later introduced another brand of loyalist teachings to the court through Motoori Norinaga (1730–1801). The Ancient Way, as reconstructed by Norinaga from his literary studies of the past, first indicated its political potential in 1787. Norinaga was then asked by Tokugawa Harusada (1728–89), the lord of Kii (one of the Three Houses), for his views on politics and economy in relation to the current social crisis.[36] In 1788, Yokoi Chiaki, an elder (*karō*) of the lord of Owari, another of the Three Houses, tried to introduce Norinaga's writings to Sadanobu in order that he might base his policies on the Ancient Way rather than on Neo-Confucianism, but the attempt failed.[37] Loyalist ideology was thus widespread among the three principal collaterals. (In Mito, the third of the Three Houses, loyalism had taken the form of historical scholarship with the publication of the *Dai Nihon-shi, Great History of Japan*, written from a loyalist and revisionist standpoint.)[38]

Norinaga's influence at the court took longer to take root. In his later years, Norinaga took three trips to Kyoto. The first, in 1790, was made on the occasion of emperor Kōkaku's ceremonial move into the new palace. In that year Norinaga held a *waka* poetry party, attended by twenty-seven people. In 1793, he was again in Kyoto and gave several lectures at the inn where he stayed. His audience consisted mostly of samurai and townsmen. At that time, however, he made friends with a court noble, Shibayama Mochitoyo, and prince Myō-hōin, who introduced Norinaga's ideas among the court nobility. And in 1801 Norinaga paid a last visit to Kyoto, this time staying seventy days, with the explicit purpose of furthering his influence at the court.[39] He succeeded in establishing contact with many court nobles, and Nakayama Yoshichika became his main sponsor. Nakayama even invited Norinaga to give lectures at his residence. Norinaga, in a letter to his sons, called Nakayama a hero.[40]

Within the context of the Hōreki Incident and the later reintroduction of loyalist teachings at the court by Nakayama, the Title Incident earns its true significance as another attempt to boost imperial prestige. The political overtones of a possible restoration of imperial authority were perceived only dimly at the time, if at all. Yet the court clearly showed itself as a possible incipient center of dissent and a source of political authority divergent from the bakufu. In the Title

Incident, Sadanobu proved himself a firm defender against such a possibility. His reasons were purely political and betrayed no disrespect toward the imperial institution as such (he even made the unprecedented suggestion that the shogun pay a visit to the emperor, a custom abandoned since 1634).[41] The emperor was the fountainhead of legitimate authority in the realm, but political and administrative authority was the bakufu's.

In his handling of the Title Incident, Sadanobu had requested full support from his colleagues and from the collaterals. This support had always been granted, although the three collaterals, influenced by their loyalist sympathies, may not wholeheartedly have agreed with Sadanobu's treatment of the court. They never displayed their discontent in that issue, but with his ban on heterodox doctrines Sadanobu drew considerable open opposition from them. When Sadanobu retired on 1793/7/23, only four months after the closure of the Title Incident, their displeasure was certainly an important element in the sudden and early end of his career as senior councillor.

THE THREAT FROM ABROAD

Another threat to the security of the bakufu during Sadanobu's term in office was created by the Russian approach from the north, and in particular the attempt in 1792 by Adam Laxman to open trade relations in Ezo (Hokkaido). In handling this problem, Sadanobu operated from the same premises and displayed the same tendencies that characterized his leadership in general (the primacy of politics over economics) and his solution of the Title Incident in particular. He manifested a similar sense of propriety, based upon a firm commitment to institutional conservatism. And again he shrewdly used delaying tactics in the negotiations with the Russians in order to avoid an open clash for which the bakufu was not prepared.

The question concerning Ezo was whether the island should be developed economically or used for strategic purposes as the northern defense line. Since the beginning of the eighteenth century, some scholars such as Namikawa Tenmin (1679–1718) had advocated economic development. But in the latter half of the century, scholars of Dutch learning such as Miura Baien (1723–89), or Yoshi Kōgyū (1724–1800), a translator in Nagasaki who had been warned by his Dutch contacts about Russian ambitions in the Far East, stressed the need for a defense policy.[42] The bakufu was spurred to action through a comprehensive memorial, the *Akaezo fūsetsu kō*, presented to Tanuma in 1781 by a Sendai physician, Kudō Heisuke (1734–1800). Although he argued that the colonization of Ezo would also act as a defense measure against the Russians, Heisuke was not as alarmed as

Hayashi Shihei was by the Russians. He was concerned with the economic aspect, advocating the opening of ports other than Nagasaki for foreign trade. His memorial triggered Tanuma's preparations for the colonization of Ezo, although he never envisioned lifting the seclusion controls.[43]

As is well known, Sadanobu abandoned Tanuma's plans as part of his curtailment of bakufu expenses. Underlying this decision, however, was a basic political view that rejected any alternative to the current political structure. Like Nakai Chikuzan (1730–1804), Sadanobu did not regard Ezo as an integral part of Japan.[44] He took the strategic view of the function of the island. He believed that a barren and undeveloped island would tempt the Russians less than an economically developed one.[45] On this point, Sadanobu met the opposition of his friend Honda Tadakazu, who preferred economic development and proposed to remove the Matsumae rulers and establish bakufu control.

The arrival of Adam Laxman on 1792/9/5 in Nemuro (Ezo) injected a new urgency in the policy discussions concerning Ezo conducted by the Senior Council and the collaterals.[46] Using the repatriation of castaways as an excuse, Laxman wanted to open direct trade relations with Edo. Sadanobu was convinced that this had to be avoided at any price, because the country's military preparedness was in too poor a state for a confrontation, if such were to develop from contact with the foreigners. As Commodore Perry was to prove two generations later, a confrontation in Edo would have disastrous consequences for the bakufu. Now that Laxman was in Nemuro, however, waiting for an answer from the bakufu, it was too late to bring the country to military readiness. Nevertheless, Sadanobu added new laws on maritime defense to the one of the previous year (1791/9) that provided for the repelling of all foreign ships. On 1792/11/7, all maritime domains were ordered to check their coastal defenses, and, on 12/27, measures for the defense of Edo bay were issued, followed on 1793/3/17 with provisions for all maritime domains to proceed with military exercises. In the same year, from 3/18 until 4/7, immediately after the closing of the Title Incident, Sadanobu undertook a personal inspection tour of the maritime defenses around the Kanto area, in Itō and Sagami.[47]

Meanwhile, Sadanobu's envoys to Laxman were instructed not to open any official negotiations and to make clear to the Russians that, according to the law of the land (*kokuhō*), the proper place for trade negotiations was neither Ezo nor Edo but Nagasaki.[48] Sadanobu, however, could not afford an outright confrontation with the Russians, and therefore promised them token trade in Nagasaki. The concession was meant primarily as an appeasement gesture to the Russians, in order to gain time for bringing the country to a proper state of defense. The strategy worked. On 1793/7/16, Laxman left Ezo for Okhotsk. Ten years elapsed before another envoy, Rezanov, returned to Nagasaki on 1804/9/6.[49]

Sadanobu's agreement to open trade in Nagasaki, where earlier he had reduced the Chinese yearly quota to ten ships,[50] may be said to have constituted a breach of the seclusion policy. But it was not Sadanobu's intention to open the country and reverse Tokugawa tradition. Given the possible alternatives, one has to conclude that his concession was a measure of political expediency from a flexible politician who knew how to yield on a minor point in order to save his main objective, which for Sadanobu was the preservation of the Tokugawa order.[51]

Sadanobu's assumptions about institutional stability had made him sensitive to any threat to the preservation of the political status quo in his country. In the Title Incident, the threat was one of principle and authority; in the Laxman affair, the political threat was implied in the new imbalance that would be created by the opening of a new economic center in the north or in Edo, and in the potential danger of antagonizing a foreign power.

The political threat from within to the bakufu's political autonomy had been met with the solution of the Title Incident. Confrontation with a foreign power had been staved off by opening Nagasaki for Russian trade; this had also given Japan time to strengthen its military defenses.

In bringing the problems discussed in this chapter to successful conclusions, Sadanobu, though he had his critics, was not stymied by open opposition. Criticism of his efforts to create an official bakufu ideology, however, was voiced aloud, as we shall see in chapter 6.

6 The Politics of Ideology

None of Sadanobu's measures has aroused more controversy than his ban on heterodox ideas and schools of thought. At the time of the ban, scholars who found themselves in the heterodox camp protested loudly against Sadanobu's narrow limitation of scholarship; the protest carried an urgency often sharpened by the growing defections of their own students after the ban. Later historians have often seized upon the ban as a clear example of the reactionary nature of Sadanobu's rule, and of the "feudalistic" system which, in their eyes, he eminently represented. For them, the ban suppressed freedom of thought.

A few scholars have approached the orthodoxy problem less passionately. Treating it more accurately, they have described the general background and the role official ideology played during the Tokugawa period, the political nature of the ban, and its limited scope. Before the ban of 1790 the bakufu had never identified itself in an explicit and exclusive manner with any one ideology, although Western historians of the Tokugawa period often imply that it had. Nor had the bakufu—its long association with the Hayashi School notwithstanding—ever imposed its control over one institution to foster such ideology to the exclusion of others. Sadanobu changed this situation. Following his pattern of increasing state control, he gave Neo-Confucianism the status of an official ideology and transformed the Hayashi School from a semi-private to a state institution.

Sadanobu's purpose in this double measure was limited to the bakufu and fitted into his general scheme of restoring an able bureaucracy, immune to corruption and bribery. He had no immediate intention of imposing his decision upon all 270 domains—or more precisely, upon the ninety-odd domain schools that were in existence at the time of the ban. It is doubtful, in any case, whether the bakufu had sufficient power to enforce such a decision, even if Sadanobu had wanted to. Nevertheless, Sadanobu's decision had its effect throughout Japan: first on the numerous private academies that had sprung up in the previous hundred years, mainly in Edo, and also on a considerable number of daimyo who, in their domains, sooner or later followed Edo's lead.

The ultimate effect of the ban was felt during the remaining decades of the Tokugawa period. The officials that were trained in the Bakufu College contributed considerably to the improved bureaucratization of the government. The fewer but sizable number of domain teachers that studied at the college also spread the official ideology throughout Japan. When Japan became a unified, bureaucratic state following the Meiji Restoration, it could rely upon an already familiar concept and reality of a bureaucratic state with a consistent internal ideology. This officialdom, aristocratic by tradition, was subjected to an official training program for over two generations prior to the Restoration, and gave Japan's political culture an increasingly bureaucratic character.

The ban was an important political event that left a complex legacy. A crucial event of this sort, historians agree, cannot be accredited to one particular person. Behind the ban on heterodoxy stood a small group of deeply committed men, but the intellectual leadership was unquestionably in the hands of Matsudaira Sadanobu.

DECLINE OF THE HAYASHI SCHOOL

Sadanobu intended to reinvigorate the bakufu bureaucracy by reshaping the Hayashi School, founded in 1630 by Hayashi Razan (1583–1657), as a training school for bureaucrats, who were to be taught a consistent ideology as the basis of their curriculum. In fact, Sadanobu did not just renew the school but rebuilt it completely. During the preceding decades the Hayashi School had fallen into a deplorable state. The quality of its instruction was far below the intellectual level of the numerous other private academies in Edo that attracted thousands of samurai. The buildings also had been sorely neglected. Two fires in 1772 and 1786 had nearly destroyed the school.[1]

When Sadanobu came to power, it seemed that the Hayashi School had exhausted its service function to the bakufu and the domains. It had been established with official funds on public land and had enjoyed routine shogunal support during its 150 years of existence. Although the bakufu supported the school economically, however, the management of the bakufu funds and decisions on educational policies lay with the head of the Hayashi family. Thus, the Hayashi School was at most a semiofficial bakufu school, and it maintained the character of a private institution.

The school had known its golden period during the Genroku era (1688–1703), under the reign of Tsunayoshi (1680–1709), the fifth shogun. He rebuilt it on a much larger scale and relocated it. In 1691 he created the new office of rector of the university (*daigaku no kami*) for the head of the Hayashi family. Tsunayoshi's infatuation with Sung scholarship (or Neo-Confucianism) also gave scholarship a new impetus, although his own practice of it was rather dilettantish and slanted toward sermonizing. It was under his patronage that Neo-Confucianism became a major school of thought and began to exert a tangible impact upon government and politics.

Traditionally, scholars have overestimated Neo-Confucianism's contribution to the creation of the Tokugawa sociopolitical system,[2] a retrospective distortion that is largely the result of the importance Neo-Confucianism acquired after Sadanobu's ban. Its formative influence dates only from the beginning of the eighteenth century, and even then its impact was of short duration, and not a monopoly of the Hayashi School. It was Arai Hakuseki, advisor to the shogun Ienobu (1709–12) and Ietsugu (1713–16), who recast the bakufu administrative style into a Confucian mold. His *Buke shohatto* (Legal code for the warriors) of 1710, for example, in contrast to earlier codes, was definitely formulated in Neo-Confucian rhetoric. But only seven years later, Yoshimune rejected Hakuseki's code for an earlier one of 1683, which was to stay in force for the next hundred years.[3] Moreover, neither of Yoshimune's advisers, Muro Kyūsō (1658–1734) and Ogyū Sorai (1666–1728), had studied in the Hayashi School. Kyūsō, like Hakuseki, was a disciple of Kinoshita Jun'an (1621–98), who belonged to the Fujiwara Seika (1561–1619) school, from which Hayashi had branched off; Kyūsō had also studied under Haguro Yōsen (1629–1702), a disciple of Yamazaki Ansai. Sorai was the founder of a new branch of the School of Ancient Learning that vigorously rejected the Neo-Confucian view of history and the universe.

Under Yoshimune, a new development took place with regard to Neo-Confucianism and the Hayashi School. In 1717 Yoshimune made an attempt to use Neo-Confucianism as a vehicle for "mass" education by introducing daily public lectures at the school, given by the students for the benefit of anyone interested: samurai, merchants, peasants, shopkeepers. These lectures continued until the fire of 1786 and were revived by Sadanobu. From the outset, however, the lectures drew little enthusiasm. In 1719, it is reported, there were only seven auditors.[4] But they did mark the start of the use of Neo-Confucianism for educational purposes.

Although famous for his promotion of culture and military arts (*bumbu*), Yoshimune showed little understanding of the politico-ideological potential of educational institutions. Someone, it is said, suggested to him that the moral effect of building a school would be very beneficial to the country. But Yoshimune took negative advice from Muro Kyūsō (who may have feared an expansion of the Hayashi School) as a confirmation of his own opinion, and rejected the idea.[5]

Neither was Yoshimune concerned with fostering one particular philosophy as the bakufu's creed. By Yoshimune's time, the deeper acquaintance of scholars with Chinese texts had greatly diversified the branches of learning, leaving Neo-Confucianism as only one of more than half a dozen schools of thought in the rapidly expanding world of scholarship. Besides Hayashi's school, but still within the confines of the Neo-Confucian creed, there were Fujiwara Seika's Kyoto School, Hayashi's parent branch; the school founded by Keian (1427–1508) in Satsuma (Southern Kyūshū); and the Kainan School from Tosa (Shikoku), from which Yamazaki Ansai in the 1660s had developed his own combination of Neo-Confucianism and Shinto. Competition between these schools was already fairly strong at the beginning of Yoshimune's rule, but the sharpest lines were between the Neo-Confucian tradition and the new schools: the Wang Yang-ming School of Nakae Tōju (1608–48) and Kumazawa Banzan (1619–91); and in particular the three Schools of Ancient Learning, represented by Yamaga Sokō, Itō Jinsai (1627–1705), and Ogyū Sorai. Yoshimune showed no interest in these scholastic rivalries, except that he made full use of the variety of the prevailing philosophies. His two advisors belonged to opposite schools, and when the public lectures at the Hayashi School proved a failure, Yoshimune ordered Muro Kyūsō, Kinoshita Kikutan (son of Jun'an), and Ogyū Hokkei (a disciple of Sorai), all of whom were outspoken critics of the Hayashi School, to open competitive lectures at the Takakura mansion in 1718.[6]

During Yoshimune's reign and the Tanuma period, the balance in the world of scholarship shifted dramatically in favor of the new schools, whose ranks were joined by a number of eclectic schools that gleaned their doctrines from the various teachings of the day. This trend is convincingly documented by Ishikawa Ken, a scholar of the development of the school system in the Tokugawa period, who examined the affiliation of the 2,228 scholars that are known to have been employed by the daimyo as personal councillors or teachers in the domain schools.

Table 6 shows how these scholars were spread over the various schools of thought and periods of the Tokugawa era. The schools outside the Neo-Confucian tradition took the lead in the middle of the eighteenth century. With 345 teachers versus 152, they more than doubled the Neo-Confucians, who at the turn of the century had dominated the field. If one compares the figures of the Hayashi school (55) with the most aggressive of the heterodox schools (Jinsai, Sorai, and Kochū), totaling 179, the insignificance of the Hayashi school in the Yoshimune-Tanuma period becomes evident.

A closer examination of the composition of the student population at the Hayashi School sheds further light upon the function played by the institution, prior to Sadanobu's reform. First it should be noticed that the enrollment at the school did not keep up with the expanding academic world of the middle period of eighteenth-century Japan (see table 7). The yearly average number of entering students climbed from

TABLE 6 Teachers of Chinese Scholarship per School and per Period

Schools	1630–1687	1688–1715	1716–1788	1789–1829	1830–1867	1868–1871	Total
Neo-Confucian							
Hayashi school	43	31	55	98	82	3	(311)
Shōhei school	—	—	5	55	160	10	(230)
Kyoto school	40	20	29	7	1	2	(99)
Others	31	27	63	115	197	26	(459)
Total	(113)	(78)	(152)	(275)	(440)	(41)	(1099)
Ansai school	12	20	121	85	47	7	(292)
Wang Yang-ming school	6	2	6	2	4	1	(21)
Jinsai school	3	11	49	10	4	—	(77)
Sorai school	—	6	118	56	13	1	(194)
Kochū school	—	—	12	28	10	—	(50)
Eclectic schools	2	4	27	63	64	7	(167)
Mito school	—	—	4	10	4	1	(19)
Others	7	—	8	12	11	3	(41)
Total	(30)	(43)	(345)	(266)	(157)	(20)	(861)
Affiliation unknown	20	15	64	85	60	24	(268)
Grand total	(163)	(136)	(561)	(626)	(657)	(85)	(2228)

To the Shōhei School belong those scholars that graduated from the *Shōheizaka gakumonjo*, the Bakufu College that after Sadanobu's reform developed as an independent institution from, but within the precincts of, the Hayashi School.

The Ansai School, although not listed as Neo-Confucian, was a mixture of Neo-Confucian thought and Shinto tradition.

The Kochū School was very much akin to Sorai's brand of Ancient Learning (representatives of this school are Minogawa Kien and Tsukada Taihō).

(From Ishikawa Ken, "Rinke-juku narabi Shōhei-kō ga hanritsu gakkō ni ataeta eikyō," *Ochanomizu Joshi Daigaku jimbun kagaku kiyō*, VIII (1956), 78–79.

6.2 under the first two Hayashis to 9.4 under the third (1681–1732), but then, under the next three rectors (1733–92), the average dropped to 8.1. The real average for this period is several points lower still, since the student population increased substantially during Sadanobu's rule. Matsudaira Sadamitsu, a scholar and descendant of Sadanobu, gives a further breakdown of 5.7 for 1732–58; 6.8 for 1759–73; and 7.69 for 1774–86.[7]

If, with table 7 at hand, one further analyzes the background of the students entering the Hayashi school, it becomes very clear that the school was not a training place for bakufu functionaries. Before Sadanobu's time, this group constituted a negligible part of the student population—only 5.2 percent in the 1733–92 period. During the same period, however, the school was 30 percent filled with students from fifty-five different domains. Must one then conclude that the main function of the institution was to turn out Neo-Confucian teachers for the domain schools? The statistics at first seem to support this interpretation, but a closer look at the data reveals that the Hayashi School was not significant in spreading Neo-Confucian doctrines to the domain schools.

Ishikawa Ken's calculations show that 31 percent from among the

TABLE 7 Students Entering the Hayashi School

Period	Total	Bakufu Retainers			Domains		
(No. of Years)	(Yearly Average)	Hata./ Goken.	Lower Ret.	Total	Daim./ Heirs	Retainers	Total
1630–1680 (50)	310 (6.2)	5	—	5	—	106	106
1681–1732 (51)	482 (9.4)	14	—	14	2	120	122
1733–1792 (59)	479 (8.1)	25	—	25	4	138	142
1793–1838 (45)	796 (17.7)	128	119	247	46	302	348
1839–1867 (26)	517 (18.4)	71	96	169	18	244	262
Total	2585	243	243	458	70	910	980

The periods are broken down according to the tenure periods of the Hayashi rectors:
Razan and Gahō (1630–80); Hōkō (1681–1732); Ryūkō, Hōkoku, Hōtan and Kimpō
(1733–92); Jussai (1793–1838); Baisai, Kansai, Fukusai and Gakusai (1839–67). (The school
existed until 1888.)

The total number of students and the bakufu retainers were computed from the *Shōdō-ki*,
the official record of the Hayashi School.

The students from the domains were computed from the *Shōdō-ki* and other records. The
980 students represent 180 domains; the *Shōdō-ki*, instead of 910 retainers, has only 797,
representing 170 domains. These 170 domains break down over the five periods as follows: 41,
65, 55, 114, 89.

Besides the Bakufu retainers and the students from the domains, there were some 220
commoners, and about 1,000 whose origin is not clear.

Hata = *hatamoto*, bannermen or upper office-holding retainers;
Goken = *gokenin*, housemen;
Daim = daimyo.

(Compiled from Ishikawa, "Rinke-juku," pp. 43, 48, 50, 55.)

daimyo's retainers studying at the school returned to their domains as
Neo-Confucian scholars.[8] What is the significance of that percentage in
terms of the philosophical affiliation of the domain schools during the
Yoshimune-Tanuma period? For the 1716–89 period, Ishikawa lists
twenty-four domains where one or several Hayashi graduates (totaling
fifty-six) were employed.[9] If one now checks these domains against the
data collected by Kasai Sukeharu, another scholar of the Tokugawa
schools and their philosophical affiliations—data which he recently
published in an exhaustive, two-volume study of all domain and
district (*gō*), schools—then one comes to the following conclusions.[10]
Exactly half of the twenty-four domains employing Hayashi graduates
had no domain school. In these domains, the graduates functioned as
private advisors or tutors to the daimyo and to some of their retainers.
After 1790, these domains did establish schools, but only half of them
chose Neo-Confucianism as their main philosophy. Of the twelve
domains with established schools prior to 1790, only four taught
exclusively Neo-Confucianism; three combined it with heterodox
doctrines; and five were purely heterodox. Hence, during this middle
period of the eighteenth century, Hayashi graduates propagated their
teaching in a politically significant way (that is, at schools where their
philosophy prevailed) at only four domain schools, although they were
spread over twenty-four domains.

To determine the philosophy of a particular domain school, therefore, it is not sufficient to establish the affiliation of its teachers. Kasai Sukeharu, in his study of the domain schools, checked the affiliation of each school's staff against the textbooks that were used. He discovered the changing affiliation patterns of 260 domain schools and twenty-three district schools over the whole Tokugawa period, but unfortunately he did not analyze or tabulate his data. By relying on Kasai's study it is possible to calculate the ratio of orthodox versus heterodox schools before and after Sadanobu's ban (see table 8). For the time being, let us consider the situation at the moment of the ban. From Kasai's total we left out schools whose foundation dates or affiliation pattern (or both) were unclear, and a few schools without Chinese studies. This leaves us with a total of ninety-three domain, and fourteen district, schools established prior to 1790. Of these, twenty-eight and five, respectively, belonged to the orthodox tradition, and, as mentioned above, only four promoted Hayashi teachings. It should be noted that "orthodox" is here defined as Neo-Confucian in the broad sense. It therefore includes eclectic schools that accepted the importance of Neo-Confucianism but not to the exclusion of other systems of thought. The remaining sixty-five (and nine) schools belonged to heterodox traditions.

TABLE 8 Orthodoxy and Heterodoxy in Domain and District Schools

	Tot.	Schools Founded: Before 1790			:	Change after '90		Before 1868 1790–1868			:	Change		1868–71		
		Tot.	O	H	:	→H	→O	Tot.	O	H	:	→H	→O	Tot.	O	H
Shimpan	3	2	—	2	:	2	—	1	1	—	:	—	—	—	—	—
Kamon	16	8	2	6	:	6	—	8	3	5	:	2	3	2	—	2
Fudai	114	40	18	22	:	14	8	74	29	45	:	33	12	19	12	7
Tozama	81	43	8	35	:	15	20	38	17	21	:	18	3	6	2	4
Total	214	93	28	65	:	37	28	121	50	71	:	53	18	27	14	13
Gōkō (a)	23	14	5	9	:	4	5	9	2	7	:	6	1	—	—	—
Total	237	107	33	74	:	41	33	130	52	78	:	59	19	27	14	13

(a) District schools, all in tozama domains.

The above figures differ slightly from the totals given by Kasai on p. 72, because they include only those schools whose founding dates with relation to the ban are known, and whose philosophical affiliations were clear. It also leaves out a few schools which specialized exclusively in the martial arts.

The philosophical affiliation of the schools was decided upon not only by the affiliation of its teachers, but also by the textbooks used; where certain schools of thought at a particular institution were present only as a minority, the institution was catalogued under its more representative affiliation.

"Orthodoxy" and "heterodoxy" represent only the major trend of an institution in 1790. Changes from heterodoxy to orthodoxy (→O) include all changes occurring between 1790 and 1868.

Border cases where heterodoxy and orthodoxy were difficult to define were solved as follows: of the many eclectic schools only the ones that explicitly centered around Neo-Confucianism were considered orthodox.

Compiled from Kasai, Kinsei hankō, pp. 89–1958.

With the heterodox schools setting the intellectual tone around the middle of the eighteenth century, the nature of scholarship underwent considerable change. While Neo-Confucian scholarship was marked by the didactic and reverential assimilation of established truths about the ethicopolitical order, the new schools launched an outright attack on these assumptions, often in an atmosphere of iconoclastic and free polemic. In the domains, the new teachings were institutionalized in the schools. In Edo they carried the day in the numerous private academies where students flocked by the thousands, while the Hayashi School stood virtually empty.

Before turning to a closer examination of these two opposed views of learning and scholarship, and of Sadanobu's position on the matter, it is worth noting one of many well-known anecdotes of the time illustrating the low ebb of the Hayashi School. In the 1770s there was an economy plan which called for pulling down the *Seidō*, the shrine to Confucius that formed the center of the Hayashi School. It is reported that neither the senior councillor Mizuno Tadatomo nor the chamberlains knew what the *Seidō* was. They asked the chief clerk of the shogun, one Ōmae Sombei, whether the shrine was Shinto or Buddhist. When Ōmae informed them that it was dedicated to Confucius, they asked what kind of man he was. Upon further enlightenment, the senior councillor exclaimed: "Ah, now I understand why Hayashi, the rector, was opposed to the plan. If we pulled it down, he said, and the news got abroad, our reputation in China would suffer."[11]

Sadanobu's View of Scholarship

Some authors have argued that Sadanobu's view of scholarship changed drastically, from a broad, eclectic one to a political utilitarian outlook, during the process that led to the ban on heterodox ideas.[12] Others, to the contrary, have demonstrated with quotations from Sadanobu's writings, both before and after the ban, that his views remained unchanged.[13] Both interpretations concede that the ban was political in nature. In discussing Sadanobu's view and use of scholarship, it is important to acknowledge this fact as central, for Sadanobu —though an intellectual and a scholar in his own way—was primarily a statesman.

In eighteenth-century Japan there were two basic attitudes toward scholarship and learning. The older one could be called didactic and normative. Its purpose was the moral cultivation of the individual, and scholarship was carried on in this tradition by sermonizing and pontificating on Neo-Confucianism in a thoroughly uncritical way. The Hayashi School of thought was the most prestigious expression of this authority-oriented tradition. Its most extreme branch, although not purely Neo-Confucian, was represented by Yamazaki Ansai's Kimon School. Ansai had no room for the study of history and poetry and had reduced the area of scholarship to little more than the exposition of three Sung commentaries, all of which were ready-made distillations and detailed political applications of Neo-Confucian philosophy. They were like vade mecums or companion manuals for the true believers—or, better, the true rulers. These three commentaries were the *Kinshiroku* (Reflections on things at hand), a selection from four Sung commentators whose sayings had been arranged according to 622 pertinent topics; the *Hakurokudō-shōin keiji* (Regulations for the Academy of the White Deer Cave), an explanation of the rules of Confucius' academy; and the *Shōgaku* (The lesser learning), an elementary introduction to Neo-Confucianism. Its simplified content and doctrinaire tone had made the Kimon school particularly apt for political purposes. In 1790, there were sixteen domain schools of the Kimon tradition. By then, however, the Kimon school together with all Neo-Confucian schools were increasingly under the pressure of the schools of Ancient Learning, especially that of Ogyū Sorai. These schools dominated thirty-seven of the existing ninety-three domain schools.

The schools of Ancient Learning and the eclectic schools took a broad view of education. Their approach was analytical and individualistic, and almost inductive when they engaged in comparative studies of government. The syncretic tolerance and the reliance upon the human mind that underpinned the methodology of this flexible view of learning was highly iconoclastic of the normative and authoritarian Neo-Confucian tradition. In these new schools, the purpose of education was not the moral formation of subjects as proper members of the polity. Learning consisted rather of the individual's intellectual cultivation and, in relation to politics, of understanding and acquiring the necessary techniques to keep society in good order. While Neo-Confucian scholars concentrated their efforts on improving society and bettering the function of political institutions, and on improving the individual through moral education, the Sorai branch of Ancient Learning constantly criticized the shortcomings of institutions in their efforts at controlling and regulating the passions of men. Scholars in this tradition, such as Dazai Shundai (1680–1747), held that nothing could be done to change human nature from what it is. Historical decline was not caused by moral decadence so much as by the deterioration of political structure.[14]

In the latter half of the eighteenth century, this tradition had produced scores of brilliant intellects, poetry critics such as Hattori Nankaku (1683–1759), and pragmatic scientists such as Sugita Gempaku (1733–1817), who in the eyes of the Neo-Confucians displayed irreverent and dilettante arrogance and intellectual hubris that threatened the unity of society. In several domains (to be discussed below in more detail), the radically but narrowly orthodox Kimon school had therefore reacted by banning all other doctrines. It is significant that the line between orthodoxy and heterodoxy was first drawn by the followers of Yamazaki Ansai with their high concern for ideological integration.

Sadanobu was not, strictly speaking, a follower of the Kimon school. His traditionalism was more broad-minded, although, as noted earlier (in chapter 2), he certainly was influenced by ideas attributable to Yamazaki. Sadanobu firmly believed in the need for core values that serve as absolutes for society. Beyond that political necessity, he did not set rigid limits in one's moral, intellectual, or aesthetic education. This was also true for training in government and administration. His definition of education could thus be described as broadly conceived. Strict adherence to certain unalterable truths about man and society, however, was absolutely necessary. For those who plunged into pedantic sophistry without having first assured themselves a basic moral foundation, Sadanobu felt nothing but scorn. Such men were, in his eyes, not properly developed human beings and certainly unfit to lead others. It was to save this moral basis, at least for bakufu functionaries, that Sadanobu issued his ban.

Sadanobu defined scholarship as "the activity whereby a person learns to become a full human being."[15] Hence to guarantee the moral education of his officials and to save scholarship were one and the same thing for Sadanobu. Scholarship ought to provide the basis whereby one trains oneself in virtue and the great ethical ideas in the Confucian tradition.[16] A person without moral training, he wrote, lives a drunken life and dies in a dream. Although he possesses the form of a human being, his heart and mind are of a lesser order.[17]

Scholarship in the sense of bookish knowledge Sadanobu saw not as an asset but as a real danger. The true purpose of scholarship is to practice the moral truths one learns.[18] This involves the rectification of one's heart and body (*seishin-shūshin*), in order to provide peace and well-being in the country (*chikoku-anmin*).[19] If one does not approach the classics with that state of mind, then one reads them like *jōruri* or popular ballads.[20] In his own works, Sadanobu is critical of the didacticism and seemingly idle talk of Neo-Confucian scholars[21] as well as the followers of Jinsai and Sorai, who, in his eyes, used scholarship for their own fame and profit.[22]

Sadanobu's criticism of the different schools, including Neo-Confucianism, was related to their unpracticality. Neo-Confucianism was limited in scope and often too theoretical. The Kimon school, which Sadanobu considered Neo-Confucianian,[23] was also much too narrow. Followers of Sorai concentrated too much on textual problems. The Wang Yang-ming school did not distinguish between good and evil. In short, they all lost sight of the essence of learning, which Sadanobu defined as an active internalization of the wisdom of the sages.[24]

Why then did Sadanobu decide upon Neo-Confucianism as the bakufu's official doctrine? In Sadanobu's own justification of his choice, one meets again with the two elements that shape his behavior as a statesman: emotional, nonempirical commitment and rational practicality. Four years after the ban, Sadanobu, then retired, wrote in his notes about his fundamental belief in the value of Neo-Confucianism (his mild criticism notwithstanding):

> You ask me what I value. I value only Yao, Shun, and Confucius, but it is very difficult to appreciate them without the glosses and commentaries. If it comes to the question as to which commentator one has to follow, I have since my childhood learned Neo-Confucianism, and I am not going to change now. It is not so much that I have a deep knowledge of these texts. *It is simply that a man without doubts does not think of changing.* [Italics mine.][25]

Neo-Confucianism, moreover, was not a harmful teaching. It had proved itself a valuable political ethic in the past and had commanded the respect of many. One was therefore unlikely to err by putting one's trust in it.[26]

Under this commonsensical and low-keyed choice of "the least harmful teaching" ran the strong conviction that someone had to put some order in the variegated world of scholarship—a conviction that should come as no surprise from someone who casts himself in the role of political "savior" of the realm. In 1812, Sadanobu wrote:

> In Neo-Confucianism there are few things that one can doubt. Now, however, there are dozens of theories—cartloads of them—and dozens of scholars abusing each other. *Someone had to unify this.* These scholars are like the bubbles of boiling water or the entangled strands of thread. *Someone had to support scholarship. . . .* In this, Ieyasu showed us the example by appointing Hayashi Razan, whose teachings, in contrast to all other theories, have not changed over the years. [Italics mine.][27]

Sadanobu's reference to Razan's teachings, as we have seen already, represents a distorted view of the establishment of Neo-Confucianism as the bakufu's official doctrine. But the view of the present situation as perilous to the official belief system made a political unification measure more acceptable. In fact, what Sadanobu and others were arguing was the loss of an ideological uniformity that never existed. The anthropologist Clifford Geertz calls such an attitude "ideological retraditionalization." "One constructs arguments for tradition," Geertz writes, "only when its credentials have been questioned."[28]

Yet the legitimation of Neo-Confucianism through an appeal to bakufu tradition, although present in the text of the ban, appears in Sadanobu's writings only years later. It was thus probably not the main factor in Sadanobu's decision. For Sadanobu, Neo-Confucianism was primarily a convenient ideology for a political system based on authority to assure political integration without altering established institutions. Unlike Sorai's followers, Sadanobu never seriously questioned the adequacy of the political system. Once, in his *Kankodōri*, he proposed to alter the system of alternate attendance, but he never did anything to implement his own proposal.[29]

The limitations Sadanobu put on scholarship were thus purely political. There were works that he preferred, considering them basic and indispensable, but he always maintained that there were no books one ought not read. In 1782 he wrote that all schools of thought had their good and bad points, and that retainers should be able to learn from any school.[30] In 1786 he recommended to a daimyo in his *Ōmu no kotoba* the Four Books, the Five Classics, the Commentary on the Great Learning, the *Nihongi*, the *Shiki*, and writings of Kumazawa Banzan and Muro Kyūsō.[31] Sadanobu gave the same advice during his tenure as chief councillor, and again in 1826, toward the end of his life.[32] Learning should be broad, but it should be based upon the classics: if one starts from the proper basis, then one can read any book with profit.[33]

THE ORTHODOX CLIQUE

The decree of the ban on heterodoxy was handed over to Hayashi Kimpō on 1790/5/24. It was worded as follows:

> Since the Keichō era (1596–1614), all generations have put their trust in Neo-Confucianism, and your house has been ordered to support that doctrine. Therefore, you should watchfully encourage that orthodoxy and promote its students. Recently, however, the world has witnessed the rise of several new doctrines; heterodoxy has become a fashion; customs have suffered from it; and orthodoxy [*seigaku*, written with the characters, meaning "correct learning" or "sacred learning"] has declined. This is a deeply regrettable situation. Even among your pupils, it is said, impure doctrines have spread. I hereby order you to discipline the school strictly. A similar order has been issued to Shibano Ritsuzan and Okada Kanzen. In

consultation with them, you should quickly proceed to prohibit
heterodoxy among the pupils. Regardless of whose students they
are, they should study orthodoxy, and in this way you should apply
yourself to promoting the formation of talented men.[34]

Kimpō complied quickly but bitterly complained about the limitations
put on scholarship at the Hayashi School. In the same year he tried to
circulate a protest memorandum among all daimyo retainers and
rōnin (masterless samurai) studying at the school, but Ritsuzan, the
newly appointed academic supervisor, prevented him from so doing.[35]
In the following year, Kimpō addressed a memorandum to Sadanobu.
The main point of his criticism was that the school had fallen into the
hands of narrow-minded Ansai followers. Exclusive emphasis was
being given to the *Shōgaku* and the *Kinshiroku*, at the expense of
neglecting other branches of learning. According to Kimpō, the
tradition of broad learning of the Hayashi School—under Razan, he
pointed out, there had been Wang Yang-ming scholars at the school—
was being destroyed by a Kimon conspiracy. He accused Shibano
Ritsuzan and Okada Kanzen of being the main culprits.[36] Was it true
that, despite Sadanobu's own moderate views, he was being side-
tracked by more radical elements, or was Kimpō's accusation merely
the frustrated complaint of an administrator who had fallen in
disgrace, against newly appointed executives who enjoyed the chief
councillor's special favor? The answer may have been that Sadanobu,
the politician, could afford to hold moderately traditional views,
while his reform was being carried out by radical lieutenants.

Kimon elements and sympathizers, as Kimpō rightly complained,
were endowing Sadanobu's reform with increasing rigidity. The new
appointees and those about to be made were either Ansai devotees or
orthodox minded Neo-Confucians. Together they formed a clique that
had been very active before 1790 in promoting Kimon or Neo-
Confucian teachings in certain domains and banning other doctrines.
Some of these scholars had been introduced to Sadanobu by his own
tutors as early as 1784.

Undoubtedly the concern of these scholars with the public state of
scholarship, and their eagerness to do something about it, had
touched a very sensitive cord in Sadanobu, who, in 1784, had just
brought to a successful end his first yonaoshi enterprise in Shirakawa.
They confirmed and strengthened his belief that it was his mission to
put the country on the right scholarly path. When he proceeded with
his ban six years later, it would have been strange indeed, if he had not
relied upon this group of "public-minded" scholars. And it was their
public-mindedness and activism that appealed more to Sadanobu than
their Kimon sympathies per se. Ultimately Sadanobu was not inter-

ested in the doctrinal differences between the more extreme Kimon school and the Neo-Confucians of the center—after all, he considered the Kimon school a full member of the Neo-Confucian fold. Kimon scholars were thus the natural allies of Sadanobu's political concerns, because over the last decades they had been the most active and successful in the politics of ideology.

All seven bans against heterodoxy that were issued in domain schools prior to 1790 were the work of Kimon scholars.[37] The first had occurred in Himeji han (fudai) in 1691, one year after the inauguration of the new Hayashi School in Edo. The domain school that was founded that year was run by Hayashi and Kimon scholars, who prohibited the teaching of all other doctrines.[38] The next domain to take similar action (in 1764) was Kōchi (tozama), where Ansai had started his career. It was, however, in the 1770s and 1780s that most bans were issued: Shibata (fudai) in 1772, Kagoshima (tozama) in 1773, Saga (tozama) in 1781, Obama (fudai) and Hiroshima (tozama) in 1782.[39] The Kagoshima domain was not strictly speaking of the Kimon tradition since the school was run by disciples of Muro Kyūsō. Kyūsō, however, had studied under a Kimon teacher and shared some of the ideas of Kimon; notably the idealization of a sage emperor who would ban pernicious doctrines and burn immoral books.[40]

All three bans of the 1780s involved scholars who were later to become close associates of Sadanobu. The ban in Saga was the work of Koga Seiri (1750–1817), whom Sadanobu invited in 1792 to lecture at the Bakufu College or *Gakumonjo* (as one part of the Hayashi School was called after Sadanobu's reform). In 1796/5 Sadanobu extended a permanent appointment to Seiri at the college.[41] Seiri had studied under Nishiyori Seisai (1702–97), an aggressive Kimon scholar whose nephew and adopted son, Bokuzan (1726–1800) was the scholar behind the ban of heterodox thought in Obama han in 1782.

In that same year, Rai Shunzui (1748–1816) started a struggle in Hiroshima han that led to the victory of the Kimon party over the scholars of Ancient Learning, who were forced to continue their activities in a private school. Shunzui was a friend and relative of Bitō Nishū (1745–1813), whom Sadanobu appointed to the Bakufu College on 1791/9. Both had studied in Osaka under Katayama Hokkai (1722–90), and had married daughters of Iioka Yoshinari, an Osaka scholar and admirer of Ansai.[42] Shunzui's earlier training had been in the Kimon tradition.[43] Much later, he also found his way to the Bakufu College as a guest lecturer in 1800/10–1801/4 and 1803/1–3.[44] Shunzui's nephew Rai Sanyō (1780–1832), a historian, exercised great influence on loyalists in the *bakumatsu* period who would topple the order Sadanobu so vigorously upheld. In 1827 Sanyō dedicated his famous history of Japan, the *Nihon gaishi* (Unofficial history of Japan), to none other than Sadanobu himself.[45]

Sadanobu's association with Rai Shunzui began quite early. In 1784/4, a close, personal tutor of Sadanobu at Tayasu and later at the Matsudaira mansion, named Kurosawa Chikō (1714–97), a scholar of Neo-Confucianism, introduced Shunzui to Sadanobu.[46] Sadanobu and Shunzui discussed the recent ban of all non-Kimon teachings in Hiroshima and the general political problem of heterodox doctrines. When Sadanobu left for Shirakawa two months later, Shunzui sent him a note of thanks for the invitation, in which he praised Sadanobu's admiration for Neo-Confucianism and his clear and detailed understanding of the origins of heterodoxy. Shunzui added that his hopes for promoting orthodox teachings rested now on Sadanobu.[47] In short, Sadanobu cultivated close relations with a very active group of scholars with a cause, just as in the political world he had assumed the leadership of the disgruntled fudai daimyo.

This group of scholars became friends at Osaka's *Kontonsha*, a poetry academy founded by Katayama Hokkai. All the key members of the group figured prominently in Sadanobu's ban on heterodox doctrines. Bitō Nishū began as a student of Ancient Learning, but then turned to Neo-Confucianism through the influence of his brother-in-law Shunzui and the writings of Muro Kyūsō.[48] He displayed the fervor of a neophyte: in 1772, twenty years before Sadanobu's ban, he had already written about the need to unify scholarship around Neo-Confucianism.[49] Koga Seiri started with Wang Yang-ming idealism and then turned to the Kimon school under Nishiyori Seisai. Influenced by Bitō Nishū, Shunzui, and Nakai Chikuzan (1730–1804), Koga became an outstanding scholar of Neo-Confucianism.[50] Nakai Chikuzan was a well-known Neo-Confucian scholar, who held more moderate views concerning the orthodoxy of doctrine than some of his *Kontonsha* friends. On the recommendation of Shibano Ritsuzan, Sadanobu made a point of meeting Chikuzan on 1788/6/3 on his return trip from Kyoto, and requested him to write an economic treatise. The result was Chikuzan's *Sōbō kigen*, which spelled out solutions for contemporary economic and financial problems along the same lines as in Sadanobu's own works.[51]

Shibano Ritsuzan, recommended to Sadanobu by the latter's tutors Kurosawa Chikō and Ōtsuka Kōtaku (1719–92),[52] was also a member of the same academy and a personal friend of Nishiyama Sessai (1735–98), another convert from Sorai scholarship to Neo-Confucianism.[53] Sessai had fanatical ideas about the promotion of orthodox doctrines. After Ritsuzan's appointment to the Bakufu College in 1788/1/16, Sessai urged him to work for a bakufu ban on heterodox doctrines,[54] so that some historians blame Sessai for Sadanobu's ban. Indeed, on 1790/6/26, a month after the ban, Sadanobu sent Sessai a letter expressing his joy over the measure he had just taken.[55] Ritsuzan, however, does not seem to have shared Sessai's narrow-mindedness. He was undoubtedly the most gifted and widely read scholar among the whole group. Having studied among others under Nakamura Ranrin (1697–1761), a disciple of Muro Kyūsō, he inherited some of the rigorism of that tradition; for instance, he lamented the existence of more than twenty different interpretations of the Analects.[56]

The only scholar connected with Sadanobu's ban on heterodox doctrines who was not from Osaka was Okada Kanzen (1740–1818).[57] The son of a samurai of the Isezaki domain in the Kantō area, he was a disciple of the Kimon scholar Muraji Gyokusui (1727–76). He was also a friend of Rai Shunzui, and Sadanobu appointed him to the college on 1789/9/10, upon the recommendation of Kurosawa Chikō and Shibano Ritsuzan. His tenure was short. In 1797/12, possibly because of an examination scandal involving his nephew,[58] Kanzen was given a post as daikan over 5,000 koku of bakufu territories of Hitachi province (Ibaraki prefecture), where he later was worshiped as a living god for his exemplary administration. Koga Seiri replaced Kanzen at the college in 1796/2.

The orthodox clique was thus a brotherhood of strongly motivated, dogmatic, and public-minded scholars. Some of them had been active in the politics of ideology, and quite a few displayed the fresh zeal of new converts. It was over this group that Sadanobu, through his tutors, assumed leadership precisely at a time when the rivalry between the different world views of the various schools had hardened into issues of orthodoxy and heterodoxy, and when the need for a publicly supported ideology was being increasingly felt in some intellectual quarters.

How can one now explain this growing need for the politicization and unification of ideology at the period when it occurred, namely in the 1770s and 1780s? The mere existence of a plurality of doctrines cannot account for the occurrence of this movement at that point, because most of these contending doctrines had been active for more than half a century. The crucial development of the Tanuma period, however, occurred in the political system when it began to depart from the immediate control of received tradition. It is precisely at such a point, Clifford Geertz contends, when conventional morality loses its integrative power, that formal ideologies emerge to maintain the political order.[59]

The emergence of numerous contending philosophical schools in the eighteenth century, and the rise of ostensibly untraditional values governing the political process under Tanuma, suggest a crisis in political ethics of the sort Geertz describes. The need for ideological order was stated first in purely philosophical terms in the middle of the century. In the 1750s, as we have seen, Takenouchi Shikibu—a follower of Suika Shinto, the religious branch of the Ansai tradition— proposed to unify teachings around the emperor. The eclectic schools, which grew in importance from that time, can be regarded as another philosophical attempt at ideological unification, though the eclectics were interested primarily in ethical unity for the individual, not in the political implementation of a unified ideology. They were even to prove themselves the strongest of the various schools in withstanding the pressure for ideological unification from above, following the ban on heterodox ideas.

The first effort to promote ideological uniformity through political means occurred during the Tanuma regime. At that time political practices in the bakufu seemed openly to flaunt traditional values; natural disasters and social upheaval reinforced the fear of social disintegration. The ruling elite in the country felt an urgency to develop learning and to reorder the world by redressing men's hearts and minds through cultivating the correct values.

The acceleration of school building in the domains provides evidence for this concern over moral decline. Before 1683 there were only seven domain schools in Japan (see table 9), but during the next hundred years, fifty-nine new schools were built, averaging six per decade. In the crucial decades of the 1770s and 1780s, however, the average rose to twelve and twenty-one respectively. The trend continued throughout the 1790s, the decade after the ban, when the number reached twenty-six.[60] These data convincingly disprove the suggestion made by some scholars that the "sudden" increase of school building after 1790 was triggered by Sadanobu's proscription of heterodox ideas and his promotion of learning.[61] The previous momentum, of course, gave concrete institutional visibility to the

TABLE 9 Foundation of Domain Schools

Periods & No. of Years	Aver./ Year	Total	Shimpan	Kamon	Fudai	Tozama
1624–1683 (60)	0.117	7	1	2	—	4
1684–1750 (67)	0.507	34	1	2	16	15
1751–1780 (30)	0.833	25	—	5	10	10
1781–1803 (23)	2.565	59	1	1	29	28
1804–1843 (40)	1.800	72	2	3	45	22
1844–1867 (24)	1.375	33	—	2	21	10
1868–1871 (4)	12.000	48	1	2	28	17
Total		278	6	17	149	106

Source: Kasai, *Kinsei hankō*, p. 72.

great number of philosophical positions that had developed in the last hundred years.

The Kimon school played an extremely important role in advocating ideological unification through political action. This school offered a very detailed and sharply focused application of Neo-Confucianism to the needs of government and administration. Its tradition, moreover, was authoritarian and left little room for discussion or speculation about ultimate truths. It did not concern itself with an objective examination of political institutions, since it saw institutions as metaphysically established normative entities. Its principal aim was to foster an attitude of devotion and *action* within institutional norms. The Kimon school was thus the first to understand how important politics was for enforcing ideological uniformity. At first, scholars of this school saw the need for ideological unity in some of the domains; they then envisioned the same on a wider national scale.

Sadanobu clearly shared the ideals and political concerns of Kimon. Even in his private life, as we have seen in chapter 2, he adopted a belief in ascetic training and spiritual autolatry as well as a general world view that was typical of the Ansai tradition. He saw religious meaning in institutional conformity because it was the way par excellence to actualize men's divine potential in themselves. It was only natural that Sadanobu would rely on the scholarly ideas and leadership of Ansai's Kimon school to implement his plans for ideological unification.

THE BAN ON HETERODOXY

As he did with his economic and financial measures, Sadanobu prepared his educational reform well in advance. He issued the ban on heterodoxy in the middle of his six-year tenure, but his first directive concerning scholarship dates from his first month in office. During the intervening three years, Sadanobu came to understand that a thorough reform was needed, and so he made the necessary appointments during this time to assure that the reform, once launched, would be durable.

It should be remembered that Sadanobu was working at the same time on his economic and financial programs, and also that the greater part of his first year as chief councillor was taken up with purging the bureaucracy and establishing his hold over the Senior and Junior Councils. Moreover, although he was aware that his role as regent to the shogun was only of a limited duration by the nature of the office, he did not know that his power as councillor would be withdrawn after only six years. But he succeeded in giving his reform a lasting basis during this short period. His sense of the urgency of his mission

explains the thoroughness of his measures and the determination and
tempo with which he implemented them.

From his first weeks in office, Sadanobu indicated that his concern
for promoting the cultural and military arts (*bumbu*) was not to be
limited to exhortative encouragements. On 1787/7/21 he ordered a
complete investigation of all schools in both fields,[62] and while
waiting for the results of that survey he embarked on concrete action.
He first drew attention to the daily public lectures that had resumed at
the Hayashi School after part of its buildings, destroyed by the fire of
the previous year, had been rebuilt. He provided the school with a
core of new students in a rather original way. Setting up a symposium
at the mansion of his trusted friend Honda Tadakazu, he invited
fifteen samurai to lecture on the Chinese Classics. Sadanobu and a few
other dignitaries were present, and after the ceremony he ordered the
fifteen samurai—probably to their great surprise—to pursue their
studies at the Hayashi School.[63]

On 1788/1/16, although despairing of ever realizing his reform
with the two councils still filled with Tanuma appointees, Sadanobu
appointed Shibano Ritsuzan, the famous Neo-Confucian scholar from
the Kansai area, to a teaching position at the Hayashi School. On
1789/9/10 he called Okada Kanzen, a Kimon devotee, to the teaching
staff. But there was no significant improvement. The school was
controlled by a weak rector, Hayashi Kimpō, who held more liberal
views on education but was not concerned primarily with problems of
educational reform.

Kimpō, an adopted son of the Hayashi family, had become rector in
1787/3 at the age of twenty. His position as adopted son was
aggravated by the emotional antagonism of two strong-willed ma-
trons of the family, the widows of the fifth and sixth rectors, Hōkoku
(1721–73) and Hōtan (1761–87). Hōkoku died in 1773 and was
succeeded by his twelve-year-old son Hōtan, who died in 1787, aged
twenty-six. The two surviving widows meddled in Kimpō's marriage,
forcing him to divorce his wife, and interfered with his affairs at
the school.[64] A strong hand was clearly needed if headway was to be
made with educational reform. With this in mind, Sadanobu con-
veyed new administrative powers to his friends Ritsuzan and Kanzen
as supervisors of academic affairs in general. They were especially
charged with implementing the decree against heterodoxy. Although
they were expected to consult formally with the rector, there was no
doubt that they were in control. For example, Ritsuzan prevented the
rector from distributing to students a pamphlet that criticized the
reform. Neither Ritsuzan nor Kanzen were young men when Sadanobu appointed them. Ritsuzan was already fifty-four, and Kanzen

fifty. They had little difficulty in controlling the twenty-three-year-old rector.

In 1790/4, Sadanobu, accompanied by a senior councillor (Torii Takaoki) and two junior councillors (Ii Naoakira and Hotta Masaatsu), paid an official visit to the school.[65] The meaning of the visit was clear. It was not merely to prepare the school for the ban on heterodoxy, which would be promulgated one month later, but to impress upon Kimpō, then rector, Sadanobu's personal desire to transform the school and to entrust the project to Ritsuzan and Kanzen.

Having made his intentions clear with regard to the Hayashi School, Sadanobu turned to the control of literary publications in Edo. He issued a decree, which he reissued four months later, that all new publications must be registered with the city magistrate and that all anonymous works would be taken out of circulation.[66] Under this decree, Santō Kyōden (1761–1816), a popular writer of comic books, was punished in the following year. More famous was the case of Hayashi Shihei (1738–1793), an independent scholar much influenced by the ideas of Sorai, whose famous work on maritime defense, called *Kaikoku heidan* (Discussion of the military matters of a maritime country), was banned, and Hayashi was confined to his house.[67]

These measures have sometimes been interpreted as Sadanobu's attempt to control public opinion. In a sense they were. They reflected his paternalistic concern for the proper moral welfare of the population, but they were not meant to silence criticism of the ban on heterodoxy. Hayashi Shihei's work, for example, was judged too alarming because it might spread unnecessary fears about national security. Shihei strongly implied that bakufu institutions were not fit to defend the country. He developed his views out of the Sorai school and showed a critical stance toward existing institutions that directly countered Sadanobu's political premises. None of the criticisms directed against Sadanobu's ban itself, however, were denied publication; nor were their authors persecuted. And there were many that made abundant use of that freedom.

Harsh criticism of the ban came from numerous scholars besides Hayashi Kimpō. From the eclectic school (*Setchūgaku*), protests were written by Tsukada Taihō, Toshima Hōshū, Yamamoto Hokusan, Kameda Hōsai, Hosoi Heishū, and Akamatsu Sōshū; and from Sorai's school, scholars such as Itō Randen, Tosaki Tanen, Ichikawa Kakumei, and Kamei Nanmei registered their opposition.[68] Most prominent among these critics were Tsukada Taihō (1745–1832) and Akamatsu Sōshū (1721–1801).

Tsukada Taihō's criticism was especially weighty. He represented the view of the two collateral houses of Owari and Kii. Employed in Owari, he was a close friend of the widely known eclectic scholar, Hosoi Heishū (1728–1801), who served the lord of Kii. Immediately after the ban, Taihō drafted a strongly worded protest (dated 1790/6), which he sent to Sadanobu after receiving prior approval from his lord, Tokugawa Munechika (1733–99). His argument was historical and psychological. Taihō drew attention to the rich development and variety of different schools in the military arts, in medicine, and in religion, and contended that scholarship was no exception. Moreover, as a good eclectic he argued that, since human likes and dislikes differ from individual to individual, it is impossible to unify taste, so that variety in schools is a good and necessary thing for human society. Taihō did not give up after this first attack. A year later, in 1791/7, he wrote the *Kossendan* (The Kossen discussion), a sarcastic overall critique of Sadanobu's financial, economic and educational policies.[69] He followed this with a request to Sadanobu in 1792/10 to establish a college (*gakumonjo*) to train students in Ancient Learning. And in 1793/12, he composed a memorial to reform the examinantion system, in order to give more leeway to the selection of talent.[70]

Akamatsu Sōshū, a scholar and elder from the Akō domain (*tozama*), wrote a letter to his personal friend Shibano Ritsuzan in 1794, arguing the need for wide learning and attacking the narrowness of the Kimon school.[71] Ritsuzan never answered—out of consideration for their friendship, it is said.[72] He left this task to his more sanguine admirer Nishiyama Sessai, who had urged him, after Ritsuzan's appointment to the Hayashi School, to have the bakufu issue a ban on heterodox ideas. Sessai's reply consisted of a rather bombastic defense, invoking the political need to unify the country, extolling the "real" scholars as distinguished from the dilettantes, and pointing to the tradition of alliance between the bakufu and Neo-Confucianism.[73]

Ritsuzan's attitude was typical of the leaders of the ban, who stayed aloof from the raging controversy and left the polemic defense to lesser figures. They probably followed Sadanobu's example. Sadanobu had carefully planned his decision and had made the necessary bureaucratic appointments to assure its success. True to his own elitist perception of his role, he felt accountable to no one for the action he had taken. There is no concrete indication that Sadanobu had expected his policy would stir great controversy. Nor is there evidence that he was disturbed by it. Given the knowledge that he received from Rai Shunzui of the struggles in the Hiroshima domain, he probably anticipated some protest. In any event, as a true aristocrat and convinced of the righteousness of his cause, he never attempted to justify himself publicly. His reaction to Tsukada's

Kossendan was brilliantly diplomatic and noncommital. It was an outstanding work, he observed, full of erudition and noble intentions.[74]

Sadanobu displayed the same sagacious aloofness when he was
asked to intervene in a dispute between Okada Kanzen and Matsudaira Katanobu (1744–1805), the lord of Aizu, a relative of the
Tokugawa (kamon). The Aizu domain had been the center of the
Kimon school since the time of its foundation by Hoshina Masayuki,
Ansai's patron. Since 1781, a reformist party, headed by the elder
Tanaka Kurokami, had been in close contact with Furuya Tsunetaka
(1734–1806), an eclectic scholar with Sorai sympathies who was a
rōnin (masterless samurai) from Edo and had served for some years as
preceptor in the Kumamoto domain. Horidaira Saeimon, the elder
who led the reform in Kumamoto, had recommended Tsunetaka to
Kurokami, the reform-minded elder from Aizu.[75] At the outset, the
latter's plan to hire Tsunetaka was barred by the antireformist party.
After a struggle of six years, however, Kurokami and his reformist
allies gained approval for their reform and, under the supervision of
Tsunetaka, switched the teachings of Kimon in the domain school to
those of Sorai. On 1790/10/10, Tsunetaka was officially extended a
teaching position at the new domain school. This was only five
months after Sadanobu's ban. When Okada Kanzen in Edo heard that
a kamon domain was in the process of abandoning the Ansai tradition
for heterodoxy, he let it be known on 1791/1/20 that Tsunetaka was
an obstacle to real reform and that his invitation should be canceled.
Obviously he was worried about the negative example that was being
set by a most prestigious house.

Katanobu, the daimyo of Aizu, asked Sadanobu to intervene in the
matter, but Sadanobu knew that the reform in Aizu had gone too far
to be reversed, and so he did not force the issue. He only spoke out
indirectly against the domain's policy, saying that he did not know
about Tsunetaka's scholarly qualities but that if appointments were
made along the line established by the founder Hoshina, there would
be no problem. He also added rather meekly that, since the school had
turned to Ancient Learning, it would be proper now to teach Neo-Confucianism also.[76] One month later, Tsunetaka's appointment was completed, and the new domain school confined itself to Sorai teachings
until 1810, when another change was made to Neo-Confucianism.

This small incident shows again Sadanobu's reluctance to be
dragged into an ideological dispute in which his political sense warned
him that victory was unlikely. His real concern was with bakufu
reform in Edo, and there his educational reform had begun to gain
momentum. Teachers of private academies were alarmed by defections of their pupils to the Bakufu College. Tsukada Taihō, in his

memorandum to Sadanobu, complained about the dubious motivations of these defectors.[77] Kameda Hōsai (1752–1826), for instance, the leader of a prosperous private academy, saw his alleged thousand students dwindle away because they were interested in employment security with the bakufu, which they knew would be denied them if they pursued heterodox doctrines. Thus the master was forced to close his school.[78]

THE BAKUFU COLLEGE

In 1792/9, ten months before Sadanobu retired, the first examinations took place at the Bakufu College, which had now been rebuilt on the grand scale of Tsunayoshi's time. Sadanobu's still young reform continued to develop unhampered along the lines set by him. This progress was in great part due to the management of the new rector, Hayashi Jussai (1768–1841), with whom Sadanobu stayed in close contact, as his diary entries suggest.[79]

The rector Kimpō died in 1793/3 at the age of twenty-five, leaving no children, and Sadanobu seized the opportunity to appoint a man of his own choice. He picked Hayashi Jussai, the third son of Matsudaira Norimori from the Iwamura domain.[80] It was under Jussai's forty-five-year tenure and firm management that the Bakufu College became the most important center of learning for the coming decades. Jussai was the most enduring member of a small group of hand-picked scholar-bureaucrats who assured the continuation of Sadanobu's policies. Until the turn of the century he had the firm backing of Sadanobu's political successor, the senior councillor Matsudaira Nobuaki; and until the second decade of the nineteenth century he was assisted by Sadanobu's appointees Ritsuzan and Nishū, and by Koga Seiri, Kanzen's successor. Jussai's death in 1841 and the appointment of the famous scholar Satō Issai (1772–1859) inaugurated a new era for the college, at least as far as ideology was concerned. Issai was in his official capacity a Neo-Confucian scholar, but he simultaneously ran a private school where he lectured on Wang Yang-ming idealism, thus contributing to the semiclandestine and late revival of that school at the end of the Tokugawa period.

From 1797 on, the Bakufu College and the Hayashi School were in fact two different institutions. Both were headed by Jussai, but unlike his predecessors he merely supervised the schools without engaging in any teaching.[81] The change that occurred in 1797 was significant. Bakufu control of the school complex begun by Sadanobu was completed, and the Hayashi School became an annex to the college, which functioned as an exclusive bakufu institution. The key to the change was control of the financial funds supporting the school.

In 1791, Sadanobu inaugurated a change in financial control with regard to the ninety-five scholarships which since 1670 had been given to the Hayashi School in the form of rice rations. Sadanobu granted a hundred rations to the college and reallocated only thirty to the Hayashi School. In 1797/12, this practice was changed again: then the total of 130 rations went to the college, while the Hayashi School received 1,500 bales in rice and 3,000 koku in stipend. In the same year, control of the income of a 1,000 koku rice field—an endowment to the school since 1691—together with the management of all expenses, which had formerly been in the hands of the rector, was placed under the jurisdiction of the bakufu office of finance.[82]

In terms of its student population, too, the college became strictly a training school for bakufu bureaucrats. Traditionally the Hayashi School had catered to a wide public: lords and retainers from the domains, bakufu retainers, masterless samurai, artisans, merchants (see table 7). A major restriction was imposed in 1793/9, when rules were established to determine the nature of the school, the office and rank of its staff, and matters concerning curriculum and examination. From then on, priests, merchants, artisans, actors, or vagrant samurai were barred from the college and its precincts.[83] In 1798/2/22 the student population was further limited when it was decreed that the college was to give education only to bakufu retainers, even excluding students from the domains.

This new directive created serious problems, because some teachers, like Bitō Nishū, had their official residence in the precincts of the Bakufu College where they held private lectures. In 1801, therefore, the rule was modified so that private pupils, upon recommendation from their teachers, were allowed to enter the college; 30 of the 130 rice portions were set aside for such students.[84]

The Hayashi School greatly benefited from the Neo-Confucian revival, but in growth and importance it did not match the Bakufu College. Statistics from the last twenty years (1845–65) of the Tokugawa period show the minor position that the Hayashi School then played vis-à-vis the Bakufu College and the domains. During those twenty years, 108 domains were represented among the students enrolled exclusively at the college; among the student population of the Hayashi School, only 63 domains were represented; and 46 domains had students at both institutions. Of the 496 non-bakufu students at the college, only 101, or 20 percent, entered the college by recommendation of Hayashi teachers.[85]

Table 6, listing teachers per school of thought and per period, also shows a slight decline of Hayashi graduates, from 98 in 1789–1829, to 82 in 1830–67. The number of graduates from the Bakufu College tripled from 55 to 160.

Finally, a word should be said about the examination system.

During the Nara period (710–784) a lukewarm and short-lived attempt had been made to subject courtier-administrators to an examination system, adapted from the Chinese model.[86] For the next thousand years, however, Japan's aristocratic rulers received no public training. In this sense, Sadanobu's innovation was precedent-breaking.

The examinations at the college were reserved for bakufu retainers, and instruction was geared to the examination of scholarship (*gaku-mon gimmi*), which since 1792/9 had been held every three years for *hatamoto* and *gokenin* over fifteen years of age (280 participated the first time; 237 in 1794/2, and 249 three years later). A more elementary examination on reading (*sodoku gimmi*) was obligatory for retainers' sons under fifteen.[87] Only the most elementary classics were used in the courses: the Great Learning, the Doctrine of the Mean, the Analects, the Mencius, and the *Shōgaku* or Lesser Learning.[88] Instruction was, as Kimpō had complained, heavily slanted toward Ansai teachings. The *Shōgaku* text used at the college was Ansai's annotated version.[89] For the Four Books and the Five Classics, however, the annotated edition of 1792 by Gotō Shibayama (1721–82) was used. Shibayama was a scholar of Neo-Confucianism, and Ritsuzan's teacher from the Takamatsu domain.[90] Another indication of the influence of Kimon thought was the practice, started on 1794/1/15, of holding the inaugural lecture of the year on the *Hakuro-kudō-shōin keiji*—Chu Hsi's regulations for his academy and one of the most important works of the Ansai canon. (This work was also held in great esteem in Sadanobu's domain school of Shirakawa.)[91]

The scholarly examinations were meant to establish a clearer connection between scholastic ability and administrative aptitude. The standardization of instruction, however, and its narrow bureaucratic purpose had adverse effects upon the scholastic level of the institution. Moriyama Takamori, one of Sadanobu's lesser aides, complains that cramming for the examinations often rewarded the slick and ambitious but not necessarily the most able.[92] Nevertheless, as an official institution with the general goal of training talent for public service, the college contributed greatly to the formation of a uniform bureaucracy.

THE AFTERMATH OF THE BAN: HETERODOXY AND THE DOMAIN SCHOOLS
As the case of the Aizu domain shows, Sadanobu was unable or unwilling to apply pressure on the domains to observe the ban on heterodoxy. But the preference of the bakufu for ideological unification was unambiguous.[93]

In the absence of any coercive power from the bakufu, such unification was not likely to materialize and, as table 6 shows, did not occur. Yet the same statistics show that, in the last eighty years of its existence, the bakufu clearly reasserted its preeminence in the field of education; the ban dealt a serious blow to heterodoxy. The downward trend of Neo-Confucianism was stopped, and by 1830 the school had regained half of its lost ground; during the next thirty years there were almost three times as many Neo-Confucian teachers as heterodox teachers.

The heterodox schools that suffered most were the schools of Ancient Learning. The Kimon school, since its teachings were so close to the Neo-Confucianism of the college, was less affected. Most remarkable is the increase in the number of teachers affiliated with eclectic schools.

To explain the vitality of the eclectic schools, it is important to note first that, while rejecting the teachings of the schools of Ancient Learning, they continued the intellectual tradition of Ogyū Sorai. The eclectics attacked Sorai's followers with their own methodology of historical relativism. Sorai had criticized the claims to absolute truth of the Neo-Confucians by demonstrating that their metaphysics were historically conditioned. The eclectics accused the followers of Ancient Learning of declaring absolute the teachings of the ancient sages. Thus, using the logic of Sorai, the eclectics rejected both the historical absolutism of Ancient Learning and the metaphysical absolutism of Sadanobu's Neo-Confucianism. They were therefore radically opposed to the bureaucratic orientation of Sadanobu's scholarship, and, in the absence of any direct coercion, they were the least inclined to conform.

A similar pattern of resistance can be observed in the domain schools. These schools fall naturally into two categories: those founded before the ban and those founded after. Table 8 shows that out of a total of 93 schools founded before 1790, 65 were heterodox, and 28 of these heterodox schools switched to orthodoxy after 1790. Of the 121 schools founded after 1790, 71 were heterodox—a smaller proportion than in the earlier period—but only 18 of these switched to orthodoxy.

These statistics also suggest that there is no difference between tozama and fudai domains in their readiness to comply with bakufu preference. Of the heterodox schools founded before 1790, the proportion of tozama schools converting to Neo-Confucianism (twenty out of thirty-five) was higher than that of fudai schools (eight out of twenty-two). After 1790, however, more heterodox fudai (twelve out of forty-five) than tozama (three out of eighteen) changed affiliation. Moreover, the domains related to the Tokugawa (shimpan and kamon) stand out by their unwavering heterodoxy.

A tabulation of schools of thought, as represented in the domain schools before and after the ban, gives the results shown in table 10.

First, schools following Ansai teachings (both those founded before and after 1790), most readily changed to Neo-Confucianism. This trend is especially strong among the schools founded after 1790. A possible explanation is that the initial choice of Ansai teachings by these later schools was made in consideration of the semi-Kimon orthodoxy of the Bakufu College. But the resistance of four out of five fudai schools founded before the ban needs some explanation. These were precisely the dogmatic schools where ideological exclusivism was strong and which, in terms of ideology and manpower, had nourished the Bakufu College. Two of them (Shibata and Obama) had issued bans before 1790; Isezaki was the domain where Okada Kanzen came from; and Tanabe was the fourth domain, where a student of Koga Seiri had been unsuccessful in bringing about an ideological reform to Neo-Confucianism.

Second, the domain schools of the eclectic tradition stand out by their resistance to change. Only two out of a total of forty switched to Neo-Confucianism. The tozama domain was Yonezawa, a domain with a long Neo-Confucian tradition, both before and after the ban, but which for a reform period of forty years (1776–1818) had an eclectic interlude and therefore, at the time of the ban, was heterodox. The fudai domain was that of Tanaka, where the change was not profound; the eclectic tradition was kept alive ostensibly, although all the teachers had studied at the Bakufu College.[94] Here again one is struck by the absence of any difference between fudai and tozama behavior. Decisions on whether to follow or not to follow bakufu preference were not made in line with loyalty obligations, which one would expect to have weighed more in the case of the fudai. On the issue of orthodoxy, the type of philosophy and its view of authority and of the nature of scholarship were more decisive than traditional bonds of loyalty to the bakufu.

The facility with which domains switched allegiance may have had something to do with the nature and size of the domain schools. Domains that did not change were often small in size, with few students and lacking well-established schools. In these schools, no particular faction would profit from a shift in philosophical allegiance over a rival faction.[95] Changes were often a response to internal conditions in domains in which new power, with or without connection to domain reforms, was the possible reward for the victorious faction. Still other schools made a superficial change (like Hikone or Wakayama) but in reality continued the heterodox tradition. (These schools have been tabulated in the present study as heterodox.)

TABLE 10 The Ban's Effect on Schools of Thought: Shifts in Philosophy per Domain School and per Family Status

Schools of Thought	Grand Total Till 1868		Totals Gener.	: Unchang./Changed	Schools Founded before 1790					Totals	1790–1868			
	Han	(Gō)			Shimpan	Kamon	Fudai	Tozama	(Gō)		Kamon	Fudai	Tozama	(Gō)
Ancient Learning	64	(13)	37	U 21	1	4	8	8	(4)	27 : 19	1	10	8	(2)
				C 16	—	—	6	10	(4)	8	1	6	1	(3)
Wang Yang-ming	4	(—)	4	U 2	—	1	1	—	(—)	— : —	—	—	—	(—)
				C 2	—	—	1	1	(—)	—	—	—	—	(—)
Eclectic	40	(1)	8	U 7	—	1	1	5	(—)	32 : 31	—	22	9	(1)
				C 1	—	—	—	1	(—)	1	—	1	—	(—)
Ansai	28	(2)	16	U 7	1	—	4	2	(—)	12 : 3	1	1	1	(—)
				C 9	—	—	1	8	(1)	9	2	5	2	(1)
Totals	136	(16)	65		2	6	22	35	(9)	71	5	45	21	(7)

Source: Compiled from Kasai, Kinsei hankō, pp. 89–1958.

Finally, there were a limited number of domains which joined the orthodox ranks mainly on account of kinship with Sadanobu. Such were Matsuyama (in Shikoku), where Sadanobu's brother Sadakuni was daimyo; Matsushiro, ruled by a son of Sadanobu; Matsuyama (in Bitchū province), where one of his grandsons had been adopted; and Kameoka, where Nobuhide, a nephew of Sadanobu, succeeded in 1807 at the age of four.[96]

One has to conclude then that orthodoxy was not an issue of the first order in the domains. However, to the extent that the ban of 1790 declared Neo-Confucianism, as understood and interpreted under Kimon influence, the official ideology of the bakufu, Sadanobu established an important tradition of scholarship and education for bureaucratic training.

It is ironical that Sadanobu, directing his prohibition on heterodox thought mainly against the Sorai school on grounds that institutions ought to be fixed and sacrosanct, implemented his decree through an institutional reform of his own. Next to the bakufu's financial recovery, the establishment of the Bakufu College was the single most effective aspect of the Kansei Reform.

The college was a manifestation of Sadanobu's basic political view of, and his effort to meet, the needs of his time. It was an institution to enhance political integration and to ensure the commitment of the elite to government. Sadanobu's stress on the practicality of doctrines notwithstanding, the curriculum of the college was geared not so much to teaching practical government skills as to shaping the bakufu elite into devoted public functionaries. Sadanobu imposed a consistent public philosophy on the warrior bureaucrats. He was the first conscious creator of an "ideology" for Japan.

7   *Retirement and Retrospect*

    In the middle of 1793, Sadanobu prepared himself for retirement. He had settled the Title Incident, completed his inspection tour of coastal defenses, and sent Laxman back to Russia. The future of his reform seemed secure. He had put the bureaucracy back into shape, created the Bakufu College for training functionaries, and established firm bakufu control over the economy in Edo. Yet Sadanobu also was aware that, with the special powers of chief councillor and the shogun's regent, he had enforced unpopular sumptuary laws, offended loyalist sensibilities among the collaterals during the Title Incident, and created enemies among scholars with his ban of 1790. This awareness convinced him of the wisdom of an early retirement.

    The full extent of personal opposition to Sadanobu had not become clear to him, however. On 1793/5/25 he petitioned to be relieved of his duties as regent, arguing that the responsibility of that office should be entrusted to the Senior Council rather than concentrated in one person. His petition was rejected in a perfunctory manner (on 7/4), but Sadanobu resubmitted it on the following day. Less than three weeks later, on 7/23, he was relieved of his duties both as regent and as senior councillor.[1] Although Sadanobu was granted a hereditary seat in the Antechamber and it was decreed that the termination of his office did not mean the rejection of his policies, he was disappointed, for he had hoped to retain his seat in the Senior Council.

    Historians have usually linked Sadanobu's dismissal to the opposition that his strict sumptuary laws aroused in the Interior. Feelings against him were especially strong, it is said, after he banished (on 1792/8/22) a priest and several ladies-in-waiting because of a scandal in the shogunal court.[2] It seems very unlikely, however, that Sadanobu's dismissal from the Senior Council would have occurred without the endorsement of the collaterals, who had played an important role in his rise to power. In his stern treatment of the imperial court, Sadanobu had alienated the Three Houses to a greater degree than he suspected. Two of the Houses had also been deeply displeased with the ban on heterodoxy. This contextual evidence strongly suggests that his dismissal was due to the Three Houses' antagonism toward Sadanobu, although not necessarily toward his reform.

    Little is known of Sadanobu's political activity after his retirement. He stayed in close contact with his political successor, Matsudaira Nobuaki, and with the new rector of the Bakufu College, Hayashi Jussai; in 1810, together with the lord of Aizu, Sadanobu took charge of the maritime defense of Edo bay on the Bōsō peninsula. In Shirakawa, he continued to rule until 1819. Here he devoted much attention to the new enterprises he established, and to the education of his retainers and their children in the domain school. The latter half of his career, however, was decidedly an anticlimax to his first years in Shirakawa and to his tenure as chief councillor and regent in Edo—but an anticlimax that made good sense to him.

Sadanobu suggests in his autobiography that one should retire before discontent sets in. Criticism and discontent inevitably follow the initial successes of a new regime, but with a timely retirement one will be remembered as a precious sword, which one unsheathes only on rare occasions. After the blade has done its work, it is put away for a later occasion. It was his task, now, to keep himself ready for such an eventuality.[3]

With the proud sense of his own historical importance still intact, Sadanobu retired almost completely from politics. He spent most of his time in the ascetic training of Kitō and in the pursuit of cultural ideals, writing poetry and essays, transcribing numerous literary works, and supervising the collation of historical encyclopediae. In his later years, he called himself *Rakuō-kō*, which one may render as the "wise old gentleman given to leisurely pursuits." Somewhere he explains *raku* as "to enjoy the heart of heaven and earth."[4] After a busy career in the Confucian world of political affairs, he withdrew into a Taoist quiet of private enjoyment of culture and nature. During these years Sadanobu also kept diaries, wrote memoirs,[5] and further cultivated his image in his autolatric rites.

The fame of Sadanobu as a model ruler was already well established during his own time. In his domain, he was honored in local shrines, and a contemporary admirer suggested that Sadanobu was as great as Ieyasu, pointing out that both the founder of the bakufu and its restorer were born on the same day of the year.[6] After his death, Sadanobu's son—following his father's desire as expressed in his will —made an official application with the Yoshida family in Kyoto for the divine title of *Shukoku daimyōjin*, "Great Diety and Protector of the Land," which was granted in three stages between 1833 and 1855. And when Mizuno Tadakuni (1794-1851) led the third and last reform of the Tokugawa period in the Tempō era (1830-43), he referred to his reforms as a return to the times of Matsudaira Sadanobu.

Undoubtedly Sadanobu enabled the bakufu to survive a crisis which, at some points, threatened to destroy it. He solved the financial difficulties and laid solid foundations for an economic recovery that continued for decades. He unambiguously reasserted bakufu authority and, most important, reformulated and gave new vigor to its political value system, which was in serious jeopardy when he took office.

The regime that Sadanobu had supported fell ignominiously in 1868 and was discredited together with all that was feudal and antimodern in Japan's past. Sadanobu's fame, however, continued undiminished. In historical studies and biographies until the end of the Pacific War he was held up as a model. Since ambitious service to the country had guided him throughout his life, there was great interest during the Pacific War in Sadanobu's ethical ideals, and very specifically in his world view based on *Shimbu no michi* for the spiritual mobilization of Japan. Since then, as can be expected, Sadanobu and even his Kansei Reform have been conspicuously neglected by historians.[7]

Still, important historical and theoretical insights may be gained from the study of Sadanobu's career and reforms. First they show the magnitude of the bakufu crisis. At the top, the system was subjected as never before to the strains of faction building. Antagonisms were fierce, and assassination was often considered the only means left to bring about change. The purge of the ruling elite conducted by Sadanobu was unprecedented in its thoroughness. At the bottom, social unrest had taken on such proportions as to have a noticeable impact upon the political process and policy formulation. The violence of the 1787 Edo riot was partly responsible for Sadanobu's rise to power and for the form of his subsequent economic measures.

Sadanobu restored the bakufu through an uncompromising defense of its political structure. All aspects of the Kansei Reform, financial, economical, political, and ideological, had this as their purpose. Admittedly, certain institutional innovations were necessary, but the main thrust of the reform was undoubtedly a revitalization of the political culture, a restoration of the political process, and a reassertion of political values and commitments.[8]

The revival of political and cultural values was bound up with a strengthened commitment to a particular metaphysical world view. Both in Sadanobu's private life and in the kind of ethos he prescribed for the bakufu functionaries, the intensity of his commitment was religious. For Sadanobu, leadership meant acquiring divine status; for the bureaucrats, normative compliance meant realizing their own divine potential through active service in the polity.

Sadanobu was a selfless ruler. He actively sought power and fame but, unlike Tanuma, did not turn his rule into a profitable enterprise for himself or his associates. His "virtue" was never questioned by his critics. Despite his idealism, Sadanobu also showed the practical flexibility of a true political ideologue. His politico-ethical ideology was not a monolithic ideology, which he inherited and enforced as such. Although called Neo-Confucianism, it was a practical amalgam of that doctrine with elements of the narrower Ansai tradition and of the more secular Sorai teachings.

In the light of recent studies of the function of charisma, specifically by Edward Shils, Matsudaira Sadanobu may well be called a charismatic leader.[9] According to Shils, charisma lies in the intensity that connects a person with central and crucial features of man's existence and his cosmos. A charismatic figure needs an intense conviction, and the object of his belief must be a worthy cause. Charisma is a matter of perception and psychology. Hence, a leader can be charismatic through the particular self-perception he has of his own role. His impact on others need not necessarily be expressed through mass followings as modern history has led one to assume, though he often displays highly persuasive powers. Moreover, charismatic actors are always the source of order, and the order they generate is seen, even in modern societies, as continuous with something ultimate. The social order which they stand for, whether by creating or defending it, must point to a transcendental moral order. The connection of charismatic leaders to order always occurs in a situation of crisis in which they act with a sense of mission. Their performance invariably has salvationist appeal. They need not, however, be rebels or prophets, attacking the old order. The establishment is not without its own charismatic defenders. Finally, the form in which charisma lives on is in the cult of the departed leader.

This view of charisma goes a long way in explaining Matsudaira Sadanobu's political personality, and in clarifying the obscure link in his career between ethics and politics. Sadanobu lived in a time of serious crisis, and he had a strong sense of mission even before he cast himself in the role of a political savior. As a political leader, he cultivated an image of moral righteousness, which he used to great advantage to offset his relatively young age, and which explains his lasting fame in subsequent Japanese history as a model ruler.

In modern societies, as Shils points out, personal charisma—though often in an attenuated form—is still essential to the sustained affirmation of the central value system upon which the political order rests.[10] Sadanobu consciously applied a brand of Neo-Confucianism with its Shinto and Kimon psychological and religious emphasis to restore faith in bureaucratic service within the bakufu. He therefore reinvigorated a secular administrative apparatus with his ethical belief that bureaucratic efficiency is a "virtue" whereby man can actualize his divine potential. Probably the last effective defender of the Tokugawa order, Matsudaira Sadanobu gave new life to a faltering regime.

Appendix A

History of the Shirakawa Domain until Sadanobu's Rule

For centuries Shirakawa[1] had been the most important cultural outpost in the north, and during the Tokugawa period its castle town (also called Sirakawa) was designated the last checkpoint for the bakufu on the Ōshūkaidō, the highway leading to the north.[2] Located on the northern perimeter of the Tokugawa territories of the Kanto plain, the domain had great strategic significance for the early bakufu. It functioned as a buffer between the bakufu and the powerful outside daimyo of northern Japan, and had therefore been entrusted to a loyal vassal daimyo. As a vassal domain it was also subject to frequent transfers of ruling houses, arranged by the bakufu in order to prevent its great vassals from building strength in the provinces.

Eight daimyo houses ruled successively over Shirakawa over a period of 241 years, 1627-1868 (see table 11). In the first sixty-five years, (1627-92), four houses succeeded each other: the Niwa house, ruling for two generations (sixteen years); the Sakakibara (Matsudaira), one generation (six years); the Honda, two generations (thirty one years) and the Okudaira (Matsudaira), again for one generation (eleven years). The next three houses ruled for considerably longer periods: the Yūki (Matsudaira) for three generations (1692-1741); the Hisamatsu (Matsudaira) for four generations (1741-1823; Sadanobu ruled 1783-1819); and the Abe for nine generations (1823-1868; all eight successions in the Abe house were by adoption, a matter each time to be decided by the bakufu).

TABLE 11 Ruling Houses in Shirakawa Domain

Ruling House	Years	(a)	(b)	Came from (c):	Went to (c):
Niwa	1627–43	2	100	Tanakura (50)	Nihonmatsu (100)
Sakakibara (M)(d)	1643–49	1	140	Tatebayashi (110)	Himeji (150)
Honda	1649–81	2	120	Murakami (100)	Utsunomiya (100)
Okudaira (M.)	1681–92	1	150	Utsunomiya (100)	Yamagata (100)
Yūki (M.)	1692–1741	3	150	Yamagata (100)	Himeji (150)
Hisamatsu (M.)	1742–1823	4	110	Takata (110)	Kuwana (100)
Abe	1823–66/6	8	100	Oshi (100)	Tanakura (100)
Abe (e)	1868/1–3		60	Tanakura (100)	

a   Number of generations.
b   Aggregate of Shirakawa in thousands of koku.
c   Aggregate in thousands of koku.
d   M = Matsudaira.
e   Between the two Abe rules, the domain became bakufu territory under the supervision of the Nihonmatsu domain (100,000 koku).

Vassal daimyo, unlike the lords who ruled the same domain for centuries, looked upon their domain as a piece of property, leased by the bakufu to them for their own private use. They knew that their identification with one particular domain was only temporary. None of the administrative features was therefore considered to belong permanently to the domain. They were private property of the ruling house. Thus, when a lord left the domain, he took with him not only the rules of the domain (for instance, its tax quotas), but also the administrative records, and even pieces of real estate such as the family's tombstones or the domain's school, textbooks, staff, and buildings.[3]

This tenuous association of one warrior house with a particular domain also encouraged greater exploitation of the peasants, because each transfer increased the financial burden on the domain. Incoming lords often brought with them old debts, sometimes incurred by earlier transfers, while outgoing lords at times succeeded in making the domain carry the burden of their move.[4]

Many of these transfers were accompanied by territorial adjustments made by the bakufu. Although the bakufu had no direct control over the administration of the domains (their taxation or the use of their financial and other resources), in the case of vassal daimyo the bakufu decided—with greater freedom than for the outside lords—who ruled where, and over how much territory.[5]

The domain began under Niwa with 110,000 koku. When Sakakibara moved in, 30,000 koku were added, but his rule in Shirakawa was merely a short phase in his rising career. After only six years he moved further upward to become daimyo of Himeji (150,000 koku). When Honda came to Shirakawa from Murakami (100,000 koku, a domain located in today's Niigata prefecture), 20,600 koku were incorporated into the bakufu territories.[6] Honda added, however, 15,000 koku of newly developed land and, through a thorough land survey in 1650-51, another 37,000 koku. This allowed him to distribute 20,000 koku as two independent fiefs to his second and third sons, while keeping still 150,000 koku for himself and his successor.

The next lord, Okudaira, after a rule of only eleven years was punished by the shogun Tsunayoshi for his inability to cope with a power struggle between two factions led by two elders, and was sent to Yamagata (100,000 koku). During the Yūki's rule, the size of the domain did not change, but when in 1742 the Hisamatsu were enfeoffed, 84,000 koku were incorporated as a separate parcel of the Takata domain and 20,000 koku became bakufu territory. Other villages, mainly in the Date and Shinobu districts were attached to the Shirakawa domain as separate parcels. Then the domain counted

110,000 koku and did not change until the end of the Tokugawa period.[7] Its population during Sadanobu's rule was about 111,000.[8]

The change of 1742 was very drastic: the new domain (40,000 koku smaller) consisted of one contiguous part (only 55 percent of the whole domain) and of nine scattered parcels. Table 12 documents this change and the new composition of the domain in numbers of villages; figures in parenthesis give the aggregate in 10,000 koku.

TABLE 12 Composition of Shirakawa Domain in 1662 and 1742

Districts	Domain in 1662 (a)	Domain (b)		1742 Loss to Takata Domain (c)		Loss to Bakufu	
Shirakawa	68 (d)	42	(2.4)	50	(3.0)	—	
Ishikawa	31	15	(0.7) (e)	42	(2.8)	12	(0.7)
Iwase	46	34	(3.2) (e)	17	(1.5)	—	
Tamura	26	—		9	(0.6)	17	(1.3)

a *Fukushima-ken shi*, III, 416.

b *Ibid.*, III, 442; VIII, 520. To this column should be added nine separate parcels. Some of them were part of the domain from before; others were added in 1742. (See, among others, *ibid.*, III, 1235; X, part 1, 931). The total of the domain was 110,000 koku.

c A total of 84,000 koku.

d Thirty-one villages were received from the bakufu in 1649 (*ibid.*, VIII, 522). The thirty-seven remaining ones are the same as the forty-two of the next column (some villages split up). In 1662 Honda Tadayoshi gave two independent apanages to two brothers of his successor, Tadahira (*ibid.*, III, 416). These two fiefs, each of the size of 10,000 koku, were taken from Shirakawa and Ishikawa districts and were later reincorporated in the domain. This explains the figures in the third and fourth columns under these two districts.

e Respectively 12 and 25 according to *Fukushima-ken shi*, VIII, 520. See correct figures in *ibid.*, III, 442; VIII, 526–27.

The tax system that had taken shape under the rules of Sakakibara (1642-49) and Honda (1649-81) was very heavy. It amounted to about 50 percent of the rice production (about 29 percent as land tax; 12 percent as miscellaneous taxes; and cash taxes equivalent to another 7 percent of the rice production), and scores of other taxes in kind. The details are as follows (calculated per 100 koku unit of production).[9]

1. *Taxes in rice:*
   land tax: 29 koku
   kuchimai: 6 koku
   betsudawara: 2 koku
   soybeans: 2 koku (convertible into rice at the rate of 2 koku of beans for 1 koku of rice)
   deccan grass: 1 koku (convertible into rice at the rate of 5 koku grass per 1 koku of rice)
   dog rice tax: 0.05 koku
   fee for rice store keepers: 0.001 koku
   obligatory seed grain loans: 2.5 per koku at 30 percent interest is 3.25 koku

(*kakemai*: 6 to 10 koku for the 5,000 koku of castle rice)

2. *Taxes in cash:*
   fusen: 1 ryō (doubled in times of extraordinary expenses
     such as building projects or journeys)
   yonaikin: 1.5 ryō
   firewood fee: 400 mon
   fee for the rice store keepers: 25 mon
   Total: 2.5 ryō and 425 mon (= about 0.12 ryō); at the
     rate of 3 koku per ryō, this equals 7 koku.

3. *Taxes in kind:*
   soybeans: 0.02 koku
   potatoes: 2 percent
   miscanthus reed (*kaya*): 16 sheaves
   reed (*ashi*): 2 sheaves
   persimmon juice: 0.01 koku
   firewood: 30 sheaves
   rice bran straw: 10 percent
   servants: 1 servant
   (tatami, dogs as hawk food, etc., according to the
     need of the moment)

Kuchimai, betsudawara, and *kakemai* were taxes meant to make up for the loss of rice during its transportation (the *betsudawara* tax in Shirakawa was twice as high as the one in bakufu territories); *fusen* was a tax for the upkeep of the roads, etc; and *yonaikin* was a tax originally meant to replace corvée duties of servants. The *yonaikin*, however, together with the dog rice tax, the firewood fee, and the rice storehouse keeper's fee were service taxes or taxes in kind which had been commuted into cash taxes, but after their conversion, the original taxes were reintroduced without cancelation of the commuted tax. Under Hayakawa's reform the total rice tax was cut to about 34 percent (about 28 percent for the land tax and 6 percent for the *kuchimai*); almost all miscellaneous taxes were abolished.

Under the Matsudaira Hisamatsu rule, *betsudawara, fukin,* and *yonaikin* were reintroduced. From the middle of the seventeenth century the land tax was paid half in kind, half in cash (gold and copper coins). The following table gives the land tax and some miscellaneous taxes for one village, Yumoto, during the early Honda rule, during the Matsudaira Yūki rule, and during the Hisamatsu rule. The 1656 statistics contain miscellaneous rice taxes under the 44 percent of the land tax; the 1740 figures reflect the Hayakawa reform: a decrease in the land tax and an increase in new land. The basic aggregate of 224.8 koku was set by a thorough land survey conducted by one of Honda

TABLE 13 Taxation in the Yumoto Village

a	1656				1740			1743		
	b	c	d	e	c	d	e	c	d	e
Honden	224.8	224.8	44.2	98.62	200.5	33.5	67.17	201.9	33.5	67.63
Shinden	2.4	—	—	—	1.3	15.0	0.19	1.3	15.0	0.19
Shinden	5.3	—	—	—	5.3	11.0	0.59	5.3	11.0	0.59
Miscel. taxes:										
kuchimai			6.0	5.9			4.07			4.10
betsudawara							—			0.72
fukin (cash)							—			1 ryō 476 mon
yonaikin (cash)				—			—			1 ryō 905 mon
Grand total (minus cash tax.):				104.5			72.03			72.53
Amount paid in rice (koku)				52.2			36.01			36.99
Amount paid in gold (ryō)				17.0			11.5			14.5
Amount paid in copper (mon)				60.0			861.0			1,593.0

a Types of fields: *honden* (original fields); *shinden* (new fields)
b Official aggregate in koku (there were no *shinden* in 1656)
c Yearly adjusted taxable aggregate in koku
d Tax percentage
e Tax amount in koku
Calculated from information communicated to me by letter dated September 28, 1971, by Sukama Zenkatsu, local historian from Shirakawa.

Tadayoshi's ministers in 1650–51: then the aggregate doubled from its previous level of 112.3 koku. That survey was the object of peasant complaints even as late as 1868, when the peasants ascribed their hardships to their being overtaxed since 1650.[10] The Yumoto village counted fifty households.

The tax rates did not change much over the years. Table 14 is a list of the tax rates from the same village from 1665 to 1856 (with some gaps). To the entries of the Honda years should be added the various miscellaneous taxes, which almost doubles the percentage. Under the Yūki rule, after the victory of the Hayakawa reform around 1720 (see chapter 1), taxes rose gradually from 30 to 33 percent; under the Hisamatsu they climbed to 34 percent, but they were cut one point by Sadanobu (except for the disastrous Tenmei years and the year 1800); they kept the same level under the Abe.

One additional financial burden for the Shirakawa domain had to do with its honor of being a prestigious vassal domain. Sometimes the daimyo were requested by the bakufu to undertake and finance honorary missions on its behalf. At different points in Shirakawa's history such missions and other extraordinary bakufu levies ruined attempts at financial reform.[11]

TABLE 14 Land Tax in Percentage of Assessed Crop Yield
for the Village of Yumoto

HONDA		HISAMATSU (M)		(SADANOBU)	
1665:	29.6	1742:	33.5	1783:	34.4
1666:	28.8	1743:	33.5	1784:	34.4
1667:	17.1	1744:	33.5	1789:	33.5
1669:	24.0	1745:	33.8	1790:	33.5
1674:	7.0	1749:	33.0	1791:	33.5
		1752:	33.8	1792:	33.5
YUKI (M)		1754:	33.8	1795:	33.5
1714:	24.7	1756:	33.8	1796:	33.5
1715:	26.9	1759:	33.8	1797:	33.5
1718:	29.0	1763:	34.0	1798:	33.5
1719:	29.0	1764:	34.0	1799:	33.5
1720:	28.0	1765:	34.0	1800:	35.5
1721:	28.0	1766:	34.0	1801:	33.5
1722:	30.0	1768:	34.2	1802:	33.5
1723:	26.0	1778:	34.4	1804:	33.5
1724:	29.0	1779:	33.4	1805:	33.5
1725:	27.5	1780:	34.4	1807:	33.5
1728:	28.0	1781:	34.4	1808:	33.5
1729:	31.0	1782:	34.4		
1730:	31.0			ABE	
1731:	31.0			1824:	33.5
1732:	31.8			1829:	33.5
1733:	33.0			1832:	33.5
1734:	33.0			1853:	33.5
1735:	31.5			1856:	33.5
1737:	33.2				
1740:	33.5				

Compiled from the letter mentioned in note to table 13 and from *Shirakawa-shi shi*, II, 140.

Appendix B
The Succession Problem of Tayasu

When Haruaki, Munetake's successor, died in the summer of 1774, only months after Sadanobu had been assigned to the Matsudaira family, Tayasu remained without an heir for thirteen years until Narimasa, a son of Hitotsubashi Harusada, was adopted on 1787/6/13. It was most likely one of the first acts of Sadanobu as chief councillor to provide Tayasu with an heir, because the decision on Narimasa was made between the informal announcement of Sadanobu's election as chief councillor on 1787/6/9 and his official appointment on 6/19.

In all probability, however, it was not Tanuma who kept the Tayasu family for such a long time without a successor. In his autobiography, Sadanobu writes how he had been unable for all those years to win the women of Tayasu over for his plans to adopt a boy from Hitotsubashi (*Uge*, pp. 42–45). One of the reasons for their opposition was the family pride and political ambition of his stepmother.

In the beginning, she kept her plans secret, and maintained an indifferent front: "She understood that one could not hope that the house would exist and flourish forever, and thus she was content with living an unconcerned life day by day. However, she was an astute woman and had a secret plan, but she kept this for herself because there was nobody to make arrangements with."

In 1778, Sadanobu discovered that she was waiting for the shogun Ieharu or his heir, Iemoto, to beget a boy whom she could adopt. The women were jealous of the numerous offspring of Hitotsubashi. Tanuma's choice, in 1781, of a Hitotsubashi as the new heir apparent (the later shogun Ienari) only added to the animosity of the women of Tayasu toward Hitotsubashi.

In 1785 new efforts by Sadanobu failed again. It seems that he had to wait until he could sway the authority of chief councillor to settle this matter. It should be noted that the opposition in Tayasu weakened considerably with the death of his stepmother in 1786/1.

Appendix C
Document on the Antechamber

The following is a translation of a document that I found at the house of a descendant of a deputy (Ichiharu Tadashiichi) of Sukagawa city, Fukushima prefecture. The document is entitled "Tamarizume on-rei ōseagerare sōrō setsu" (Note on the ordered gifts for the seat in the Antechamber.) I have added between brackets the number of incumbents of each office (established with the help of Totman, *Politics*, pp. 270–77, and Mitamura Engyo, *Buke jiten* [Tokyo: Aokaeru bōkan, 1958]).

[1] *Shogun*   1 sword
                 30 reels of cotton
                 10 ryō as horse fee
[1] *Grand councillor (Dainagon)*
                 1 sword
                 20 reels of cotton
                 10 ryō as horse fee
[1] *Wife of shogun*
[6] *Ladies of collaterals*
                 5 pieces of silver (*mai*) each
[?] *Grand elder lady of the Central Citadel (Honmaru rōjoshū)*
[?] *Elder ladies of the Western Citadel (Nishimaru rōjo): Manrinokoji dono, Hamaoka dono*
                 2 pieces of silver each
[?] *Elder couriers (Honmaru omote zukaishū)*
                 1 piece of silver each
[5] *Senior councillors*
                 1 sword
                 5 reels of embroidered gossamer
                 10 ryō as horse fee each
[1] *Kyoto deputy*
                 1 sword
                 10 ryō as horse fee
[1] *Grand chamberlain of the Western Citadel*
[1] *Keeper of Osaka castle*
[3] *Junior councillors*
                 1 sword
                 5 pieces of silver each
[4] *Superintendents of temples and shrines*
                 1 sword
                 2 pieces of silver each

[14] *Chamberlains*
        1 sword
        3 pieces of silver each (?)
[5] *Keepers of Edo castle*
[5] *Inspector generals*
[2] *City magistrates*
[8] *Superintendents of finance*
[4] *Superintendents of works*
[2] *Superintendents of public works*
[16] *Inspectors*
        1 sword
        1 piece of silver each
[9] *Seats of the Antechamber* (?) (*naisekisama*)
        1 sword
        10 ryō as horse fee
        5 reels of gossamer
        1 box of dried sea bream
        1 box of sea tang
        10 *kan* of coppercoins as barrel fee

The swords, horse fees, and barrel fees of the above document were standard bribery fees, in lieu of real swords, horses, or barrels of sake. The above amounts approximately to a total of:

        82 "swords,"
        50 reels of cotton,
        170 ryō,
        163 pieces of silver,
        70 reels of gossamer,
        18 boxes of fish,
        90 *kan* in copper coins.

Notes

Introduction

1. Max Weber, *Max Weber: On Charisma and Institution Building*, The Heritage of Sociology, ed. S. N. Eisenstadt (Chicago: University of Chicago Press, 1968), pp. 48, 52.

2. *Ibid.*, pp. 51-52.

3. Edward Shils, "Center and Periphery," in *The Logic of Personal Knowledge: Essays Presented to Michael Polanyi* (London: Routledge and Kegan Paul, 1961), pp. 117-30. Reprinted in *Center and Periphery: Essays in Macrosociology*, Selected Papers of Edward Shils, II (Chicago: University of Chicago Press, 1975).

Chapter One: Political Legacy

1. For my treatment of the Kyōhō Reform, I relied on Tsuda Hideo, *Hōkenshakai kaitaikatei kenkyūjosetsu* (Tokyo: Kōshobō, 1970); on Tanuma there exists an excellent English work: John Whitney Hall, *Tanuma Okitsugu, 1719-1788: Forerunner of Modern Japan*, Harvard-Yenching Institute Monograph Series (Cambridge: Harvard University Press, 1955); Matsudaira Sadanobu's standard biography is: Shibusaba Eiichi, *Rakuō-kō den* (Tokyo: Iwanami shoten, 1937).

2. Tsuda, *Hōkenshakai*, pp. 55-56.

3. The growing importance of the merchants is shown, for instance, in the increasing percentage of the total cash income of the bakufu that came from sources other than the land tax: in the 1722–25 period, this percentage was 44; in the 1736–40 period, it had almost doubled to 75. See Furushima Toshio, "Bakufu zaisei shūnyū no dōkō to nōmin shūdatsu no kakki," in *Nihon keizai-shi taikei*, ed. *idem* (Tokyo: Tokyo Daigaku shuppankai, 1965), IV, chart between pp. 14 and 15.

4. Conrad Totman, *Politics in the Tokugawa Bakufu: 1600-1843*, Harvard East Asian Series (Cambridge: Harvard University Press, 1967), p. 199.

5. Hall, *Tanuma*, pp. 35-37.

6. James Murdoch, *A History of Japan*, Vol. III, *The Tokugawa Epoch 1652-1868* (New York: Greenberg, 1926), p. 411.

7. During the Yoshimune years, the high percentage of cash income from sources other than the land tax, reached in the five-year period of 1736–40, was not maintained. Under Tanuma, however, during the three five-year periods between 1775 and 1790, the percentages were: 70, 68, and 72. Notice that during the last period Tanuma was in power for only two years and a half. In the 1790–95 period, the percentage dropped to 36. See Furushima, "Bakufu zaisei," chart between pp. 14 and 15, and pp. 33-34.

8. Thomas C. Smith, *The Agrarian Origins of Modern Japan* (Stanford: Stanford University Press, 1959), p. 77.

9. Hall, *Tanuma*, p. 120.

10. Furushima Toshio, "Shōhin ryūtsū no hatten to ryōshu keizai," in

Nihon rekishi: Kinsei, IV, Vol. XII of *Iwanami kōza Nihon rekishi* (Tokyo: Iwanami shoten, 1963), pp. 78–79.

11. Hall, *Tanuma*, pp. 119–22; see also Arakawa Hidetoshi, *Kikin no rekishi*, Nihon rekishi shinsho (Tokyo: Shibundō, 1967), pp. 17–27; 64–65.

12. Chihō-shi kenkyū kyōgikai, ed., *Kinsei chihō-shi kenkyū nyūmon* (Tokyo: Iwanami shoten, 1955), pp. 296–99.

13. Between 1600 and 1700, there were only two years with more than ten disturbances; in the 1700–1780 period, however, there were thirty-two years with more than ten. Aoki Kōji, *Hyakushō ikki no nenjiteki kenkyū* (Tokyo: Shinseisha, 1966), pp. 14–18.

14. See Hayashi Motoi, "Hōreki-Tenmei-ki no shakai jōsei," in *Nihon rekishi: Kinsei*, IV, Vol. XII of *Iwanami kōza Nihon rekishi* (Tokyo: Iwanami shoten, 1963), pp. 104–54; idem, *Kyōhō to Kansei*, Vol. XVI of *Kokumin no rekishi* (Tokyo: Buneidō, 1971), pp. 251–308.

15. Abe Makoto and Sakai Hajime, "Hōkensei no dōyō," in *Nihon rekishi: Kinsei*, IV, Vol. XII of *Iwanami kōza Nihon rekishi* (Tokyo: Iwanami shoten, 1963), p. 49; Hayashi Motoi, "Hōreki," pp. 147–54.

16. See Harold Bolitho, *Treasures among Men; The Fudai Daimyo in Tokugawa Japan* (New Haven: Yale University Press, 1974), pp. 34, 194–95.

17. *Tokugawa jikki*, X; Vol. XLVII of *Kokushi taikei*, ed. Kuroita Katsumi (2d ed.; Tokyo: Yoshikawa kōbunkan, 1966), pp. 244, 785; Hall, *Tanuma*, p. 77.

18. Totman, *Politics*, p. 168.

19. *Tokugawa jikki*, X, 736.

20. Furushima, "Shōhin," p. 78.

21. Hayashi, *Kyōhō*, pp. 375–77.

22. *Ibid.*, p. 377. The daimyo in question was Nabeshima (Matsudaira) Harushige, lord of the Saga domain. He was not exactly an in-law of Sadanobu. Shigemochi, the previous lord and Harushige's nephew, who had died childless in 1770 and to whom Harushige had succeeded, was married to a full sister of Sadanobu. See Shibusawa, *Rakuō-kō den*, Appendix, p. 24, and Watanabe Seyū, *Daimyō-hen*, Vol. III of *Denki Dainihon-shi* (Tokyo: Yūzankaku, 1934), pp. 461, 463.

23. That year the rice price stood at about 100 *momme* per koku; ten *momme* equal one *bu*.

24. The assassination was not motivated by this issue. The official version of this incident is that Sano Masakoto, the assassin, resented Tanuma Okitomo for having used his family's genealogical documents to alter his own genealogy. See Hall, *Tanuma*, pp. 42, 133.

25. *Ibid.*, pp. 81–82.

26. *Tokugawa jikki*, X, 803–04; Takayanagi Shinzō, Ishii Ryōsuke, ed., *Ofuregaki Tenmei-shūsei* (Tokyo: Iwanami shoten, 1936), No. 3082, pp. 916–17.

27. The document *Tenmei kōsetsu* was written in 1786, probably by a high official. It is now at the library of Keio University, Tokyo. See Yamada Tadao, "Tanuma Okitsugu no shikkyaku to Tenmei matsunen no seiji jōkyō," *Shigaku*, 43 (1970), 1–2, p. 243.

28. *Tanuma shudono gashiradono e ōse-wataserare sho,* in *Retsukō tanbiroku,* ed. Hayakawa Junsaburō (Tokyo: Kokusho kankōkai, 1914), p. 526.

29. Yamada, "Tanuma," p. 243.

30. *Ibid.;* see also the *Rintoku-ki,* the official biography of Tokugawa Harusada, the Lord of Kii (quoted in Hayashi, *Kyōhō,* p. 380).

31. *Tokugawa jikki,* X, 809.

32. *Ryūei bunin,* II, Dai Nihon kinsei shiryō (Tokyo: Tokyo Daigaku shiryō hensanjo, 1964), p. 73.

33. Yamada, "Tanuma," pp. 250-51.

34. Hayashi, "Hōreki," pp. 115-16, 128; *idem, Kyōhō,* p. 164.

35. Totman, *Politics,* p. 33.

36. Great vassal domains are domains of over 100,000 koku. The putative yield of Sadanobu's native house, Tayasu, was of the same order (*ibid.,* pp. 126, 163).

37. Tamura Eitarō, "Shirakawa-han seisō to nōmin ikki," in *idem, Ikki, kumosuke, bakuto* (Tokyo: Obatake shoten, 1933), pp. 258–61, 264.

38. Between 1681 when the first disturbance occurred, and 1742 when the Hisamatsu Matsudaira were enfeoffed in Shirakawa, there were nine peasant petitions, disturbances, and riots of significance—this leaves out disturbances in single villages. Between 1742 and 1783, a badly documented period, two more took place, the last one in the summer before Sadanobu succeeded to the house. Calculated from Aoki Kōji, *Hyakushō ikki,* pp. 28, 37–123; see also *Fukushima-ken shi* (Fukushima-ken: n.p.) III (1970), 485.

39. See Tamura, "Shirakawa-han," pp. 251-401.

40. *Fukushima-ken shi,* III, 423, 449-50; Tamura, "Shirakawa-han," pp. 258-308. Similar factional struggles also erupted in the Taira and Sendai domains (*Fukushima-ken shi,* III, 450).

41. For the *kambun* text, with a postscript by Sadanobu, and the transcript, see *Kinsei chihō keizai shiryō,* ed. Ono Takeo (Tokyo: Yoshikawa kōbunkan, 1958), III, 440–77.

42. Matsudaira Sadanobu, *Uge no hito koto,* in *idem, Uge no hito koto; Shugyō roku* (Tokyo: Iwanami shoten, 1942), p. 46. (Hereafter abbreviated as *Uge.*) Also, in references to Sadanobu's works, his name will not be mentioned. All of Sadanobu's writings, except for the two autobiographical works, were published as parts of larger collections, which will be referred to in abbreviated form. A reference to several works simultaneously, lists these works in chronological order.

43. Totman, *Politics,* pp. 126-27.

44. *Uge,* p. 27.

45. *Ibid.,* p. 29.

46. For Munetake's career and scholarship, see Doki Zenmaro, *Tayasu Munetake* (4 vols.; Tokyo: Nihon hyōronsha, 1946).

Munetake was a patron and scholar of the new School of National Learning (*Kokugaku*). Kada no Azumamaro (1669–1739), inspired by Ogyū Sorai's return to Chinese antiquity, had undertaken the study of Japan's ancient literature. His nephew and adopted son, Kada no Arimaro (1706–51) was employed by Munetake in 1731 (the year Tayasu was established) for the study of the ancient bureaucracy. It was under his patronage that Arimaro published his *Yūshoku kojitsu* (*ibid.*, I, 105). Kamo no Mabuchi, however, was Munetake's most famous protégé and collaborator.

47. *Ibid.*, I, 121.

48. *Ibid.* With Munetake and Mabuchi's interpretation of Japanese culture there started a debate—still in progress—about the essence of Japan's cultural identity. In the latter half of the century, Motoori Norinaga (1730–1801) turned within the same tradition of National Learning to the *Kojiki* and the *Tale of Genji* and, stressing feminine and aesthetic values, organized his views of Japan's cultural identity in a totally opposite way. Matsumoto Shigeru, *Motoori Norinaga: 1730-1801*, Harvard East Asian Series (Cambridge: Harvard University Press, 1970), pp. 177-93. For this debate and for Munetake's place in it, see Umehara Takeru, *Bi to shūkyō no hakken: sōzōteki Nihon bunkaron* (Tokyo: Chikuma shobō, 1967), pp. 144ff.

49. Doki, *Tayasu Munetake*, I, 34-41.

50. It was the physical debility of the shogun that had made the rise of Tanuma possible. In 1754, the adjutant Ōoka Tadamitsu, the only person who understood the utterings of the shogun, had acquired daimyo status. In 1757, he became grand chamberlain with a strong following in the Interior. Ieharu was unable to redress the wrongs of the Ieshige era, and before long relied more and more on his chamberlain Tanuma Okitsugu. Totman, *Politics*, pp. 221-22.

51. *Uge*, pp. 24, 25, 29; for the text of the *Jikyōkan* see Ema Seihatsu, ed. *Rakuō-kō isho* (3 vols.; Tokyo: Hachio shoten, 1893), I (hereafter abbreviated as *RKI*).

52. *Uge*, p. 28; Tauchi Chikasuke, *Go-gyōjō kiryō*, in *Nihon ijin genkō shiryō*, XVII (Tokyo: Kokushi kenkyūkai, 1916), p. 74 (hereafter abbreviated as *Go-gyōjō*); Hirose Mōsai, *Uringen-kō den*, in *Nihon bunkō*, V (Tokyo: Hakubunkan, 1891), 4-5 (hereafter abbreviated as *Urin*).

53. There were many houses in Tokugawa Japan with the name of Matsudaira. Originally, it was the family name of Ieyasu. He and his successors later bestowed it upon houses that thus received the honor of becoming cadet houses of the Tokugawa. Of the thirty or more related houses thus established during the Tokugawa period, twenty-four survived to 1868. (Totman, *Politics*, pp. 111, 264-69.)

54. *Uge*, pp. 30, 32.

55. For the details of Tanuma's scheme, see Yamada Tadao, "Tanuma Okitsugu no seiken dokuten o megutte," *Shigaku*, XLIV, 3 (April 1972), 91-114.

Chapter Two: Intellectual Legacy and
Psychological Development

1. *Uge*, p. 39; *Go-gyōjō*, p. 93.

2. This list, *Dokushokō karoku*, can be found in RKI, I; see also: Shibusawa, *Rakuō-kō den*, pp. 22–23, and Fukaya Kentaro, *Matsudaira Sadanobukō to keishin sonō no kyōiku* (Tokyo: Hokkai shuppansha, 1941), pp. 84–88.

3. For this brief introduction to Sadanobu's literary works and most of

their English titles, I am indebted to Robert Lee Backus, "Matsudaira Sadanobu as Moralist and Litterateur" (unpublished Ph.D. dissertation, University of California, Berkeley, 1963).

4. Matsudaira Sadakuni from Shirakawa should not be confused with Tayasu Sadakuni, Sadanobu's older brother, who, after his adoption into the Matsudaira family of Matsuyama han, was also called Matsudaira Sadakuni.

5. This visit was in connection with a shogunal procession to Ieyasu's mausoleum in Nikkō. Surrounding domains had to contribute to the preparation of this event. Sadanobu's stepfather, sick at the time, had entrusted this task to Sadanobu. It was Sadanobu's only visit to the domain before he became daimyo in 1783 (*Uge*, pp. 37-38).

6. Shibusawa, *Rakuō-kō den*, pp. 24, 25; *Uge*, p. 39. (Manuscript. Nara: Tenri University).

7. All the above works, except for one, can be found in the three volumes of *Rakuō-kō isho*. *Ōmu no kotoba* is published in *Sanjippuku* (*SJP*), compiled by Ōta Nampo (Tokyo: Kokusho kankōkai, 1917), III, 433-38. The *Shiji seiyō, Kokuhonron, Seigo* and *Shoyū hen* are also reprinted in the more readily available *Nihon keizai taiten* (NKT), edited by Takimoto Seiichi (2d ed.; Tokyo: Meiji bunken, 1967), XIII, 321-437.

For a complete list of Sadanobu's writings, consisting of some 130 titles, see: Shibusawa, *Rakuō-kō den*, pp. 358-65, 381-87, and Inamura Hiromoto, "Rakuō-kō chojutsu hensansho kaisetsu," in *Rakuō-kō yoei*, ed. *idem* (Tokyo: p.u., 1929), pp. 33-60. The latter list is briefly annotated.

In English there exists an annotated list of all published works of Sadanobu, giving all editions of each work. This is to be found as an appendix to Robert Lee Backus, "Matsudaira Sadanobu as Moralist and Litterateur" pp. 532-601. This list is complete, except for the following four items: *Shiji seiyō*, to be found in NKT, XIII; *Rō no oshie*: RKI, III, and in vol. II of *Nihon eisei bunkō* (Tokyo: Dōbunkan, 1917), pp. 109-22; *Monogatari*, and *Heibō tai-i kudensho*, both available in: Itasawa Takeo, "Matsudaira Sadanobu to Shimbu no michi," *Nihon-gaku kenkyū*, III, 2 (February 1943), 6-9 and 11-17. R. L. Backus offers also a complete translation of *Kagetsutei hikki*, pp. 134-92 passim.

8. *Uge*, p. 46.

9. *Shūshin roku*, RKI, I, 3-4; *Shiji seiyō*, NKT, XIII, 390-91.

10. *Taikan zakki*, in Vol. XIV of *Nihon zuihitsu zenshū* (Tokyo: Kokumin tosho kabushiki kaisha, 1928), p. 248. (Hereafter abbreviated as NZZ.)

11. *Shūshin*, RKI, I, 3; *Kagetsutei hikki*, RKI, III, 3.

12. *Shūshin*, RKI, I, 5; *Kanko-dōri*, RKI, I, 1.

13. *Kokuhonron*, NKT, XIII, 327; *Kagetsutei*, RKI, III, 15; *Ōmu no kotoba*, SJP, III, 435.

14. *Rakutei hikki*, RKI, II, 44; *Kokuhonron*, NKT, XIII, 330; *Ōmu*, SJP, III, 435.

15. *Ōmu*, SJP, III, 435.

16. *Kokuhonron*, NKT, XIII, 334.

17. *Seigo*, NKT, XIII, 395.

18. *Ibid.*, p. 396.

19. *Shūshin*, RKI, I, 25; *Seigo*, NKT, XIII, 411–12.

20. *Kokuhonron*, NKT, XIII, 329.

21. *Ibid.*, p. 348.

22. On the theme of heavenly retribution in one's own life, or in that of one's descendants, see *Daigaku keibun kōgi*, RKI, III, 50-53, 80-82.

23. *Kokuhonron*, NKT, XIII, 328; *Daigaku*, RKI, III, 154, 175-76; *Ōmu*, SJP, III, 434.

24. *Kagetsutei*, RKI, III, 1.

25. *Kokuhonron*, NKT, XIII, 328; *Seigo*, NKT, XIII, 396; *Ōmu*, SJK, III, 434; *Kagetsutei*, RKI, III, 1.

26. *Kokuhonron*, NKT, XIII, 328, 350.

27. *Shūshin*, RKI, I, 12.

28. *Kokuhonron*, NKT, XIII, 334; *Kanjo ronsetsu*, RKI, I, 22-23.

29. *Daigaku*, RKI, III, 62, 150-51; *Ōmu*, SJP, III, 434.

30. *Daigaku*, RKI, III, 4, 131, 137; *Rakutei*, RKI, II, 17, 35.

31. *Seigo*, NKT, XIII, 406.

32. *Kagetsutei*, RKI, III, 18.

33. *Ōmu*, SJP, III, 434.

34. *Seigo*, NKT, XIII, 396, 418; *Shisei*, NKT, XIII, 392.

35. *Shūshin*, RKI, I, 29-30; *Ōmu*, SJP, III, 436.

36. *Kagetsutei*, RKI, III, 11-13.

37. *Ōmu*, SJK, III, 437.

38. *Kanjo*, RKI, I, 2-3; *Shūshin*, RKI, I, 25.

39. *Shūshin*, RKI, I, 23.

40. *Kanjo*, RKI, I, 18, 48-49; *Kokuhonron*, NKT, XIII, 332-33; *Shūshin*, RKI, I, 2, 26-27; *Seigo*, NKT, XIII, 404; *Kagetsutei*, RKI, III, 6.

41. *Kanjo*, RKI, I, 2; *Seigo*, NKT, XIII, 410; *Kagetsutei*, RKI, III, 10.

42. *Shūshin*, RKI, I, 16, 21.

43. *Sekizen shū*, I, 16 (RKI, II); *Rakutei*, RKI, II, 61. See also the instructions for his retainers, delivered two months after Sadanobu took office as daimyo: "Matsudaira Etchū no kami Sadanobu ason, go-kerai e go-kyōjisho." (Manuscript; Tokyo: Tokyo Daigaku shiryō hensanjo, dated 1783/12) p. 68 (pagination mine). Copies of this manuscript are widespread, often bearing a different title: "Shirakawa-ke seiroku" (Kyoto: Kyoto Daigaku), "Shirakawa-kō denshinroku" (Tokyo: private collection of Yamauchi Ichiro), or Shira-kawake-rei denshinroku" (Shirakawa: private collection of Ishioka Seiichi).

44. *Tōzen manpitsu*, RKI, I, 13.

45. *Shūshin*, RKI, I, 15; *Daigaku*, DKI, III, 143-45; *Seigo*, SJK, III, 404, 406; *Kagetsutei*, RKI, III, 15-16.

46. *Kagetsutei*, RKI, III, 14-15, 28.

47. *Tōzen*, RKI, I, 16-19; *Daigaku*, RKI, III, 50.

48. *Seigo*, NKT, XIII, 397.

49. Backus, "Matsudaira Sadanobu," pp. 138-39.

50. *Kagetsu sōshi*, NZZ, XIII, 586; *Kagetsutei*, RKI, III, 2.

51. *Rakutei*, RKI, II, 8; *Kagetsutei*, RKI, III, 8.

52. *Kasumi no tomo*, RKI, I, 33; *Kanjo*, RKI, I, 19, 22-23; *Shūshin*, RKI, I,

32-33; *Seigo*, NKT, XIII, 416; *Tōzen*, RKI, I, 12; *Sekizen*, Vol. III, 58 (RKI, II); "Go-kerai e go-kyōjisho," Manuscript, 1783 (p. 42). See also instructions to his retainers, dated 1789/3: Shirakawa-ko mitsugo" (Manuscript; Tokyo: Tokyo Daigaku shiryō hensanjo), p.9. The same manuscript is also to be found as the last section of "Shirakawa jinsei-roku" (Kyoto: Kyoto University), and as "Matsudaira Etchū no kami seikan" (Tokyo: Keio University).

53. *Daigaku*, RKI, III, 179, 184-87; *Sekizen*, III, 11-13 (RKI, II).
54. *Rakutei*, RKI, II, 6.
55. *Seigo*, NKT, XIII, 403.
56. *Kokuhonron*, NKT, XIII, 336, 338.
57. *Rakutei*, RKI, II, 43.
58. *Kokuhonron*, NKT, XIII, 337; *Seigo*, NKT, XIII, 413.
59. *Kokuhonron*, NKT, XIII, 374-77; *Seigo*, NKT, XIII, 415-16.
60. *Kagetsutei*, RKI, III, 24-27.
61. *Kokuhonron*, NKT, XIII, 344-45.
62. *Seiji*, NKT, XIII, 391.
63. *Seigo*, NKT, XIII, 401.
64. *Shūshin*, RKI, I, 39.
65. *Seigo*, NKT, XIII, 411-12.
66. *Ōmu*, SJP, III, 437; *Kagetsutei*, RKI, III, 21.
67. *Seigo*, NKT, XIII, 411-12.
68. *Kagetsutei*, RKI, III, 26.
69. *Shūshin*, RKI, I, 40.
70. *Tōzen*, RKI, I, 28-29.
71. *Uge*, pp. 38-39; *Rō no oshie*, RKI, III, 5, 11; *Go-gyōjō*, pp. 90-91; *Urin*, p. 7.
72. Erik H. Erikson, *Identity: Youth and Crisis* (New York: W. W. Norton & Co. Inc., 1968), p. 144.
73. Elsewhere, Sadanobu suggests that he was interested in governmental affairs from age nine (*Uge*, p. 29) or ten (*Jisho ryakuden*, composed in 1820; see Fukaya, *Matsudaira Sadanobu-kō*, p. 265).
74. *Uge*, p. 28. For the exact reference of the passage, see *Hou Han shu* (Taipei: I wěn, n.d.), Ch. 96 (lieh-Chuen, 56), p. 1a.
75. Erikson, *Identity*, pp. 16, 96; idem, *Young Man Luther: A Study in Psychoanalysis and History* (New York: W. W. Norton & Co. Inc., 1958), p. 14.
76. At ages sixteen and twenty-six, Munetake suffered from dropsy; in his later years a chronic kidney disease developed and he began suffering from rheumatism. At thirty-two he had to be excused from attendance at the shogun's court for a whole year, and at forty-five, he used a cane to walk. The year after, he was ill again. (Doki, *Tayasu*, IV, 163-70.)
77. Sadanobu's stepmother was the sister of the *kampaku* (imperial advisor) Konoe Uchisaki.
78. By 1758 one daughter had probably already been married off to the lord of the Saga domain in Hizen. Three others were later married to: the lord of the Tottori domain in Inaba, the lord of the Hagi domain in Nagato, and the lord of the Shōnai domain in Dewa. For a genealogy of the Tayasu house, see

Shibusawa, *Rakuōkō-den*, Appendix, and Arai Hakuseki, *Hankampu*, I (2d ed.; Tokyo: Jimbutsu ōraisha, 1967), 508-09.

79. *Uge*, pp. 23-24, 46-47; *Shugyō roku*, p. 181; *Go-gyōjō*, p. 72; *Urin*, p. 4.

80. *Uge*, p. 30.

81. *Shugyō roku*, p. 181; *Go-gyōjō*, p. 72.

82. *Uge*, p. 37.

83. *Ibid.*, p. 42.

84. *Uge*, p. 46; see also *ibid.*, pp. 52-53, and *Go-gyōjō*, p. 95.

85. *Shūshin*, RKI, I, 33-34.

86. See, e.g.: *Uge*, p. 53; *Shugyō roku*, pp. 181-83; *Jisho ryakuden*, p. 265.

87. Suzuki was holder of the military post of superintendent of muskets and cabinets. *Ryūei bunin*, IV, 174, 290.

88. *Shugyō roku*, p. 182; *Monogatari*, in: Itasawa Takeo, "Matsudaira Sadanobu to Shimbu no michi," *Nihon-gaku kenkyū*, III, 2 (February 1943), 7-8. See also one letter of the *Sōrishū*, a collection of 124 letters, addressed to Sadanobu after he was adopted by the Matsudaira and before he became chief councillor. One of the letters is from Suzuki, and Sadanobu added a note, giving some information about the master. The *Sōrishū* is now at the library of Tenri University in Nara prefecture. For an introduction to the collection, see: Matsudaira Sadamitsu, "Matsudaira Sadanobu o chūshin to suru shokō no kyōyō: Sōrishū o chūshin to shite," in *Kinsei Nihon no Jugaku*, ed. Fukushima Kashizō (Tokyo: Iwanami shoten, 1939), pp. 141-56. The letter in question is quoted in Itasawa, "Shimbu no michi," p. 10.

89. *Shugyō roku*, pp. 182, 188; *Monogatari*, Itasawa, "Shimbu no michi," p. 9.

90. Backus, "Matsudaira Sadanobu," p. 214.

91. *Shugyō roku*, pp. 183, 186; *Monogatari*: Itasawa, "Shimbu no michi," p. 6.

92. *Jūjutsu* was founded in the middle of the seventeenth century by a Chinese immigrant, Ch'en Yüan-pin (1587–1671), who was patronized by the lords of Kii. A third-generation disciple, but a contemporary of the founder, was later employed by the lord of Matsue, where he developed the Kitō school. See *Dokushi sōran* (Tokyo: Jimbutsu ōrai-sha, 1966), p. 1331, and *Nihon budō zenshū*, ed. Imamura Yoshio, V (Tokyo: Jimbutsu ōrai-sha, 1966), pp. 14, 19-24.

93. *Nihon budō zenshū*, I, 26; V, 19.

94. *Ibid.*, V, 25, 369-70.

95. The influence of *Shimbu no michi* on Sadanobu's thinking is most prominent in his *Daigaku keibun kōgi* (1784) and in his *Taikan zakki*, a collection of miscellaneous notes, observations and reflections, covering the first seven years after his chief councillorship, from 1794 until 1800. Ema Seiichi edited one edition (Tokyo: Hachio shoten, 1892); references, however are to the more available vol. XIV of *Nihon zuihitsu zenshū*, pp. 161-438.

Shimbu no michi's philosophy is the direct object of a set of small scrolls, written half a year before Sadanobu's death: *Hai no zō, Tai kuden, Gōri, Kisetsu, Katachi no oshie*, (the last three grouped together as "Shimbu no michi") all of which, except the first one are now at the library of Tenri

University, Nara prefecture. *Hai no zō* may still be at the house of Sadanobu's direct descendant in Kamakura or at the Chinkoku-Shukoku shrine in Kuwana, Mie prefecture, although both places denied to be in possession of the document. Two more scrolls, *Monogatari* (date unknown) and *Heibō tai-i kudenshō* (1787), are published in the above mentioned article by Itasawa Takeo. Besides the article by Itasawa, there exists, to my knowledge, only one work on *Shimbu no michi*: Satō Kenji, *Shimbu no michi* (Tokyo: Kōdansha, 1942). I could not find it, however, at any major library in Tokyo or Kyoto.

96. *Daigaku*, RKI, III, 1; *Sekizen*, I, 14–15 (RKI, II).

97. *Daigaku*, RKI, III, 10, 27.

98. *Ibid.*, p. 20.

99. *Ibid.*, p. 33; *Sekizen*, II, 50, 61 (RKI, II).

100. *Heibō*: Itasawa, "Shimbu no michi," p. 12.

101. *Taikan zakki*, NZZ, XIV, 313.

102. *Daigaku*, RKI, III, 146-47; *Taikan*, NZZ, XIV, 184-85.

103. *Daigaku*, RKI, III, 80.

104. *Ibid.*, pp. 32, 37, 50; *Heibō*: Itasawa, "Shimbu no michi," p. 11.

105. *Daigaku*, RKI, III, 21; *Taikan*, NZZ, XIV, 242.

106. *Sekizen*, II, 31, (RKI, II).

107. *Ibid.*, Vol. I, RKI, II, 14; *Taikan*, NZZ, XIV, 242; *Kagetsu sōshi*, NZZ, XIII, 594; *Heibō*: Itasawa, "Shimbu no michi," p. 15.

108. *Daigaku*, RKI, III, 15, 82, 86-87, 174-78; *Sekizen*, I, 14 (RKI, II); II, 31, 43 (RKI, II).

109. *Daigaku*, RKI, III, 22, 33-34, 91.

110. *Heibō*: Itasawa, "Shimbu no michi," p. 13; *Taikan*, NZZ, XIV, 279; "Katachi no oshie," Manuscript.

111. *Rō no oshie*, RKI, III, 7; *Taikan*, NZZ, XIV, 279, 338; "Gōri," Manuscript; *Heibō*: Itasawa, "Shimbu no michi," p. 14; *Shugyō roku*, pp. 183, 203.

112. *Shugyō roku*, pp. 186-87.

113. *Heibō*: Itasawa, "Shimbu no michi," p. 14.

114. For this definition of religion as a model for action and an image of the world, see Clifford Geertz, "Religion as a Cultural System," in Michael Banton, ed., *Anthropological Approaches to the Study of Religion*, A. S. A. Monographs (London: Tavistock publications, 1966), pp. 1-46.

115. We know of this ritual aspect of Sadanobu's self-deification through an unpublished manuscript, drafted in 1840 by Okamoto Jishō, probably a personal attendant of Sadanobu, and completed in 1850. The manuscript, *Kantoku roku* (Tokyo: Naikaku bunkō), is quoted in part in Fukaya, *Matsudaira Sadanobu-kō*, pp. 266-67 (see for a partial translation in Backus, "Matsudaira Sadanobu," pp. 256-59) and in Katō Genchi, *Hompō seishi no kenkyū: seishi no shijitsu to sono shinri bunseki* (Tokyo: Meiji seitoku kinen gakkai hakkō, 1932), p. 90. The pages devoted to Matsudaira Sadanobu in Katō's study (pp. 87-102) were first published as an article: Katō Genchi, "Kami no jikaku ni jūshite mizukara seishi o mōketa Matsudaira Rakuō-kō," *Meiji seitoku kinen gakkai kiyō*, XXXIII (1930), 1-10.

116. Katō, *Hompō seishi*, p. 90.

117. *Kagetsu sōshi*, NZZ, XIII, 617; *Shugyō roku*, p. 183; *Jisho ryakuden*, Fukaya, *Matsudaira Sadanobu-kō*, p. 265.

118. Matsumoto, *Motoori Norinaga*, p. 184.

119. Katō, *Hompō seishi*; see also: Katō Genchi, "Shinto Worship of Living Human Gods in the Religious History of Japan," *The Asiatic Review*, XXVI (1930), 575-80.

120. These three examples appear in Katō's study (Katō, *Hompō seishi*, pp. 118-20, 350-51); Okada is also mentioned in his English article (Katō, "Shinto Worship," p. 576).

121. *Uge*, p. 58.

122. Satō Tahei, *Rakuō Matsudaira Sadanobu* (Tokyo: Miyakoshi tai-yōdō shobō, 1942), pp. 110-11; Asano, *Matsudaira Sadanobu*, p. 93.

123. Katō, *Hompō seishi*, p. 381.

124. *Ibid.*, pp. 49-54. In the application to the authorities for this cult, the precedent of O-ana-muchi is used as an argument.

125. *Ibid.*, pp. 54–58; Maeda Kōji, *Aizu-han ni okeru Yamazaki Ansai* (Tokyo: Nishizawa shoten hakkō, 1935), pp. 94, 124, 196.

126. E.g.: "The gods are the spirit of heaven and earth, human beings are the gods of creation. In sum, Heaven and Man are one; and the essence of their Way is found exclusively in the teaching of Reverence." Quoted in David Magarey Earl, *Emperor and Nation in Japan: Political Thinkers of the Tokugawa Period* (Seattle: University of Washington Press, 1964), p. 55.

127. Satō, *Rakuō*, pp. 25-26; Asano, *Matsudaira Sadanobu*, p. 149; "Go-kerai e go-kyōjisho," Manuscript, 1783 (pp. 2-4, 12).

128. Totman, *Politics*, 210.

129. Sadanobu is aware of his status as adopted successor, since he asks his retainers special loyalty, disregarding the fact that he is only an adopted son. "Go-kerai e go-kyōjisho," Manuscript, 1783 (p. 138).

130. Ishikawa, *Kinsei kyōiku*, p. 55.

131. Nishida Taichirō, ed., *Fujiwara Seika, Nakae Tōju, Kumazawa Banzan, Yamazaki Ansai, Yamaga Sokō, Yamagata Daini-shū*, Vol. XVII of *Nihon no shisō* (Tokyo: Chikuma shobō, 1970), p. 14.

Chapter Three: Savior and Politician

1. Tsuda Sōkichi, *Nihon no Shinto*, Vol. IX of *Tsuda Sōkichi zenshū* (Tokyo: Iwanami shoten, 1964), pp. 49, 53-55.

2. *Uge*, p. 57.

3. *Iwase-gun shi* (Fukushima-ken: Iwase-gun yakusho, 1922), pp. 43–44.

4. Hayashi Motoi (*Kyōhō*, p. 371) is the first to draw attention to this riot. The only material I could find concerning this riot is an indirect reference to it in the records of the neighboring Aizu domain (*Aizu-ke seikeki*, vols. 218-20) as quoted in Nagakura Tamotsu, "Aizu-han ni okeru hansei kaikaku," in *Hansei kaikaku no kenkyū*, ed. Horie Hideichi (Tokyo: Ochanomizu shobō, 1955), p. 88. The riot was serious enough for Aizu han to make it close its borders to all travelers or *rōnin* from other domains.

5. *Go-gyōjō*, p. 113. It is very unlikely that Sadakuni was in Shirakawa at the time of the riot, as Hayashi thinks.

6. In the material on Sadanobu's rule in Shirakawa, very few names of retainers are mentioned, and hence it is impossible to document the existence of factions. One retainer house that must have been very close to Sadanobu is the Yoshimura house. Matazaeimon brought the request of Sadanobu's succession to Edo and returned with Sadanobu's first directives to the domain (*Go-gyōjō*, pp. 113-14); in a document from 1785, he is also mentioned as the source of information concerning criticism on Sadanobu's frugality laws (*ibid.*, p. 190); and his eightieth birthday is celebrated with special fanfare for his loyal services (*ibid.*, 179). Another Yoshimura (Mataichi) was employed in the important office of inspectors (*yokome yakusho*) (*Uge*, p. 66), and was steward to Sadanobu on his Kyoto journey. See Sugano Wātarō, "Kansei no kaikaku to Nakai Chikuzan," *Keizai-shi kenkyū*, XV (1936), 1, 72. On Sadakuni's retirement, see *Go-gyōjō*, pp. 113-14.

7. *Iwase-gun shi*, pp. 44-45.

8. *Uge*, p. 65.

9. *Iwase-gun shi*, pp. 43-45.

10. *Ibid.*

11. Ten *gō* is the equivalent of 1.92 quarts. In the domain of Yonezawa, also ruled by a famous, young daimyo, Uesugi Yōzan (then thirty-two, and much admired by Sadanobu), the rations were even smaller: 3 *gō* for male retainers, 2 *gō* for females. See Sugita Gempaku, *Nochimigusa*, partially reprinted as an appendix to Arakawa, *Kikin no rekishi*, p. 159.

12. *Shirakawa-shi shishiryōshū*, I, 10.

13. "Matsudaira Etchu no kami kanai" (manuscript).

14. "Shunnōō" in *Kinsei chihō keizai shiryō*, III, 319. *Shunnōō* (meaning "Dark Nightingale of Spring") is a small collection of documents concerning the first months of Sadanobu's rule. It contains some instructions to his retainers, directives for the peasants (both from 1783/11), details on relief measures of 1784/1 and further instructions on agriculture from the fourth month of the same year. Manuscript copies (with more appropriate names) are preserved at several institutions in Japan—another indication that Sadanobu's relief program was well publicised in his days. These manuscripts can be found in Tokyo (Kyōiku Daigaku) under the title *Shirakawa kokusei*, or in Kyoto (Kyoto Daigaku): *Shirakawa jinsei roku*.

15. *Fukushima-ken shi*, III, 79.

16. Calculated from *Dokushi biyō*, comp. Tokyo Daigaku shiryō hensanjo (Tokyo: Kōdansha, 1966), p. 769.

17. Calculated from "Matsudaira Etchū no kami kanai" (manuscript. Shirakawa: private possession of Kobayashi Kakuzaeimon).

18. See Tamura, "Shirakawa-han."

19. *Uge*, p. 54.

20. *Go-gyōjō*, p. 128.

21. Tokutomi Iichirō, *Kinsei Nihon kokumin-shi* (Tokyo: Jiji tsūshinsha, 1964), XXIV, *Matsudaira Sadanobu jidai*, p. 23.

22. The private wealth of daimyo or collateral houses is an obscure topic on which no data is as yet available. The main reason is that private capital of the lords was never an item in the official bookkeeping of the domains. One

document, however, shows that some lords put their money to clever use through some kind of banking activities. Thus Ii Naoaki (the older brother of the famous Ii Naosuke), Lord of Hikone, left a note on the interests farmers paid him on loans he had granted them on a private basis. See Yamaguchi Keiji, "Shiryō shūshū fukumeisho—Shiga-ken," Vol. II (Unpublished mimeographed manuscript; Tokyo Daigaku shiryō hensanjo, November 1967), pp. 40-41.

23. *Urin*, p. 13.

24. *Uge*, p. 75.

25. *Go-gyōjō*, p. 120.

26. *Ibid.*, p. 114.

27. *Ibid.*, pp. 114-16; for the complete text, see "Shunnōō" pp. 315-16.

28. "Shunnōō," pp. 316–18.

29. In his directives to officials and peasants of 1783/11 ("Shunnōō," pp. 315-16); in his speech when he entered the domain for the first time (*Go-gyōjō*, p. 141).

30. *Go-gyōjō*, pp. 140, 139; *Uge*, p. 59.

31. The number of incumbents is calculated from "Matsudaira Etchū no kami kanai" (manuscript).

32. *Rakutei*, RKI, II, 61-63; *Go-gyōjō*, pp. 122.

33. *Rakutei*, RKI, II, 17.

34. *Ibid.*, p. 27.

35. *Ibid.*, pp. 30-31.

36. *Fukushima-ken shi*, III, 69.

37. *Go-gyōjō*, p. 131.

38. "Gokerai e go-kyōjisho" (manuscript), pp. 13, 17, 26, 27, 29, 35, 69, 70.

39. Shibusawa, *Rakuō-kō den*, p. 60.

40. "Shunnōō," p. 318.

41. Certain village records, however, show no cancelation of taxes; see *Shirakawa-shi shi*, II, 131-36, 140; see also Appendix A.

42. *Go-gyōjō*, p. 142.

43. *Ibid.*, pp. 142, 147.

44. *Ibid.*, pp. 172-74.

45. Sato, *Rakuō*, pp. 109-10.

46. The reformer Hayakawa Mōzaeimon had initiated this policy. See *Shirakawa-shi shi*, II, 155; and *Fukushima-ken shi*, III, 439.

47. *Shirakawa-shi shi*, II, 155.

48. *Go-gyōjō*, p. 144; see also a letter to a superintendent, dated 1799/1/11, quoted in Matsudaira Sadamitsu, "Matsudaira Sadanobu no kyōgaku," *Nihon-gaku kenkyū*, III (1943), 2, 35–36. Also: Ōmori Shirō, "Matsudaira Rakuō-kō no jinko seisaku," *Tōhoku bunka kenkyū*, I, 5 (1929), 81-90.

49. *Fukushima-ken shi*, III, 452; Kanazawa Harutomo, "Shirakawa chihō no hōkōnin seido," *Shakai keizai shigaku*, III (1934), 10, 71.

50. *Go-gyōjō*, p. 144. This population transfer was a success in the southern part of the domain around Shirakawa, but not in the northern region around Sukagawa. This difference had to do with the religious beliefs of the

peasants from Echigo, all followers of the eastern branch of the New Pure Land sect (*Jōdo Shinshū, Higashi honganji*). This branch had temples around Shirakawa but not in Sukagawa. This seems to have been the reason why the settlers in the north disappeared from the population registers after a while. (Communication by Sukama Zenkatsu in a letter of 1971/3/16.)

51. *Ibid.*
52. Asano, *Matsudaira Sadanobu*, p. 38.
53. "Yōikukin kankei bunsho," in "Sukagawa-shi shihenshū shiryō: XII, Sukagawa-machi daikan Naitō-ke bunsho," comp. Sukagawa-shi shihenshū iinkai (mimeographed; Fukushima-ken: Sukagawa-shi, 1970), pp. 1–12.
54. *Urin*, p. 25.
55. *Ibid.*, p. 27. See also Honjō Eijirō "Rakuō-kō no jinko zōshoku seisaku," *Keizai ronsō*, VII, 5 (1918), 131–36.
56. Asano, *Matsudaira Sadanobu*, p. 156.
57. "Go-kerai e go-kyōjisho" (manuscript), p. 69.
58. Fukushima-ken shi, III, 496.
59. Asano, *Matsudaira Sadanobu*, pp. 66-69.
60. *Go-gyōjō*, p. 146.
61. *Fukushima-ken shi*, III, 439.
62. *Go-gyōjō*, p. 133.
63. Takeuchi Makoto, "Matsudaira Sadanobu," in: *Daimyo retsuden*, ed. Kodama Kōta and Kimura So, III *Bakkaku-hen*, Part 2 (Tokyo: Jimbutsu ōraisha, 1967), 263.
64. Asano, *Matsudaira Sadanobu*, pp. 123-40.
65. *Ibid.*, pp. 85-88.
66. Shibusawa, *Rakuō-kō den*, p. 335.
67. *Shirakawa-shi shishiryō*, VI (1966), 1. The document reprinted here carries the date of 1788, which is probably a mistake for 1784, the date on a manuscript in Tokyo Daigaku shiryō hensanjo ("Matsudaira Rakuō-kō on-kakikudashi shorui," p. 30). According to *Iwase-gun shi*, p. 44, however, the stipends were canceled and not cut in half in 1783: *go-chigyō nokorazu on-kariage nite.*
68. Shibusawa, *Rakuō-kō den*, p. 335.
69. *Go-gyōjō*, p. 132.
70. "Go-kerai e go-kyōjisho" (manuscript), pp. 136-38.
71. *Shirakawa-shi shi*, II, 138.
72. *Uge*, p. 65.
73. Shibusawa, *Rakuō-kō den*, p. 69.
74. *Go-gyōjō*, p. 160. Sadatsuna (1592–1651) was the youngest son of Hisamatsu (Matsudaira) Sadakatsu, a milk brother of Tokugawa Ieyasu. Ieyasu and Sadakatsu's mother was the famous Dentsū-in. Sadatsuna was allowed to found a new house: in 1635 he became daimyo of Kuwana. In 1710 the house moved to Takata until 1741, when it was enfeoffed in Shirakawa. (Shibusawa, *Rakuō-kō den*, pp. 33–35.)
75. *Ibid.*, p. 169.
76. See chap. 2, p. 43n.

77. *Go-gyōjō*, pp. 162-64.
78. *Uge*, p. 63.
79. *Shirakawa-shi shi*, II, 153-54.
80. *Go-gyōjō*, pp. 153-54; Asano, *Matsudaira Sadanobu*, p. 105.
81. Sato, *Rakuō*, pp. 80-82; Asano, *Matsudaira Sadanobu*, p. 31.
82. Shibusawa, *Rakuō-kō den*, p. 335.
83. RKD, II; Fukaya, *Matsudaira Sadanobu-kō*, pp. 134-304.
84. Asano, *Matsudaira Sadanobu*, p. 46.
85. Satō, *Rakuō*, p. 117.
86. *Urin*, p. 33.
87. Totman, *Politics*, pp. 36, 167.
88. These are four senior councillors, one junior councillor, five super-intendents of temples and shrines, and all three grand chamberlains.
89. *Uge*, pp. 41-42, 49.
90. *Ibid.*, pp. 41-42.
91. *Ibid.*, p. 56.
92. The authors of the history of Izumi han, in comparing these statistics with the population level of 1784, which was 7,479, wrongly ascribe great success to Tadakazu's population policy. This increase in population to the 10,000 level was in fact caused by an increase of the domain from 15,000 to 20,000 *koku* in 1790. (*Fukushima-ken shi*, III, 106.)
93. *Ibid.*, pp. 104, 106, 118; *Shirakawa-shi shi*, II, 154.
94. The careers of Sadanobu's friends were compiled from the *Ryūei bunin*.
95. *Uge*, pp. 41, 68-70.
96. Tsuji Zennosuke, *Tanuma jidai* (Tokyo: Nihon gakujutsu fukyūkai, 1936), pp. 224-37.
97. *Ibid.*, pp. 233-34.
98. *Kyōhō*, pp. 369-70.
99. Tamura, *Yonaoshi*, p. 38.
100. Tokutomi, *Kokuminshi*, XXIV, 38-40.
101. *Ibid.*, pp. 41-44; Kikuchi Kenjirō, "Matsudaira Sadanobu nyūkaku jijō," *Shigaku zasshi*, XXVI (1915), No. 1, 1-22.
102. *Zoku Tokugawa jikki*, I, Vol. XLVIII of *Kokushi taikei*, ed. Kuroita Katsumi (2d ed.; Tokyo: Yoshikawa Kōbunkan, 1966), p. 15.
103. Tokutomi, *Kokuminshi*, XXIV, 47.
104. *Ibid.*, p. 54.
105. Hayashi, *Kyōhō*, p. 382.
106. Yamada Tadao, "Tenmei no Edo uchikowashi," *Shigaku* (Mita shigakkai), XXXVI (1963), Nos. 2-3, 249.
107. *Kinsei chihō-shi kenkyū nyūmon*, p. 298.
108. Hayashi, *Kyōhō*, p. 384.
109. Tamura, *Yonaoshi*, pp. 23, 36.
110. The two documents are: *Kumo no ito maki*, a collecton of essays and sketches of life in Edo during the Tenmei period, by Iwase Kyōsan (NZZ, XVI, 473), and *Tenmei shichi hinoto hitsuji nen Edo kikin sōdō no koto*, in Vol. XVII

of *Kaitei shiseki shūran*, comp. Kondō Heijō (Tokyo: Kondō Shuppanbu, 1912-1929), p. 646.

111. The dismissal of Yokota Noritoshi broke a career that had almost reached the top. Four weeks earlier he had been granted a stipend raise of 3,000 *koku* and was thus only 500 *koku* below the 10,000 *koku* level that would have elevated him to daimyo rank. (Hayashi, *Kyōhō*, pp. 387-88.)

112. *Go-gyōjō*, p. 197, and Shibusawa, *Rakuō-kō den*, Appendix, p. 43.

113. Tokutomi, *Kokuminshi*, XXIV, 83-85.

114. Sugita Gempaku, *Nochimigusa*, in *Kaitei shiseki shūran*, XXXVII, 720-21.

Chapter Four: Bureaucratic Reformer

1. Calculated from Mitamura, *Buke jiten*, and Watanabe, *Denki dai Nihon-shi: Daimyo-hen*.

2. In the intercalary tenth month of 1786, Tanuma had already been deprived of 20,000 koku income, of his Osaka storehouses, and of his official mansion in Edo.

3. Shibusawa, *Rakuō-kō den*, pp. 122-23.

4. *Uge*, p. 94.

5. *Ibid.*, pp. 94–95; Tsuda Hideo, "Kansei Kaikaku," in *Nihon rekishi: Kinsei, v. 4*, Vol. XII of *Iwanami kōza Nihon rekishi* (Tokyo: Iwanami, 1963), p. 242.

6. Hall, *Tanuma*, p. 27; Totman, *Politics*, p. 40.

7. Totman, *Politics*, pp. 40, 164-65.

8. Inobe Shigeo, "Matsudaira Sadanobu no hosa shūnin," in *idem, Bakumatsu-shi no kenkyū* (Tokyo: Yuzankaku, 1927), pp. 11, 16.

9. *Uge*, p. 94.

10. Mori Sugio, "Kansei kaikaku-ki no osameyado haishi," *Rekishi kenkyū*, XI (1969).

11. *Uge*, p. 132; Shibusawa, *Rakuō-kō den*, p. 137; Takeuchi Makoto, "Kansei kaikaku to komekata goyōtachi no seiritsu," *Rekishi kyōiku*, IX, 10 (1961), 54-56.

12. *Go-gyōjō*, p. 134.

13. *Uge*, p. 96.

14. A fairly complete resumé of the *Yōkun hōshi kokoroe* is given in Mikami Sanji, *Edo jidai-shi* (Tokyo: Fuzanbō, 1944), II, 356–58. Manuscript copies of the document can be found at the library of Tenri University, Tenri (Nara prefecture), and at the shrine in honor of Matsudaira Sadanobu in Kuwana city (Mie prefecture).

15. Hall, *Tanuma*, pp. 14, 141-42.

16. *Uge*, p. 75.

17. Totman, *Politics*, p. 80.

18. Shibusawa, *Rakuō-kō den*, p. 163. The deficit of 1789 was caused by the rebuilding of the imperial palace in Kyoto, ravaged by fire on 1788/1/31.

19. "*Kinkoku no tsuka ue ni ki shi-sōrō koto*" (*Uge*, pp. 71-72; this formula appears also in the vow Sadanobu made in 1788/3, to be discussed below),

and *"ima wa kinkoku no tsuka wa shōka ni ki shite ikan to mo subekarazu"* (*ibid.*, pp. 104-5.)

20. Tsuda, "Kansei kaikaku," p. 255.

21. Shibusawa, *Rakuō-kō den*, p. 120; Mikami, *Edojidai-shi*, II, 355.

22. Shibusawa, *Rakuō-kō den*, p. 160.

23. Shibusawa, *Rakuō-kō den*, pp. 106-7.

24. *Uge*, p. 170.

25. Shibusawa, *Rakuō-kō den*, pp. 108-9.

26. Anesaki Masaharu, *History of Japanese Religion: With Special Reference to the Social and Moral Life of the Nation* (Rutland, Vt.: Charles E. Tuttle Co., 1963), pp. 139, 233.

27. *Uge*, p. 114.

28. Tsuda, "Kansei kaikaku," pp. 245-46.

29. *Uge*, pp. 117–19; Shibusawa, *Rakuō-kō den*, pp. 189–90.

30. Shibusawa, *Rakuō-kō den*, pp. 134–36.

31. Tsuda, "Kansei kaikaku," pp. 250-51.

32. RKI, I, 24-25. See also Takashiro Senji, "Shirakawa Rakuō-kō no 'Bukkaron' o hyōsu," *Mita gakkai zasshi*, VI, 2 (1912), 79–107.

33. Sadanobu was greatly influenced by the *Kyūji-saku* which his mentor Ōtsuka Kōi wrote in 1788. Itō Yoshiichi, "Tanuma seiji makki no keizai-ron: 'Kyūji-saku' to 'Getaya Jimbei kakiage' ni tsuite," *Katei*, 8 (December 1960). For the text of the *Kyūji-saku*, see NKT, XXIII, 105-46.

34. Sadanobu refers explicitly to his intention to give his reform the character of a return to the Kyōhō times, from the very beginning of his rule, in his speech to the assembled officials on 1787/7/1 (Shibusawa, *Rakuō-kō den*, p. 120).

35. Hall, *Tanuma*, pp. 68-73.

36. *Uge*, p. 105.

37. Shibusawa, *Rakuō-kō den*, pp. 150–51.

38. Itō Yoshiichi, "Kansei kaikaku tōji ni okeru Osaka shōnin no dōkō: 'Shoyū hen' o megutte," *Katei*, 7 (1958), p. 5. The *Kyūji-saku* of his mentor also influenced Sadanobu's financial measures. Itō, "Tanuma seiji," pp. 5-8.

39. Shibusawa, *Rakuō-kō den*, p. 150; Tsuda ("Kansei kaikaku," p. 271) gives the date of 1793.

40. Itō, "Tanuma seiji," p. 11.

41. Tsuda, "Kansei kaikaku," p. 271.

42. *Uge*, pp. 111–12.

43. Tsuda, "Kansei kaikaku," p. 258. Sadanobu referred to this policy already in his *Bukkaron* in 1789 (RKI, I, 23).

44. Tsuda, "Kansei kaikaku," p. 274.

45. Tamura, *Yonaoshi*, pp. 44–47, 58.

46. Itō, "Tanuma seiji," p. 4.

47. Itō Yoshiichi, "'Uezaki Kyūhachirō jōsho' ni tsuite," *Katei*, 10 (March, 1962), pp. 5–6.

48. Tsuda, "Kansei kaikaku," pp. 275–76.

49. The Loan Agency and the Collectors Agency were established next to

each other in the township of Saruya in Asakusa. Other names (for reasons that will become clear below) for the Loan Agency were: *Taruya go-yakusho* (the Taruya Office), and the *Go-kaisei yakusho* (the Revision Office). My treatment of these three agencies is based upon the following studies: Takeuchi Makoto, "Kansei kaikaku to komekata"; *idem,* "Kansei kaikaku to 'kanjōsho goyōtachi' no seiritsu," *Nihon rekishi,* 128 (February, 1959), pp. 23–32; 129 (March, 1959), pp. 49–56; Kitahara Susumu, "Kansei 'kien-ryō' ni tsuite," *Rekishi hyōron,* 162 (February, 1964), pp. 66–76; 163 (March, 1964), pp. 66–77; Inamura Hiromoto, "Matsudaira Rakuō-kō no kōsei ni oyoboseru kanka-eikyō," *Nihongaku kenkyū,* III, 2 (1943), pp. 49–54; Naga-mine Mitsuyoshi, "Chōhō kaikaku to shichibu-kin shimatsu," in *Rakuō-kō yoei,* ed. Inamura Hiromoto (Tokyo: n.p., 1929), pp. 18–32; Matsuyoshi Sadao, *Daimyo yarikuri-chō: kanemochi daimyo, binbō daimyo* (Tokyo: Shin-jimbutsu ōraisha, 1970).

50. Matsuyoshi, *Daimyo,* pp. 38–41; Kitahara, "Kien-ryō," pt. I, 69.

51. On the establishment of the *fudasashi kabunakama,* see Kitahara Susumu, "Fudasashi kabunakama no seiritsu," *Rekishi kyōiku,* IX, 10 (1961), pp. 46–52. Matsuyoshi (*Daimyo,* p. 41) gives the erroneous date of 1722.

52. Matsuyoshi, *Daimyo,* p. 108. *Kuramai* allowances were calculated in bales and rations, not in koku: one bale (*hyō*) equals 0.35 koku, and one ration (*fuchi*) was five *gō* (0,005 koku) per man a day.

53. Hall, *Tanuma,* p. 110.

54. Kitahara, "Kien-ryō," pt. I, 70–71.

55. *Ibid.,* pp. 71–72. Edo had a northern and a southern magistrate, who were in charge of the overall city administration in alternate months. (Yagyū was city magistrate from 1787/9/27 until 1788/9/10, when he became superintendent of finance.)

56. Kitayama ("Kien-ryō," pt. I, 70) has ninety-six as the total number of rice brokers. He gives a breakdown of them according to the number of bales of rice, handled per house in one year: eighty-one houses handled over 30,000 bales; twelve handled over 20,000 bales, and three over 10,000 bales. It would be interesting to correlate these figures with Matsuyoshi's analysis of the solidity of their capital. On first sight, one would have to conclude that many of them were big spenders, since only seven were independent in terms of their operational capital, although eighty-one of them turn up in the upper bracket of the business turnover. And, indeed, the rice brokers set the tone of extravagant life in Edo at that time: eighteen of them were known as the "eighteen men about town" or dandies (*jūhachi daitsū*). (See Hall, *Tanuma,* p. 110.)

57. Matsuyoshi, *Daimyo,* pp. 108–9, 141.

58. Yazaki Takeo, *Social Change and the City in Japan: from Earliest Times through the Industrial Revolution* (Japan: Japan Publications Inc., 1968), pp. 230–31.

59. Matsuyoshi, *Daimyo,* pp. 139–41.

60. Kitahara, "Kien-ryō," pt. II, 73.

61. Takeuchi, "Kanjōsho," p. 28.

62. Matsuyoshi, *Daimyo,* pp. 110–12.

63. Tokutomi, *Kokumin-shi,* XXIV, 150.

64. Shibusawa, *Rakuō-kō den*, p. 184; *Uge*, p. 133.
65. Kitahara, "Kien-ryō," pt. II, 77.
66. Takeuchi, "Kanjōsho," p. 24.
67. *Ibid.*, p. 29.
68. *Ibid.*, p. 49.
69. *Ibid.*, pp. 28, 51.
70. Takeuchi, "Komekata," p. 57.
71. Kitahara, "Kien-ryō," pt. II, 76.
72. Tsuda, "Kansei kaikaku," p. 267.
73. Nagamine, "Chōhō kaikaku," p. 18.
74. Takeuchi wrongly assumes in his two articles that the Edo Township Agency was already operative in 1790 ("Komekata," p. 57, and "Kanjōsho," p. 31).
75. Inamura, "Matsudaira," p. 50.
76. Takeuchi, "Komekata," p. 57.
77. Nagamine, "Chōhō kaikaku," p. 27.
78. Inamura, "Matsudaira," pp. 51–52.
79. Shibusawa, *Rakuō-kō den*, p. 144.
80. Takeuchi, "Komekata," p. 58.
81. Takeuchi, "Kanjōsho," p. 52.
82. *Ibid.*, pp. 51–52.
83. Takeuchi, "Komekata," p. 56.
84. *Ibid.*, p. 58.
85. *Ibid.*, p. 57.
86. Takeuchi, "Kanjōsho," p. 54.

Chapter Five: In Defense of the Bakufu
1. In Tsuda's "Kansei kaikaku" for instance, the Title Incident is not even mentioned. Kitajima Masamoto, in his *Bakuhansei no kumon* (*Nihon no rekishi*, XVIII; Tokyo: Chūōkōron-sha, 1966), refers to the incident in one paragraph in connection with Sadanobu's retirement (p. 126).
2. Herschel Webb, *The Japanese Imperial Institution in the Tokugawa Period*, Studies of the East Asian Institute, Columbia University (New York: Columbia University Press, 1968), p. 77.
3. *Nihon-shi jiten*, ed. Kyoto Daigaku Bungakubu Kokushi Kenkyūshitsu (rev. and enl. ed.; Tokyo: Sōgensha, 1960), pp. 639, 641.
4. Webb, *The Japanese Imperial Institution*, pp. 117–19.
5. *Ibid.*, pp. 93–94.
6. Tokutomi, *Kokumin-shi*, XXIV, 224–25.
7. *Uge*, p. 81.
8. Tokutomi, *Kokumin-shi*, XXIV, 222, 230.
9. *Uge*, p. 144. Sadanobu made it a point to keep his correspondence with the kampaku and the deputy, and he had planned to attach these documents to his autobiography (which only mentions the Title Incident in passing). This, however, did not happen, but the documents were preserved and copied in three volumes in 1845 by Tauchi Chikasuke, one of Sadanobu's retainers, who also wrote a biography of Sadanobu in 1835 (this is the *Go-gyōjō kiryō*). Later, Tokutomi Sohō published this correspondence in slightly abbreviated

form in his *Matsudaira Sadanobu jidai* (*Kokumin-shi*, XXIV, 216–392). It is this material that gives us a detailed knowledge of the meandering development of the incident. A manuscript of the documents can be found at the library of Tenri University, Nara prefecture.

10. Tokutomi, *Kokumin-shi*, XXIV, 227–31.

11. *Ibid.*, pp. 231–38.

12. *Ibid.*, pp. 238–44.

13. *Ibid.*, p. 250.

14. *Ibid.*, p. 247.

15. *Ibid.*, pp. 255–56,

16. Shibusawa, *Rakuō-kō den*, p. 254.

17. Tokutomi, *Kokumin-shi*, XXIV, 258–64.

18. *Ibid.*, pp. 264–70, 422.

19. *Ibid.*, pp. 271–78.

20. There was one instance where the bakufu had humiliated a courtier by summoning him to Edo and ordering him to house arrest. This had happened in 1629, when emperor Go-Mizunoo (then aged thirty-three), in protest against bakufu interference with the court, abdicated without warning in favor of his six-year-old daughter, who became empress Meishō. One of the small group of courtiers behind this abdication (the messenger Nakanoin Michimura) had then been disciplined by the bakufu in Edo. See Ono Shinji, "Bakufu to tennō," in *Nihon rekishi: Kinsei*, II, Vol. X of *Iwanami kōza Nihon rekishi* (Tokyo: Iwanami shoten, 1963), pp. 335–37; Mikami, *Edo jidai-shi*, II, 470; *Dai Nihon jinmei jisho*, II (Tokyo: Dai Nihon jinmei jisho kankōkai, 1926), p. 1891.

21. Tokutomi, *Kokumin-shi*, XXIV, 283–305.

22. *Ibid.*, pp. 310–29.

23. *Ibid.*, pp. 330–56.

24. Mikami, *Edo jidai-shi*, II, 470.

25. Shibusawa, *Rakuō-kō den*, p. 263.

26. G. Sansom treats the Title Incident in one paragraph and concludes that it had "no great significance at the time" (George Sansom, *A History of Japan: 1615–1867*; Stanford: Stanford University Press, 1963, p. 199.); and H. Webb (*The Imperial Institution*, pp. 124–25) treats it in two pages but implies that the incident was "trivial."

27. Mikami, *Edo jidai-shi*, II, 471–73; Tatsui Matsunosuke, *Edo jidai-shi*, II, Vol. XX in *Sōgō Nihon-shi taikei* (Tokyo: Naigai shoseki, 1939), pp. 180–84; Tokutomi, *Kokumin-shi*, XXIV, 405–12. Mikami, in general, presents more detailed information, but very often takes over, almost literally, Tatsui's text.

28. Tokutomi, *Kokumin-shi*, XXIV, 405–9.

29. Mikami, *Edo jidai-shi*, II, 473; Tatsui, *Edo jidai-shi*, II, 184; Tokutomi, *Kokumin-shi*, XXIV, 410, 412.

30. In 1767, there had also been the Meiwa Incident, involving Yamagata Daini. Both incidents are certainly related: Takenouchi Shikibu was banished for the second time then, and Takenouchi, Yamagata and Fujii Umon all stayed at the same house in Kyoto (see Mikami, *Edo jidai-shi*, II, 341). The

Hōreki Incident, however, is more relevant for the study of the Title Incident, because it involved the court and the bakufu, while the Meiwa Incident was an internal affair of the bakufu. For this interpretation, see Tokutomi, *Kokuminshi*, XXII, 398.

31. Tokutomi, *Kokumin-shi*, XXII, 130–31, 206, 233; see also Mikami, *Edo jidai-shi*, II, 301–2.

32. The five regency houses were the only ones that could fill the offices of *sesshō* and *kampaku*. The Konoe and Takatsukasa were among them.

33. Mikami, *Edo jidai-shi*, II, 301.

34. Tokutomi, *Kokumin-shi*, XXII, 205, 212, 233.

35. Mikami, *Edo jidai-shi*, II, 302.

36. Matsumoto, *Motoori Norinaga*, p. 126.

37. *Ibid.*, p. 128.

38. On the *Dai Nihon-shi*, see Webb, *The Imperial Institution*, pp. 146–47, 183–87.

39. Matsumoto, *Motoori Norinaga*, pp. 129–34.

40. *Motoori Norinaga-ō shokan-shū*, ed. Okuyama Uhichi (Tokyo: p.u., 1933), p. 634. Quoted and translated by Matsumoto, *Motoori Norinaga*, p. 135: "Today, by invitation, we visited the residence of Honorable Nakayama after noon and left there before dark.... The audience were Honorable Nakayama, his son, Honorable Kazan'in and Honorable Sono, and also some of their attendants. Since Honorable Nakayama is a hero and intellectual of our time, whom the emperor especially trusts, and who is foremost among all the court nobles, I was particularly glad of today's lecture.... I am told to come again to lecture on the fourth (of the fifth month)."

41. *Kanko-dōri*, RKI, I, 7.

42. Maruyama Kunio, "Matsudaira Sadanobu no gaikō seisaku," *Nihongaku kenkyū*, III (1943), 6, 40.

43. Hall, *Tanuma*, pp. 102–5; Shibusawa, *Rakuō-kō den*, p. 272.

44. Maruyama, "Gaikō," p. 46.

45. *Uge*, p. 145; Shibusawa, *Rakuō-kō den*, p. 296.

46. *Ibid.*, pp. 314–16.

47. The maritime defense of the Bōsō peninsula, protecting the eastern shore of Edo bay, was in 1810 entrusted to the Aizu and Shirakawa domains (*ibid.*, p. 355).

48. *Ibid.*, p. 308.

49. Maruyama, "Gaikō," pp. 52–57.

50. Hall, *Tanuma*, p. 86.

51. Maruyama, "Gaikō," p. 58.

Chapter Six: The Politics of Ideology

1. Ishikawa Ken, "Shōhei-zaka Gakumonjo no hattatsu katei to sono yōshiki," *Ochanomizu Joshi Daigaku jimbun kagaku kiyō*, VII (1955), 8.

2. Ōta Akira, "Shūshigaku seigakuka no katei: Kansei-ki shakai shisō kenkyū no ikkiku," *Chiba Daigaku rigakubu kiyō (Bunka kagaku)*, II (1957), No. 2, 57.

3. *Ibid.*, p. 59.

4. Ishikawa, "Shōhei-zaka," p. 25.

5. Wajima Yoshio, "Kansei igaku no kin no kaishaku: Kansei no Sung-gaku-shi no shūshi," *Kobe Jogakuin Daigaku ronshū*, III (1957), No. 3, 51.

6. *Ibid.*, p. 47; Ishikawa, "Shōhei-zaka," p. 23.

7. Matsudaira Sadamitsu, "Matsudaira Sadanobu no kyōgaku," *Nihongaku kenkyū*, III (1943), No. 2, 44–45.

8. Ishikawa Ken, "Rinke-juku narabi Shōhei-kō ga han-ritsu gakkō ni ataeta eikyō," *Ochanomizu Joshi Daigaku jimbun kagaku kiyō*, VIII (1956), 70.

9. *Ibid.*, pp. 63–69.

10. Kasai Sukeharu, *Kinsei hankō ni okeru gakutō-gakuha no kenkyū*, 2 vols. (Tokyo: Yoshikawa Kōbunkan, 1969–70). (Since there is only one pagination which runs through the two volumes, volume numbers will not be mentioned in references to this work.)

11. Matsuura Seizan, *Kasshi yawa*, quoted by Ishikawa, "Shōhei-zaka," p. 8.

12. Watanabe Toshimasa, *Fukko shisō to Kansei igaku no kin*, Vol. XXX of *Kokumin seishin bunka kenkyū* (Tokyo: n.p., 1937), pp. 108–9.

13. Shibusawa, *Rakuō-kō den*, p. 205.

14. Najita Tetsuo, "Political Economism in the Thought of Dazai Shundai (1680–1747)." *Journal of Asian Studies*, XXXI (1972), 825.

15. *Rikkyōkan dōmō kun* (1797), in: *Nihon kyōiku bunko: Kunkai-hen, I*, ed. Kurokawa Masamichi and Odaki Jun (Tokyo: Dōbunkan, 1910), p. 706 (henceforeward abbreviated as NKB); *Sekizen* (1800), I, 3, 5; II, 27 (RKI, II); *Kagetsu sōshi* (1812), NZZ, XIII, 602.

16. *Rikkyōkan* (1797), NKB, *Kunkai-hen*, I, 706; *Rakutei* (1805), RKI, II, 6; *Kagetsutei* (1826), RKI, III, 3.

17. *Taikan* (1797), NZZ, XIV, 342.

18. *Shūshin* (1782), RKI, I, 4; *Rakutei* (1795), RKI, II, 16; *Sekizen* (1800), I, 4 (RKI, II).

19. *Taikan* (1794), NZZ, XIV, 177.

20. *Shūshin* (1782), RKI, I, 4.

21. *Kanjo* (1778), RKI, I, 53–54.

22. *Shūshin* (1782), RKI, I, 4; *Taikan* (1794), NZZ, XIV, 177; *Sekizen* (1800), I, 11 (RKI, II).

23. *Taikan* (1794), NZZ, XIV, 177.

24. *Shūshin* (1782), RKI, 3, 4; *Taikan* (1796), NZZ, XIV, 310.

25. *Taikan* (1796), NZZ, XIV, 177.

26. *Ibid.*, p. 178.

27. *Kagetsu sōshi* (1812), NZZ, XIII, 611.

28. Clifford Geertz, "Ideology as a Cultural System," in: *Ideology and Discontent*, ed. D. E. Apter (New York: Free Press of Glencoe, 1964), p. 75.

29. RKI, I, 2.

30. *Shūshin* (1782), RKI, I, 4.

31. *Ōmu* (1786), SJP, III, 435.

32. *Tōzen* (1787–1793), RKI, I, 1; *Kagetsutei* (1826), RKI, III, 3.

33. *Tōzen* (1787–1793), RKI, I, 1; *Sekizen* (1800), I, 7 (RKI, II).

34. *Tokugawa kinrei kō*, comp. Ishii Ryōsuke (Tokyo: Sōbunsha, 1959), 1st ser., II, 165–66.

35. Watanabe, *Fukko*, pp. 103–4.

36. This document is to be found as an appendix to Takase Daijirō, *Tsukada Taihō* (p.u.: p.u., 1919); quoted in Ōta, "Shūshigaku," pp. 62–63.

37. Yamaga Sokō's banishment from Edo and Kumazawa Banzan's house arrest in the 1760s were the result of Hoshina Masayuki's influence with the bakufu (Masayuki was the lord of Aizu and patron of Ansai), but the reasons for these measures seems to have been mainly political. See Ōta, "Shūshigaku," p. 61.

38. Kasai, *Kinsei hankō*, p. 1014.

39. *Ibid.*, pp. 1014, 1493, 413, 1921–22, 1604, 557, 1215.

40. R. P. Dore, *Education in Tokugawa Japan* (Berkeley: University of California Press, 1965), p. 23; Suzuki Masayoshi "Muro Kyūsō to Shūshigaku," in: *Kinsei Nihon no jugaku*, ed. Fukushima Kashizō (Tokyo: Iwanami, 1939), pp. 436–43.

41. Watanabe, *Fukko*, p. 105.

42. Kasai, *Kinsei hankō*, p. 2054.

43. Kinugasa Yasuki, "Setchū gakuha to kyōgaku tōsei," in: *Nihon rekishi: Kinsei*, IV, Vol. XII of *Iwanami kōza Nihon rekishi* (Tokyo: Iwanami, 1963), p. 230.

44. Watanabe, *Fukko*, p. 106.

45. Fukaya, *Matsudaira Sadanobu-kō*, pp. 250–63.

46. *Ibid.*, p. 59. (All biographical dictionaries have copied from each other the wrong dates for Kurosawa Chikō; Fukaya has the right dates.)

47. Watanabe, *Fukko*, p. 80; Tokutomi, *Kinsei*, XXIV, 115–16.

48. Iwahashi Junsei, *Dai Nihon rinri shisō hattatsu shi*, I (Tokyo: Meguro shoten, 1915), 515–16; Suzuki, "Muro Kyūsō," p. 450.

49. Morohashi Tetsuji, "Kansei igaku no kin," in: *Kinsei Nihon no jugaku*, ed. Fukushima Kashizō (Tokyo, Iwanami shoten, 1939), p. 167; Nakamura Kōya, "Kansei igaku no kin ni tsuite," *Shibun*, XVII (1934), No. 2, 9.

50. Iwahashi, *Dai-Nihon rinri*, p. 530.

51. Sugano Watarō, "Kansei no kaikaku to Nakai Chikuzan," *Keizai-shi kenkyū*, XV (1936), No. 1, 72.

52. Watanabe, *Fukko*, p. 106.

53. Iwahashi, *Dai-Nihon rinri*, p. 500.

54. *Kansei igaku-kin kanrei bunsho*, in: *Nihon jurin sōsho*, III, ed. Seki Giichirō (Tokyo: Tokyo Toshokan kōkai, 1928), p. 14.

55. Watanabe, *Fukko*, p. 81.

56. *Ibid.*

57. Kasai, *Kinsei hankō*, p. 302.

58. Watanabe, *Fukko*, p. 101.

59. "When neither a society's most general cultural orientations nor its most down-to-earth, 'pragmatic' ones suffice any longer to provide an adequate image of the political process, ideologies begin to become crucial as sources of sociopolitical meanings and attitudes." Geertz, "Ideology," pp. 63–64.

60. Compiled from Kasai, *Kinsei hankō*, pp. 89–1958.
61. Matsudaira Sadamitsu, "Matsudaira kyōgaku," p. 46.
62. Tokutomi, *Kinsei*, XXIV, 110.
63. *Ibid.*
64. Matsudaira Sadamitsu, "Matsudaira kyōgaku," p. 43.
65. Wajima, "Kansei igaku," p. 51.
66. *Tokugawa kinrei kō*, 2d ser., I, 95.
67. Tokutomi, *Kinsei*, XXIV, 210, 212–13.
68. Watanabe, *Fukko*, p. 89.
69. NKT, XXIX, 319–59.
70. Watanabe, *Fukko*, pp. 90, 91.
71. *Kansei bunsho*, pp. 2–3.
72. *Ibid.*, p. 13.
73. *Ibid.*, pp. 5, 8.
74. Watanabe, *Fukko*, p. 108.
75. Nagakura Tamotsu, "Kansei kaikaku o meguru kyōgaku tōsei no mondai: Aizu-han no 'Igaku no kin' e no taiō kara," *Rekishi hyōron*, No. 50 (1953), pp. 3–4; see also Ishikawa, *Kinsei kyōiku*, p. 107.
76. Nagakura, "Kansei kaikaku," p. 6.
77. *Kansei bunsho*, p. 27; see also Morohashi, "Kansei igaku no kin," pp. 166, 175.
78. Morohashi, "Kansei igaku no kin," p. 166.
79. "Kagetsu nikki" (manuscript), referred to by Matsudaira Sadamitsu, "Matsudaira kyōgaku," p. 45. This diary covers the 1812–28 period and is presently at the library of Tenri University, Tenri (Nara Prefecture).
80. Watanabe, *Fukko*, p. 105.
81. Kasai, *Kinsei hankō*, p. 2054.
82. Ishikawa, "Shōhei-zaka," pp. 42–43; Watanabe, *Fukko*, p. 52.
83. Ishikawa, "Shōhei-zaka," p. 43.
84. Ishikawa Ken, *Nihon gakkō-shi no kenkyū* (Tokyo: Shogakukan, 1960), pp. 202–5.
85. *Ibid.*, pp. 206–10.
86. Robert Spaulding, *Imperial Japan's Higher Civil Service Examinations* (Princeton: Princeton University Press, 1967), Ch. I, pp. 9–19.
87. Ishikawa, "Shōhei-zaka," pp. 38–40.
88. *Ibid.*, p. 27.
89. *Ibid.*, p. 40.
90. Kasai, *Kinsei hankō*, p. 83.
91. *Ibid.*, p. 2054; Fukaya, *Matsudaira Sadanobu-kō*, pp. 123–24.
92. Moriyama Takamori, *Ama no takumo*, quoted by Watanabe, *Fukko*, p. 119. For a partial translation of this passage, see Dore, *Education*, pp. 201–2.
93. Among all scholars that have written about the ban on heterodoxy, only Kinugaki Yasuki reports that in 1795 the ban was expanded to all domains (Kinugaki, "Setchūgakuha," p. 225). He gives no reference for this information, and an investigation of the *Tokugawa jikki* and compilations of decrees and laws of the period did not reveal the existence of any such

measure. A correspondence with Kasai Sukeharu yielded no information either. It does not seem likely that the ban was expanded to all domains.

94. For details, see Kasai, *Kinsei hankō*, under the appropriate domains.
95. *Ibid.*, p. 2094.
96. See *ibid.* under the appropriate domains.

Chapter Seven: Retirement and Retrospect

1. Shibusawa, *Rakuō-kō den*, pp. 327–31.
2. *Ibid.*, pp. 324–25.
3. *Uge*, p. 125.
4. *Kagetsu sōshi*, quoted in Shibusawa, *Rakuō-kō den*, p. 409.
5. Out of all his memoirs and notes, Sadanobu had designated his autobiographical *Uge no hito koto* together with some other documents for those of his descendants who might hold the office of senior councillor. Since none was ever appointed, the sealed box containing these manuscripts was preserved intact until 1894, when the seal broke of itself. Sadanobu had three sons and nine daughters by two wives after his first two wives had died childless. The direct line of his descendants was plagued with premature deaths. Sadanaga, his eldest son, died at forty-seven in 1838; his grandson, Sadakazu, ruled for only three years until he was twenty-nine, to be succeeded by his own son, Michi, who died at twenty-five in 1859. Another of Sadanobu's sons, Yukitsura (1791–1852) succeeded in the Sanada house to the Matsushiro domain (100.000 koku) in 1815. Sadanobu's numerous daughters were married off to various daimyo families. Among the most prestigious of these are Katō from Ōsu (60.000 koku), Makino from Nagaoka (74.000 koku), Matsudaira (Hisamatsu) from Matsuyama (150.000 koku), Ii from Hikone (350.000 koku), Suwa from Takashima (80.000 koku), and Matsuura from Hirado (61.000 koku). (For a complete genealogy, see Shibusawa, *Rakuō-kō den*, Appendix.)
6. *Go-gyōjō*, p. 70.
7. The Kansei Reform is the least studied of all three Tokugawa reforms, and Sadanobu has been neglected almost to the point of oblivion. So much so that present-day publishers in Japan, looking for writers for a postscript to a reprinted edition of Sadanobu's memoirs, and for a new biography that has been scheduled for over ten years, have to rely on scholars who did some minor research on Matsudaira Sadanobu during the war years. Yamaguchi Keiji, who wrote his graduation paper on Matsudaira Sadanobu for the University of Tokyo, is author of the postscript, dated 1969, to the *Uge no hito koto;* and Kodama Kōta is scheduled for a new biography, to appear in the series *Jimbutsu sōsho*, edited by the *Nihon rekishi gakkai* and published by Yoshikawa kōbunkan. He is the author of "Matsudaira Sadanobu to sono jidai," *Nihon-gaku kenkyū*, III (1943), No. 8, 34–66.
8. This, of course, raises all the more sharply the question of how the descendants of these committed bureaucrats, two generations later, dismantled that same political structure. Obviously, they had to rely on a different ideology.
9. The theory of charisma discussed here owes much to the following three

articles: Edward Shils, "Centre and Periphery," in *The Logic of Personal Knowledge: Essays Presented to Michael Polanyi* (London: Routledge & Kegan Paul, 1961), pp. 117–30; *idem*, "Charisma, Order, and Status," *American Sociological Review*, XXX (1965), 199–213; Robert C. Tucker, "The Theory of Charismatic Leadership," *Daedalus*, Journal of the American Academy of Arts and Sciences, XCVII, No. 3 (Summer 1968: "Philosophers and Kings: Studies in Leadership"), 731–56. See also S. N. Eisenstadt, "Charisma and Institution Building: Max Weber and Modern Sociology," Introduction to *Max Weber: On Charisma*, pp. ix–lvi. Exactly 100 years after Matsudaira Sadanobu, China produced a charismatic politician, K'ang Yu-wei, much akin in vision and behavior to Sadanobu. See Richard C. Howard, "K'ang Yu-wei (1858–1927): His Intellectual Background and Early Thought," in *Confucian Personalities*, ed. Arthur F. Wright and Denis Twitchett (Stanford: Stanford University Press, 1962), pp. 294–316.

   10. Shils, "Charisma," pp. 202–3; *idem*, "Centre," p. 124.

Appendix A
   1. There exist four histories of the Shirakawa domain: Shōji Kichinosuke, "Shirakawa-han," in *Tōhoku, kita Kanto no shohan*, Vol. I of *Dai niki monogatari han-shi*, ed. Kodama Kōta and Kitajima Masamoto (Tokyo: Jimbutsu ōraisha, 1966), pp. 281–331; *Fukushima-ken shi* (Fukushima-ken: n.p.) III (1970), 398–512; *Shirakawa-shi shi* (Shirakawa: n.p.), II (1971); Tamura Eitarō, "Shirakawa-han seisō to nōmin ikki," in *idem, Ikki, kumo-suke, bakuto* (Tokyo: Obatake shoten, 1933), pp. 251–401 (first partially published in *Teikoku nōkai-hō*, XXI [1931], 4, 6, 7, 9; XXII [1932], 4). Shōji's brief history is not exhaustive and not trustworthy in its detail, although based on the same material as the following two works. The second history was published as part of the third volume of the twenty-six-volume history of Fukushima prefecture; volumes VIII and X of the same series contain collections of primary sources: VIII (1965), 518–737; X, part 1 (1967), 931–82. Tamura's work is not a complete history but a study of han politics and peasant uprisings under the Yūki (Matsudaira) rule (1692–1741). Some additional primary sources can be found in: *Shirakawa-shi shishiryōshū* (6 vols. Shirakawa: Kofūdō, 1963–66).
   2. This resulted in extra burdens for the wayside villages where corvée labor was requisitioned to move official parties and their equipage. See a petition of 1747 to alleviate this burden, in *Fukushima-ken shi*, VIII, 697–98. Moreover, when in 1701–8 the domain tried to enforce circulation of paper currency, the effort failed, mainly because the domain had no jurisdiction over the thousands of travelers passing every year through the town (*Shirakawa-shi shi*, II, 71).
   3. This happened, for instance, when Sadanobu's son, Sadanaga, left Shirakawa for Kuwana in 1823. The Abe family who succeeded the Matsudaira family in Shirakawa built a new domain school on the same spot where Sadanobu had built his. These transfers had another unfortunate result, namely the loss or destruction of documents: in contrast to outside domains, who have preserved their records very well, vassal domains stand out today for the poor state of their records.

4. For Honda Tadayoshi (lord in Shirakawa, 1642–62), his appointment to Shirakawa was the third transfer in the span of ten years: from Harima (40,000 koku) to Tōtōmikakagawa (70,000 koku) in 1639; to Murakami (100,000 koku) in 1644; to Shirakawa (120,000 koku) in 1649 (See *Fukushima-ken shi*, III, 415). Okudaira Matsudaira Tadahiro (1681–92) had also been transferred twice before coming to Shirakawa. (See: Kodama Kōta and Kitajima Masamoto, ed., *Dai niki*, I, 14, 115, 452.) Yūki Matsudaira Naonori's (1692–95) enfeoffment in Shirakawa was his sixth transfer (*ibid.*, pp. 116–17; Tamura, "Shirakawa-han," pp. 251–53).

When, in August 1681, Honda Tadahira was ordered to exchange domains with the lord of Utsunomiya, he made the peasants of Shirakawa shoulder the expenses of the transfer. Taxes were normally levied in the eleventh month, but Tadahira ordered the pre-levy of taxes, the cutting of even the green rice, and the requisitioning of one man and one horse per 100 koku (*Fukushima-ken shi*, VIII, 708).

Similar measures were taken by Yūki Matsudaira Yoshinori to cover the expenses of his transfer to Himeji in 1741. Only half of the retainer's stipends were paid, with the promise that the second half would be paid from Himeji. The servants of the domain, already provided and paid by the peasants under normal circumstances, had to accompany the lord to Himeji and then return to Shirakawa, but each village had to provide three bu per servant to cover the return costs. In addition, one man and one horse were requisitioned (*ibid.*, III, 440).

5. Bolitho, *Treasures among Men*, pp. 8, 34; Kodama Kōta, "Daimyo no tempō," in *Tōhoku, kita Kanto no shohan*, ed. *idem*, pp. 14, 18.

6. Shōji, in his "Shirakawa-han," p. 289, has the wrong numbers.

7. Shōji is again mistaken on pp. 285–86 of his "Shirakawa-han."

8. Tauchi Chikasuke, a contemporary biographer of Sadanobu, reports 111,016 for around 1795 (*Go-gyōjō*, p. 144). For a further breakdown of the population one has to rely on earlier documents, when the total population was around 90,000. In 1660, the population consisted of: 82,500 peasants, 2,000 footsoldiers, guild members, and servants in the countryside, and 7,500 inhabitants of the castle town: 700 footsoldiers, guild members and servants, and 6,800 members of the warrior class. *Shirakawa-shi shishiryōshū*, I, 5, 10. According to a payroll from Sadanobu's time, there were 1,503 retainers ("Matsudaira Etchū no kami kanai").

9. Calculated from *Fukushima-ken shi*, III, 420; VIII, 553, 709.

10. *Fukushima-ken shi*, VIII, 524.

11. In 1705, an extraordinary levy was prescribed by the bakufu in order to help finance the dredging of Edo's Honchō river; in 1710, contributions were asked for the building of a reception hall (*fukiage goden*) in the Chiyoda castle, and there were further occasions in 1714, 1715 and 1736. See Tamura, "Shirakawa-han seisō," pp. 262–64, 273 ff.

Glossary

bakufu. The government or administrative structure of the Tokugawa house, headed by the shogun, whose lands covered about one-fourth of Japan.

bakuhan. The administrative system of the whole of Japan during the Tokugawa period, consisting of the *bakufu* (baku-) ruled by the shogun, and the domains (han) of the daimyo.

bakumatsu. Refers to the end of the Tokugawa period, roughly 1853–68.

bu. Gold coin, equals one-fourth of a *ryō*; also weight measure for silver, equals ten *momme*.

daikan. Deputy or intendant in charge of a district of shogunal or daimial land.

daimyo. Ruler of a feudal domain (*han*); there were four categories of daimyo: *shimpan, kamon, fudai, tozama*.

daimyōjin. Divine title, meaning "Great August Deity."

fudai. Vassal daimyo, comprising all daimyo whose ancestors were vassals of Ieyasu, the founder of the Tokugawa house, before the decisive battle of Sekigahara in 1600.

goyōtachi. Government purveyors, created by Matsudaira Sadanobu.

gundai. District deputy; the same as *daikan*.

han. Feudal domains ruled by the daimyo; the 280 *han* covered about three-fourths of Japan, while the bakufu was in control of the remaining one-fourth.

hatamoto. One category of liege vassals of the shogun, called bannermen; they held offices in the bakufu and ruled portions of shogunal land.

jinsei. Benevolent government, usually the regime of a model ruler who has the welfare of his subjects at heart.

kammon. One thousand pieces of one-*mon* copper coins.

kamon. Daimyo related to the shogun (*shimpan*) other than the six collaterals (*sanke, sankyō*).

kampaku. Advisor to an adult emperor.

koku. A measure of capacity (5.1 bushels), used to assess the rice yield of a domain; *koku* assessment of a daimyo was thus an indication of his wealth and status within the Tokugawa system.

momme. Standard unit of weight to measure silver; ten *momme* of silver equal one silver *bu*.

myōjin. Divine title, meaning "August Deity."

ryō. The unit of gold coin, its subdivisions being the *bu* and the *shu* (6 *shu* equal 1 *bu*; 4 *bu* equal 1 *ryō*).

sanke. "The Three Houses"; name for the three senior collateral houses of the Tokugawa, created in the seventeenth century: Mito, Owari, Kii.

sankyō. "The Three Lords"; name for the three junior collateral houses of the Tokugawa, created in the eighteenth century: Tayasu, Hitotsubashi, Shimizu.

shimpan. Collective name for all daimyo related to the Tokugawa: *sanke, sankyō, kamon.*

shu. Gold coin; see *ryō.*

taigi meibun. Confucian ethical imperative requiring that rank, status, and title correspond with the proper office and duty.

tozama. Outside daimyo, refering to the descendants from the daimyo who accepted Ieyasu's suzerainty only after the Sekigahara battle of 1600.

yonaoshi. "Correction of the world"; name of popular reformist movements with an egalitarian philosophy; they arose toward the end of the eighteenth century and were very prevalent toward the end of the Tokugawa period and during the early Meiji period.

Bibliography

English Language Works

Anesaki Masaharu. *History of Japanese Religion: With Special Reference to the Social and Moral Life of the Nation*. Rutland, Vt.: Charles E. Tuttle Co., 1963.

Backus, Robert Lee. "Matsudaira Sadanobu as Litterateur and Moralist." Unpublished Ph.D. dissertation, University of California, Berkeley, 1963.

Bolitho, Harold. *Treasures among Men: The Fudai Daimyo in Tokugawa Japan*. New Haven: Yale University Press, 1974.

Dore, Ronald P. *Education in Tokugawa Japan*. Berkeley: University of California Press, 1965.

Earl, David Magarey. *Emperor and Nation in Japan: Political Thinkers of the Tokugawa Period*. Seattle: University of Washington Press, 1964.

Erikson, Erik H. *Identity: Youth and Crisis*. New York: W. W. Norton & Co., 1968.

_____. *Young Man Luther: A Study in Psychoanalysis and History*. New York: W. W. Norton & Co., 1958.

Geertz, Clifford. "Religion as a Cultural System." In *Anthropological Approaches to the Study of Religion*, edited by Michael Banton. A. S. A. Monographs. London: Tavistock publications, 1966.

_____. "Ideology as a Cultural System." In *Ideology and Discontent*, edited by D. E. Apter. New York: Free Press of Glencoe, 1964.

Hall, John Whitney. *Tanuma Okitsugu, 1719–1788: Forerunner of Modern Japan*. Harvard-Yenching Institute Monograph Series. Cambridge: Harvard University Press, 1955.

Howard, C. Richard. "K'ang Yu-wei (1858–1927): His Intellectual Background and Early Thought." In *Confucian Personalities*, edited by Arthur F. Wright and Denis Twitchett, pp. 294–316. Stanford: Stanford University Press, 1962.

Katō Genchi. "Shinto Worship of Living Human Gods in the Religious History of Japan." *Asiatic Review* 26 (1930): 575–80.

Lifton, Robert Jay. *Revolutionary Immortality: Mao Tse-Tung and the Chinese Cultural Revolution*. New York: Random House, Vintage Books, 1968.

Matsumoto Shigeru. *Motoori Norinaga: 1730–1801*. Harvard East Asian Series. Cambridge: Harvard University Press, 1970.

Murdoch, James. *A History of Japan*. 3 vols. New York: Greenberg: 1926.

Najita Tetsuo. "Political Economism in the Thought of Dazai Shundai (1680–1747)." *Journal of Asian Studies* XXXI (1972), 821–39.

Nihongi: Chronicles of Japan from the Earliest Times to A.D. *697.* Translated by William George Aston. London: Allen & Unwin, 1956.

Sansom, George. *A History of Japan.* 3 vols. Stanford: Stanford University Press, 1958–63.

Shils, Edward. "Charisma, Order, and Status," *American Sociological Review* XXX (1965), 199–213. Reprinted in *Center and Periphery. Selected Papers of Edward Shils II.* Chicago: University of Chicago Press, 1974.

_____. "Centre and Periphery." In *The Logic of Personal Knowledge: Essays presented to Michael Polanyi,* pp. 117–30. London, Routledge & Kegan Paul, 1961. Reprinted in *Center and Periphery. Selected Papers of Edward Shils II.* Chicago: University of Chicago Press, 1974.

Smith, Thomas C. *The Agrarian Origins of Modern Japan.* Stanford: Stanford University Press, 1959.

Spaulding, Robert. *Imperial Japan's Higher Civil Service Examinations.* Princeton: Princeton University Press, 1967.

Totman, Conrad. *Politics in the Tokugawa Bakufu: 1600–1843.* Harvard East Asian Series. Cambridge: Harvard University Press, 1967.

Tucker, Robert C. "The Theory of Charismatic Leadership," *Daedalus* XCVII, 3 (summer 1968: "Philosophers and Kings: Studies in Leadership."), pp. 731–56.

Webb, Herschel. *The Japanese Imperial Institution in the Tokugawa Period.* Studies of the East Asian Institute, Columbia University. New York: Columbia University Press, 1968.

Weber, Max. *Max Weber: On Charisma and Institution Building,* edited by S. N. Eisenstadt. The Heritage of Sociology. Chicago: University of Chicago Press, 1968.

Yazaki Takeo. *Social Change and the City in Japan: From Earliest Times Through the Industrial Revolution.* Japan: Japan Publications Inc., 1968.

Works by Matsudaira Sadanobu
Referred to in the Text and Notes

*Bukkaron*物 価 論(Treatise on commodity prices). In Vol. I of RKI.

Daigaku keibun kōgi 大 学 経 文 講 說 (Lectures on the classic "The Great Learning"). In vol. III of RKI.

*Dokushokō karoku*読 書 功 課 錄(List of achieved readings). In vol. I of RKI.

Genshishu 言志集 (Anthology of poems). In vol. I of RKI.

"Gōri 合離 (On the bringing together and separation of ether)." Manuscript. 1828/9/20. Nara: Tenri University.

"Hai no zō 肺の臓 (On the lung as visceral center)." Manuscript. 1828/9/21. Private collection of Matsudaira Sadayasu 松平定康 in Kamakura, or Chinkoku-Shukoku Shrine in Kuwana, Mie prefecture.

Heibō tai-i kudenshō 兵法大意口伝抄 (Summary of the oral tradition concerning the great meaning of martial arts). In "Matsudaira Sadanobu to Shimbu no michi," by Itasawa Takeo, pp. 11–16.

Jikyōkan 自教鑑 (Mirror of self-instruction). In Vol. I of RKI.

Jisho ryakuden 自書略伝 (Curriculum vitae). In Fukaya, *Matsudaira Sadanobu-kō*, p. 265.

"Kagetsu nikki 花月日記 (Blossoms and moonlight diary)." Manuscript. 1812–28. Nara: Tenri University.

Kagetsu sōshi 花月草紙 (Blossoms and moonlight notes). In Vol. XIII of NZZ, 563–671.

Kagetsutei hikki 花月亭筆記 (Random notes from the pavilion of blossoms and moonlight). In Vol. III of RKI.

Kanjo ronsetsu 漢書論説 (A dissertation on the "Han History"). In Vol. I of RKI.

Kanko-dōri 諫鼓鳥 (Birds on the admonitory drum). In Vol. I of RKI.

Kasumi no tomo 霞の友 (Companion of the mist). In Vol. I of RKI.

"Katachi no oshie かたちの教 (On the teaching of postures)." Manuscript. 1828/9/20. Nara: Tenri University.

"Kisetsu 気説 (On the meaning of the ether)." Manuscript. 1828/9/20. Nara: Tenri University.

Kokuhonron 国本論 (On the basis of the country). In Vol. XIII of NKT, 325–77.

"Koshi-itsu 古史逸 (Anecdotal ancient history)." Manuscript. Nara: Tenri University.

Kyūgenroku 求言録 (A record of the search for opinions). In Vol. III of RKI.

"Matsudaira Etchū no kami Sadanobu ason, go-kerai e go-kyōjisho 松平越中守定信朝臣御家来江御教示書 (Book of instructions by Matsudaira Sadanobu, Governor of Etchū, of the rank of Ason, to his retainers)." Manuscript. 1783/12. Tokyo: Tokyo Daigaku shiryō hensanjo.

"Matsudaira Rakuō-kō on-kakikudashi shorui 松平楽翁公御書下書類 (Writings of Matsudaira, Lord Rakuō)." Manuscript. Tokyo: Tokyo Daigaku shiryō hensanjo.

*Migiri no yanagi*細 の 柳(Willows by the eaves-stones). In Vol. I of RKI.

*Monogatari*物 語(Tale). In "Matsudaira Sadanobu to Shimbu no michi," by Itasawa Takeo, pp. 6–9.

*Naniwa-e*難 波 江(The Naniwa estuary). In Vol. I of RKI.

*Ōmu no kotoba*鸚 鵡 の 詞(Parroted words). In Vol. III of *Sanjippuku* 三 十 輻. Compiled by Ōta Nampo太 田 南 畝Tokyo: Kokusho kankōkai, 1917, pp. 433–38.

*Rakutei hikki*楽 亭 筆 記(Random notes from the pavilion of leisure). In Vol. II of RKI.

*Rikkyōkan dōmō kun*立 教 館 童 蒙 訓(Precepts for the young pupils of the Rikkyōkan). In NKB, *Kunkai-hen*訓 誡 篇, I, 706–12.

RKI *Rakuō-kō isho*楽 翁 公 遺 書(Literary legacy of Lord Rakuō). Edited by Ema Seihatsu 江 間 政 發 . 3 vols. Tokyo: Hachio shoten, 1893.

*Rō no oshie*老 の 教(Teachings of an old gentleman). In Vol. III of RKI.

*Seigo*政 語(Discourse on government). In Vol. XIII of NKT, 395–424.

*Sekizen shū*責 善 集(Collected themes for mutual encouragement toward good). 3 parts. In Vol. II of RKI.

*Shiji seiyō*資 治 清 要(Vade mecum for government). In Vol. XIII of NKT, 381–92.

"Shirakawa-kō mitsugo白 河 侯 密 語(Secret words of the Lord of Shirakawa)." Manuscript. 1789/3. Tokyo: Tokyo Daigaku shiryō hensanjo.

*Shoyū hen*庶 有 編(Section on possession by the masses). In Vol. XIII of NKT, 427–37.

*Shugyō roku*修 行 録(Record of self-training). In *Uge no hito koto; Shugyō roku*宇 下 人 言 ; 修 行 録. Iwanami bunko, Tokyo: Iwanami shoten, 1942. pp. 179–206.

*Shūko jisshu*集 古 十 種(Ten categories of collected antiquities). 4 vols. Compiled by Matsudaira Sadanobu. Tokyo: Kokusho kankōkai, 1908.

*Shunnōō*春 濃 鶯(Dark nightingale of spring). In Vol. III of *Kinsei chihō keizai shiryō*近 世 地 方 経 済 史 料. Edited by Ono Takeo 小 野 武 夫. Tokyo: Yoshikawa kōbunkon. 1958. pp. 315–22.

*Shūshin roku*修 身 録(A record for the cultivation of the person). In Vol. I of RKI.

"Tai kuden体 口 伝(An oral tradition about the body)." Manuscript. 1828/11/12. Nara: Tenri University.

*Taikan zakki*退 閑 雑 記(Random notes of my retirement). In Vol. XIV of NZZ, 159–438.

*Tōen-in no miya no tatekata sono hoka no sadamegaki*東 圓 悦 宮 建 方 其 外 定 書 (Provisions concerning the erection of a shrine in the Tōen cloister and other matters). In Fukaya, *Matsudaira Sadanobu-kō*, pp. 268–71.

*Tokuhitsu yokyō*禿 筆 餘 興 (Amusement with a frayed brush). In Vol. I of RKI.

*Tōzen manpitsu*燈 前 漫 筆 (Stray notes by lamplight). In Vol. I of RKI.

*Uge no hito koto*宇 下 人 言 (Words of a man under the eaves). In *Uge no hito koto; Shugyōroku*宇 下 人 言 ; 修 行 錄. Iwanami bunkō. Tokyo: Iwanami shoten, 1942. pp. 3–178.

"Yōkun hōshi kokoroe幼 君 奉 仕 心 得(Directives for service of the young shogun)." Manuscript. 1788/10. Nara: Tenri University; Mie prefecture: Kuwana Chinkoku-Shukoku shrine.

*Zokugaku mondō*俗 楽 問 答(A discussion of profane music). In Vol. II of RKI.

Documents and Secondary Works in Japanese

Abe Makoto阿 部 真 琴and Sakai Hajime酒 井 一. "Hōkensei no dōyō 封 建 制 の 動 揺 (Unrest in the feudal system)," *Nihon rekishi: Kinsei*日 本 歴 史 ： 近 世 (Japanese history: Early modern period), IV. Vol. XII of IKNR, 1–52.

Abe Yoshio 阿 部 吉 雄. "Yamazaki Ansai to sono kyōiku山 崎 闇 斎 と 其 の 教 育 (Yamazaki Ansai and his education)," *Kinsei Nihon no jugaku*, pp. 335–56.

"Aizu-ke seikeki会 津 家 世 家 紀 (Family records of the ruling houses of Aizu)." Quoted in Nagakura Tamotsu, "Aizu-han ni okeru hansei kaikaku," p. 88.

Aoki Kōji 青 木 虹 二. *Hyakushō ikki no nenjiteki kenkyū* 百 姓 一 揆 の 年 次 的 研 究(Chronological study of peasant uprisings). Tokyo: Shinseisha, 1966.

Arai Hakuseki新 井 白 石. *Hankampu*藩 翰 譜(*Han* genealogies). 5 vols. 2d ed. Tokyo: Jimbutsu ōraisha, 1967–68.

Arakawa Hidetoshi荒 川 秀 俊. *Kikin no rekishi*饑 饉 の 歴 史(A history of famines). Nihon rekishi shinsho日 本 歴 史 新 書(New publications on Japanese history). Tokyo: Shibundō, 1967.

Asano Genko浅 野 源 吾. *Matsudaira Sadanobu, Ninomiya Sontoku-hen*松 平 定 信 二 宮 尊 徳 扁(Matsudaira Sadanobu, Ninomiya Sontoku). Suppl. vol. to *Tōhoku sangyō keizai-shi*東 北 産 業 経 済 史 (History of the industry and economy of the Tōhoku region). Tokyo: Tōhoku Shinkōkai, 1943.

Chihō-shi kenkyū kyōgikai地 方 史 研 究 協 議 会(Council for the study of local history), ed. *Kinsei chihō-shi kenkyū nyūmon*

近世地方史研究入門 (Introduction to the study of local history in the early modern period). Tokyo: Iwanami shoten, 1955.

Dai Nihon jinmei jisho 大日本人名辞書 (Biographical dictionary of Japan). 3 vols. Tokyo: Dai Nihon jinmei jisho kankōkai, 1926.

Doki Zenmaro 土岐善麿. *Tayasu Munetake* 田安宗武. 4 vols. Tokyo: Nihon hyōronsha, 1946.

Dokushi biyō 読史備要 (Historical vade mecum). Compiled by Tokyo Daigaku shiryō hensanjo 東京大学史料編纂所 (Tokyo University office for compilation of historical materials). Tokyo: Kōdansha, 1966.

Dokushi sōran 読史総覧 (Comprehensive historical directory). Tokyo: Jimbutsu ōraisha, 1966.

Fukaya Kentarō 深谷賢太郎. *Matsudaira Sadanobu-kō to keishin sonnō no kyōiku* 松平定信公と敬神尊皇の教育 (Matsudaira Sadanobu and education in respect for the gods and reverence for the emperor). Tokyo: Hokkai shuppansha, 1941.

Fukushima-ken shi 福島県史 (History of Fukushima prefecture). Fukushima-ken n.p. Vol. III: *Kinsei* 近世 (Early modern period) 2 (1970). Vol. VIII: *Kinsei shiryō* 近世資料 (Documents on the early modern period) 1 (1965). Vol. X, part 1: *Kinsei shiryō* 近世資料 3 (1967).

Furushima Toshio 古島敏雄. "Bakufu zaisei shūnyū no dōkō to nōmin shūdatsu no kakki 幕府財政収入の動向と農民収奪の画期 (Trends in the financial revenue of the bakufu and periods of squeeze of the peasants)," *Kinsei* 近世 (Early modern period). II. Edited by *idem*. Vol. IV of *Nihon keizai-shi taikei* 日本経済史大系 (Outline of Japanese economic history) 6 vols. Tokyo: Tokyo Daigaku shuppankai, 1965.

―――. "Shōhin ryūtsū no hatten to ryōshu keizai 商品流通の発展と領主経済 (The growth of commercial activity and the economy of the domainial lords)," *Nihon rekishi: Kinsei* 日本歴史：近世 (Japanese history: Early modern period), IV. Vol. XII of IKNR, 53–101.

Hayashi Motoi 林基. "Hōreki-Tenmei-ki no shakai jōsei 宝暦天明期の社会情勢 (Social conditions during the Hōreki and Tenmei eras)," *Nihon rekishi: Kinsei* 日本歴史：近世 (Japanese history: Early modern period), IV. Vol. XII of IKNR, 103–54.

―――. *Kyōhō to Kansei* 享保と寛政 (The Kyōhō and Kansei eras). Vol. XVI of *Kokumin no rekishi* 国民の歴史 (A people's history). Tokyo: Buneido, 1971.

Hirose Mōsai 広瀬蒙斎. *Uringen-kō den* 羽林源公伝 (Biography of the Lord Minamoto of the Plumed Forest). In Vol. V of *Nihon bunkō* 日本文庫 (The Japan Library). Tokyo: Hakubunkan, 1891, pp. 1–60.

Honjō Eijiro本庄栄治郎 *Kinsei Nihon no san dai kaikaku* 近世日本 の三大改革 (The three great reforms of early modern Japan). Tokyo: Tatsumisha, 1944.

———. "Rankuō-kō no jinkō zōshoku seisaku楽翁公の人口増殖 政策(Lord Rakuō's policy of population growth)," *Keizai ronsō* 経済論叢(Collection of economic treatises), VII (1918), 5, 131–36.

*Hou Han shu*後漢書(History of the Later Han Dynasty). Taipei: I wên, n.d.

IKNR *Iwanami kōza Nihon rekishi*岩波講座日本歴史(Iwanami lectureship Japanese history). 23 vols. Tokyo: Iwanami shoten, 1963.

Imamura Yoshio, ed.今村嘉雄. *Nihon budō zenshū*日本武道全集 (Complete works of the Japanese martial arts). 7 vols. Tokyo: Jimbutsu ōraisha, 1966–

Inamura Hiromoto稲村坦元. "Matsudaira Rakuō-kō no kōsei ni oyoboseru kanka-eiyō松平楽翁公の後世に及ぼせる感化 影響(Matsudaira, Lord Rakuō's posthumous influence)," *Nihon-gaku kenkyū*日本学研究(Studies in Japonology), III (1943), 2, 49–54.

———. "Rakuō-kō chojutsu hensansho kaisetsu楽翁公著述編纂 書解説(Interpretation of compilations of Lord Rakuō's works)," *Rakuō-kō yoei*楽翁公餘影(Lord Rakuō's posthumous influence). Edited by *idem*. Tokyo: p.u., 1929, pp. 33–60.

Inobe Shigeo井野辺茂雄. "Matsudaira Sadanobu no sokumenkan 松平定信の側面観(A new view on Matsudaira Sadanobu)," *Risshō Daigaku ronsō (Rekichi)*立正大学論叢歴地 (Collected treatises of Risshō University: History and Geography), III (1946), 5–15.

———. "Rakuō-kō to gaikoku kankei 楽翁公と外国関係 (Lord Rakuō and relations with other countries)," *Rekishi kyōiku*歴史教 育(History education), X (1935), 10, 1–12.

———. "Matsudaira Sadanobu no hosa shūnin 松平定信の輔 佐就任(Matsudaira Sadanobu's appointment as regent to the shogun)," *Bakumatsu-shi no kenkyū mokuji*幕末史の研究目次 (Topical studies in the history of the end of the Tokugawa period), by *idem*. Tokyo: Yūzankaku, 1927, pp. 1–17.

Inoue Tomoichi井上友一. *Rakuō to Sutain*楽翁と須多因(Rakuō and Karl vom Stein, 1757–1831). Tokyo: Ryōsho, 1908.

Ishii Ryōsuke石井良助, comp. *Tokugawa kinrei kō* 徳川禁令考 (Study of Tokugawa edicts) 11 vols. Tokyo: Sōbunsha, 1959–61.

Ishikawa Ken石川謙. *Kinsei Kyōiku ni okeru kindaikateki keikō: Aizu-han kyōiku o rei to shite* 近世教育に於ける近代化的

傾向　会津藩教育を例とし て(Modernizing trends in education of the early modern period, as exemplified by the education in the Aizu domain). Tokyo: Kōdansha, 1966.

————. *Nihon gakkō-shi no kenkyū* 日本学校史の研究 (A study of the history of schools in Japan). Tokyo: Shogakukan, 1960.

————. "Rinke-juku narabi Shōhei-kō ga hanritsu gakkō ni ataeta eikyō 林家塾ならびに昌平黌が藩立学校に与えた影響 (The influence of the Hayashi School and the Bakufu College upon domain schools)," *Ochanomizu Joshi Daigaku jimbun kagaku kiyō* お茶の水女子大学人文科学紀要, VIII (1956), 41–82.

————. "Shōheizaka Gakumonjo no hattatsu katei to sono yōshiki 昌平坂学問所の発達過程とその様式 (Form and development of the Bakufu College)" *Ochanomizu Joshi Daigaku jimbun kagaku kiyō* お茶の水女子大学人文科学紀要, VII (1955), 1–46.

Itasawa Takeo 板沢武雄. "Matsudaira Sadanobu to shimbu no michi 松平定信と神武の道 (Matsudaira Sadanobu and the Way of Psychic and Martial Power)," *Nihon-gaku kenkyū* 日本学研究 (Studies in Japonology), III, 2 (February, 1943), 2–18.

Itō Yoshiichi 伊藤好一. "Tanuma seiji makki no keizai-ron: 'Kyūji-saku' to 'Getaya Jimbei kakiage' ni tsuite 田沼政治末期の経済論「救時策」と下駄屋甚平衛書上」について (Essay about economic theories toward the end of the Tanuma regime: The "Plan to rescue society" and "Getaya Jimbei's memorial"), *Katei* 過程 (Process), VIII (December, 1960), 1–15.

————. "'Uezaki Kyūhachirō jōsho' ni tsuite 植崎九八郎上書」について (About 'Uezaki Kyūhachirō's memorial)," *Katei* 過程 (Process), X (March, 1962), 1–9.

————. "Kansei kaikaku tōji ni okeru Osaka shōnin no dōkō: 'Shoyū hen' o megutte 寛政改革当時における大阪商人の動向「庶有編」をめぐって (Study of trends among the Osaka merchants at the time of the Kansei Reform, as reflected in "Section on possession by the masses")," *Katei* 過程 (Process), VII (December 1958), 1–9.

Iwahashi Junsei 岩橋遵成. *Dai Nihon rinri shisō hattatsu-shi* 大日本倫理思想発達史 (History of the development of ethical thought in Japan). 2 vols. Tokyo: Meguro shoten, 1915.

Iwase-gun shi 岩瀬郡史 (History of Iwase district). Fukushima prefecture: Iwase-gun yakusho, 1922.

Iwase Kyōsan 岩瀬京山. *Kumo no ito maki* 蜘蛛の糸巻 (The spider's thread). In vol. XVI of NZZ, pp. 441–501.

Kanazawa Harutomo 金沢春友. "Shirakawa chihō no hōkōnin seido

白 川 地 方 の 奉 公 入 制 度 (The day laborer system of the Shirakawa region);" *Shakai keizai shigaku*社 会 経 済 史 学(Social and
economic history), III (1934), 10.

*Kansei igaku-kin kankei bunsho*寛 政 異 学 禁 関 係 文 書(Documents concerning the ban on heterodoxy of the Kansei era). In
*Nihon jurin sōsho*日 本 儒 林 叢 書(Series on Japanese Confucianism). Edited by Seki Giichirō 関 儀 一 郎 . 6 vols. Tokyo: Tokyo
Toshokan kōkai, 1928.

*Kansei jūshū shokafu*寛 政 重 修 諸 家 譜(Genealogies of all major
ruling houses of the Kansei era). 9 vols. Tokyo: Eishinsha, 1917–18.

"Kansei kaikaku寛 政 改 革(The Kansei Reform)." *Kantō kinsei-shi
kenkyūkai kaihō* 関 東 近 世 研 究 会 会 報 (Reports of the study
group for the study of the early modern history of the Kanto era).
Tokyo: Meiji Daigaku daigakuin, 2 (September 1964), 1–20.
(Mimeographed.)

Kasai Sukeharu 笠 井 助 治 . "Kansei igaku no kin to hangaku
寛 政 異 学 の 禁 と 藩 学 (The Kansei ban on heterodoxy and
learning in the domains)." (Mimeographed.)

———. *Kinsei hankō ni okeru gakutō-gakuha no kenkyū*近 世 藩 校
に 於 け る 学 統 学 派 の 研 究 (A study of schools of thought
and scholarly affiliations in the domain schools of the early modern
period). 2 vols. Tokyo: Yoshikawa kōbunkan, 1969–70.

Katō Genchi加 藤 玄 智. *Hompō seishi no kenkyū: seishi no shijitsu to
sono shinri bunseki*本 邦 生 祠 の 研 究 生 祠 の 史 実 と 其 心 理
分 析 (A study in living gods in Japan: A historical and psychological analysis of living gods). Tokyo: Meiji seitoku kinen
gakkai hakkō, 1932.

———. "Kami no jikaku ni jūshite mizukara seishi o mōketa Matsudaira Rakuō-kō 神 の 自 覚 に 住 し て 自 ら 生 祠 と 設 け た 松
平 楽 翁 公 (On Matsudaira, Lord Rakuō, who through his own
divine learning made himself into a living god)," *Meiji seitoku kinen
gakkai kiyo*明 治 聖 徳 記 念 学 会 紀 要(Minutes of the learned
Meiji memorial society), XXXIII (1930), 1–10.

Kikuchi Kenjirō菊 池 謙 二 郎. "Matsudaira Sadanobu nyūkaku jijō
松 平 定 信 入 閣 事 情 (The circumstances of Matsudaira
Sadanobu's entrance into the Senior Council)," *Shigaku zasshi*
史 学 雑 誌(Journal of history), XXVI (1915), 1, 1–22.

Kinsei Nihon no jugaku 近 世 日 本 の 儒 学(Confucianism of early
modern Japan). Edited by Fukushima Kashizō 福 島 甲 子 三. Tokyo:
Iwanami, 1939.

Kinugasa Yasuki衣 笠 安 喜. "Setchū gakuha to kyōgaku tōsei 折 衷
学 派 と 教 学 統 制(The eclectic schools and the control of learning)," *Nihon rekishi: Kinsei*日 本 歴 史 : 近 世 (Japanese history:

the early modern period), IV. Vol. XII of IKNR, 199–232.

Kitahara Susumu北原進. "Kansei 'kien-ryō' ni tsuite寛政棄捐令
について(About the Kansei cancelation of debts)," *Rekishi
hyōron*歴史評論 (Historical review), 162 (February 1964), 66–76;
163 (March 1964), 66–77.

_____. "Fudasashi kabunakama no seiritsu札差株仲間の成立
(The establishment of the licensed guild of money brokers),"
*Rekishi kyōiku*歴史教育 (History education), IX (1961), 10,
46–52.

Kitajima Masamoto北島正元. *Bakuhansei no kumon*幕藩制の苦
悶(Agony of the *bakuhan* system). Vol. XVIII of *Nihon no rekishi*
日本の歴史(Japanese history). 31 vols. Tokyo: Chūōkōron-sha,
1966.

Kodama Kōta児玉幸多. "Daimyo no tempō大名の転封(Daimyo
transfers)." *Dainiki monogatari han-shi*第二期物語藩史(Short
historical accounts of the domains. Second series). Edited by *idem*
and Kitajima Masamoto北島正元. Vol. I: *Tōhoku, Kita-Kanto
no shohan*東北北関東の諸藩 (The domains of Tōhoku and the
northern Kanto region). Tokyo: Jimbutsu ōraisha, 1966, pp. 13–18.

_____. "Matsudaira Sadanobu to sono jidai松平定信とその時代
(Matsudaira Sadanobu and his time)," *Nihon-gaku kenkyū*日本学
研究(Studies in Japonology), III (1943), 8, 34–66.

Kondō Masatsugu近藤正治. "Seidō to Shōheizaka gakumonjo
聖堂と昌平坂学問所(The Seidō and the Bakufu College),"
Kinsei Nihon no jugaku, pp. 199–217.

Maeda Kōji前田恒治. *Aizu-han ni okeru Yamazaki Ansai*会津藩
に於ける山崎闇斎(Yamazaki Ansai in Aizu han). Tokyo:
Nishizawa shoten hakko, 1935.

Maruyama Kunio丸山国雄. "Matsudaira Sadanobu no gaikō sei-
saku松平定信の外交政策(Matsudaira Sadanobu's foreign
policy)," *Nihon-gaku kenkyū*日本学研究(Studies in Japonology),
III (1943), 6, 37–63.

"Matsudaira Etchū no kami kanai松平越中守家内(Retainers of
Matsudaira, Governor of Etchū). Manuscript. Shirakawa: collection of Kobayashi Kakuzaeimon小林寛左衛門.

Matsudaira Sadamitsu松平定允. "Matsudaira Sadanobu no kyō-
gaku松平定信の教学(Matsudaira Sadanobu's teachings),"
*Nihon-gaku kenkyū*日本学研究(Studies in Japonology), III
(1943), 8, 19–48.

_____. "Matsudaira Sadanobu o chūshin to suru shokō no kyōyō:
Sōrishū o chūshin to shite 松平定信を中心とする諸侯の
教養双鯉集を中心として(The education of daimyo around
Matsudaira Sadanobu, based on his "Collection of letters")," *Kinsei*

Nihon no jugaku, pp. 141–56.

Matsudaira Sadatsuna 松 平 定 綱. *Bokumin kōhan* 牧 民 候 判(Additional considerations on how to govern the people). In Vol. III of *Kinsei chihō keizai shiryō* 近 世 地 方 経 済 史 料(Documents on local economic history of the early modern period). Edited by Ono Takeo 小 野 武 夫. Tokyo: Yoshikawa kōbunkan, 1958, 439–77.

Matsuura Seizan 松 浦 静 山. *Kasshi yawa* 甲 子 夜 話(Kasshi evening talks). Quoted by Ishikawa, "Shōhei-zaka," p. 8.

Matsuyoshi Sadao 松 好 貞 夫. *Daimyo yarikuri-chō: kanemochi daimyo, binbō daimyo* 大 名 や り く り 帖 - 金 持 大 名 貧 乏 大 名 (Management booklet of the daimyo: Rich daimyo, poor daimyo). Tokyo: Shin-jimbutsu ōraisha, 1970.

Mikami Sanji 三 上 参 次. *Edojidai-shi* 江 戸 時 代 史(History of the Edo period). 2 vols. Tokyo: Fuzambō, 1944.

―――. *Shirakawa Rakuō-kō to Tokugawa jidai* 白 河 楽 翁 公 と 徳 川 時 代 (Lord Rakuō of Shirakawa and the Tokugawa period). Tokyo: Sōgensha, 1940.

―――. "Mohan seijika to shite no Matsudaira Sadanobu 模 範 政 治 家 と し て の 松 平 定 信(Matsudaira Sadanobu as a model politician)," *Shigaku zasshi* 史 学 雑 誌(Historical journal), XVII (1906), 11, 1085–1125.

Mitamura Engyo 三 田 村 鳶 魚. *Buke jiten* 武 家 事 典(Encyclopedia of the warrior class). Tokyo: Aokaeru bōkan, 1958.

Mori Sugio 森 杉 夫. "Kansei kaikaku-ki no osameyado haishi 寛 政 改 革 期 の 納 宿 廃 止 (The abolition of the rice collectors during the Kansei Reform)," *Rekishi kenkyū* 歴 史 研 究(Historical studies) (Osaka-furitsu Daigaku), XI (1969).

Moriyama Takamori 森 山 孝 盛. *Ama no takumo* 蜑 の 焼 藻. Quoted in Watanabe, *Fukko,* p. 119.

Morohashi Tetsuji 諸 橋 轍 次. "Kansei igaku no kin 寛 政 異 学 の 禁 (The Kansei ban on heterodoxy)," *Kinsei Nihon no jugaku,* pp. 157–78.

Motoori Norinaga-ō shokan shū 本 居 宣 長 翁 書 簡 集(Collected letters of Motoori Norinaga). Edited by Okuyama Uhichi 奥 山 宇 七. Tokyo: p.u., 1933.

Nagakura Tamotsu 長 倉 保. "Aizu-han ni okeru hansei kaikaku 会 津 藩 に 於 け る 藩 政 改 革 (The administrative reform of Aizu han)," *Hansei kaikaku no kenkyū.* 藩 政 改 革 の 研 究. (Studies in the reforms of han administrations). Edited by Horie Hideichi 堀 江 英 一. Tokyo: Ochanomizu shobō, 1955, pp. 61–117.

―――. "Kansei kaikaku o meguru kyōgaku tōsei no mondai: Aizu-han no 'Igaku no Kin' e no taiō kara 寛 政 改 革 を め ぐ る 教 学 統 制 の 問 題 : 会 津 藩 の 「 異 学 の 禁 」 へ の 対 応 か ら

(Problems concerning the control of learning around the Kansei Reform: How Aizu han coped with the ban on heterodoxy)," *Rekishi hyōron* 歴 史 評 論 (Historical review), 50 (1953), 1–8.

Nagamine Mitsuyoshi 永 峰 光 壽 . "Chōhō kaikaku to shichibu-kin shimatsu 町 法 改 革 と 七 分 金 始 末 (Study of the reform of township laws and the savings fund)," *Rakuō-kō yoei* 楽 翁 公 餘 影 (Lord Rakuō's posthumous influence). Edited by Inamura Hiromoto 稲 村 坦 元 . Tokyo: n.p., 1929, pp. 18–32.

Nakamura Kōya 中 村 芳 也 . "Kansei igaku no kin ni tsuite 寛 政 異 学 の 禁 に 就 て (About the Kansei ban on heterodoxy)," *Shibun,* 斯 文 XVII (1934), 2, 1–19.

Nihonshi jiten 日 本 史 辞 典 (Encyclopedia of Japanese history). Edited by Kyoto Daigaku Bungakubu Kokushi Kenkyūshitsu 京 都 大 学 文 学 部 国 史 研 究 室 (Research Institute of Japanese History. Department of Arts and Letters, Kyoto University). Revised and enlarged edition. Tokyo: Sōgensha, 1960.

Nihon shoki 日 本 書 紀 (History of Japan). Vols. 1–2 of *Kokushi taikei* 国 史 大 系 (Outline of Japanese history). Edited by Kuroita Katsumi 黒 板 勝 美 . 63 vols. 2d ed. Tokyo: Yoshikawa Kōbunkan, 1966–67.

Nishida Taichirō 西 田 太 一 郎 , ed. *Fujiwara Seika, Nakae Tōju, Kumazawa Banzan, Yamazaki Anzai, Yamaga Sokō, Yamagata Daini shū* 藤 原 惺 窩 中 江 藤 樹 熊 沢 蕃 山 山 崎 闇 斎 山 鹿 素 行 山 県 大 弍 集 . Vol. XVII of *Nihon no shisō* 日 本 の 思 想 (Japanese thought). Tokyo: Chikuma shobō, 1970.

NKB *Nihon kyōiku bunko* 日 本 教 育 文 庫 (Library of Japanese education). Edited by Kurokawa Masamichi 黒 川 真 道 and Odaki Jun 小 瀧 淳 . 13 vols. Tokyo: Dōbunkan, 1910–11.

NKT *Nihon keizai taiten* 日 本 経 済 大 典 (Encyclopedia of Japanese economy). Edited by Takimoto Seiichi 滝 本 誠 一 . 54 vols. 2d ed. Tokyo: Meiji bunken, 1967.

NZZ *Nihon zuihitsu zenshū* 日 本 随 筆 全 集 (Complete collection of Japanese essays). 20 vols. Tokyo: Kokumin tosho kabushiki kaisha, 1927–30.

Okamoto Jishō 岡 本 益 裝 . "Kantoku roku 感 徳 録 (In praise of _virtue)." Manuscript. 1840. Tokyo: Naikaku bunko.

Ōmori Shirō 大 森 志 郎 . "Matsudaira Rakuō-kō no jinkō seisaku 松 平 楽 翁 公 の 人 口 政 策 (The population policy of Matsudaira, Lord Rakuō)," *Tōhoku bunka kenkyū* 東 北 文 化 研 究 (Study of the culture of Tōhoku), I (1929), 5, 81–90.

Ono Shinji 小 野 信 二 . "Bakufu to tennō 幕 府 と 天 皇 (The bakufu and the emperor)," *Nihon rekishi: Kinsei* 日 本 歴 史 近 世 (Japanese history: The early modern period), II. Vol. X of IKNR, 313–56.

Ono Toshito小 野 寿 人. "Kansei igaku no kin to Soraigakuha寛 政異 学 の 禁 と 徂 徠 学 派(The Sorai School and the Kansei ban on heterodoxy)," *Nihon shogakuhakō iinkai kenkyū hōkoku*日 本 諸 学 派 興 委 員 会 研 究 報 告 (Research reports of the committee on Japanese schools of thought), IV (*Rekishigaku*歴 史 学 History) (1939), 251–57.

Ōta Akira 多 田 顕. "Shūshigaku seigakuka no katei: Kansei-ki shakai shisō kenkyū no ikkiku 朱 子 学 正 学 化 の 過 程:寛 政 期 社 会 思 想 研 究 の 一 掬 (The process by which Neo-Confucianism became an orthodoxy: A tentative study of social thought of the Kansei era)," *Chiba Daigaku rigakubu kiyō (Bunka Kagaku)*, 千 葉 大 学 理 学 部 紀 要 文 化 科 学 (Reports of the Science Department of Chiba University: Cultural Sciences), II (1957), 2, 57–67.

Ōtsuka Kōi大 塚 彦 感. *Kyūji-saku*救 時 策(Plan for rescuing society). In Vol. XXIII of NKT, 105–46.

*Rintoku-ki*隣 徳 記(Record of Rintoku). Quoted in Hayashi, *Kyōhō*.

*Ryūei bunin*柳 営 補 任(Official directory of bakufu offices and office holders). Dai Nihon kinsei shiryō大 日 本 近 世 資 料(Historical early modern Japanese documents). 7 vols. Tokyo: Tokyo Daigaku shiryō hensanjo, 1963–69.

Satō Kenji佐 藤 堅 司. *Shimbu no michi*神 武 の 道(The way of psychic and martial power). Tokyo: Kodansha, 1942.

Satō Tahei佐 藤 太 平. *Rakuō Matsudaira Sadanobu*楽 翁 松 平 定 信. Tokyo: Miyakoshi taiyōdō shobō, 1942.

Seki Giichirō関 儀 一 郎and Seki Yoshinao関 義 直. *Kinsei kangakusha chojutsu mokuroku taisei* 近 世 漢 学 者 著 述 目 録 大 成 (Complete list of early modern scholars of Chinese learning and their works). Tokyo: Tōyōtosho kankōkai, 1936.

Shibusawa Eiichi渋 沢 栄 一. *Rakuō-kō den*楽 翁 公 伝(Biography of Lord Rakuō). Tokyo: Iwanami shoten, 1937.

*Shirakawa-shi shi*白 河 市 史(History of the town of Shirakawa). Vol. II. Shirakawa: n.p., 1971.

*Shirakawa-shi shishiryōshū*白 河 市 史 資 料 集(Collected historical materials on the town of Shirakawa). 6 vols. Shirakawa: Kofūdō, 1963–66.

Shōji Kichinosuke庄 司 吉 之 助. "Shirakawa-han白 河 藩." *Dai niki monogatari han-shi*第 二 期 物 語 藩 史 (Short historical accounts of domains, second series). Edited by Kodama Kōta児 玉 幸 多and Kitajima Masamoto北 島 正 元. Vol. I: *Tōhoku, Kita-Kanto no shohan*東 北 , 北 関 東 の 諸 藩(The domains of Tōhoku and the northern Kanto region). Tokyo: Jimbutsu ōrai-sha, 1966, pp. 281–331.

"Sōrishū 双 鯉 集 (Collection of letters)." Manuscript. Nara: Tenri University.

Sugano Watarō 菅 野 和 太 郎. "Kansei no kaikaku to Nakai Chikuzan 寛 政 の 改 革 と 中 井 竹 山 (The Kansei Reform and Nakai Chikuzan)," *Keizai-shi kenkyū* 経 済 史 研 究 (Studies in economic history), XV (1936), 1, 71–84.

Sugita Gempaku 杉 田 玄 白. *Nochimigusa* 後 見 草 (Afterthoughts). In Vol. XVII of *Kaitei shisekishūran* 改 定 史 籍 集 覧 (Revised collection of historical works). Compiled by Kondō Heijō 近 藤 瓶 城. 42 vols. Tokyo: Kondō shuppanbu, 1912–29, pp. 658–721.

Suzuki Masayoshi 鈴 木 直 治. "Muro Kyūsō to shūshigaku 室 鳩 巣 と 朱 子 学 (Muro Kyūsō and Neo-Confucianism)," *Kinsei Nihon no jugaku*, pp. 427–52.

Tahara Tsuguo 田 原 嗣 郎. "Kansei kaikaku no ikkōsatsu-igaku no kin to kanryōseika no mondai kara 寛 政 改 革 の 一 考 察 : 異 学 の 禁 と 官 僚 制 化 の 問 題 か ら (A study of the Kansei Reform: the problem of the ban on heterodoxy and bureaucratization)," *Rekishi-gaku kenkyū* 歴 史 学 研 究 (Historical studies), 178 (1954), 9–21.

Takase Daijirō 高 瀬 代 次 郎. *Tsukada Taihō* 塚 田 大 峰. p.u.: p.u., 1919.

Takashiro Senji 高 城 仙 次. "Shirakawa Rakuō-kō no 'Bukkaron' o hyōsu 白 河 楽 翁 公 の 物 價 論 を 評 す (An evaluation of the Shirakawa Rakuō Lord's "Treatise on commodity prices")," *Mita gakkai zasshi* 三 田 学 会 雑 誌 (Journal of the Mita Learned Society), VI (1912), 2, 79–107.

Takayanagi Shinzō 高 柳 真 三 and Ishii Ryōsuke 石 井 良 助, ed. *Ofuregaki Tenmei-shūsei* 御 触 書 天 明 集 成 (Collection of decrees of the Tenmei period). Tokyo: Iwanami shoten, 1936.

Takeuchi Makoto 竹 内 誠. "Matsudaira Sadanobu 松 平 定 信." *Bakkaku-hen* 幕 閣 篇 (The senior and junior council), II. Vol. VII of *Daimyo retsuden* 大 名 列 伝 (Daimyo biographies). Edited by Kodama Kōta 児 玉 幸 多 and Kimura So 木 村 礎. Tokyo: Jimbutsu ōraisha, 1967. pp. 241–302.

_____. "Kansei kaikaku to kometaka goyōtachi no seiritsu 寛 政 改 革 と 米 方 御 用 達 の 成 立 (The Kansei Reform and the establishment of the rice purveyors)," *Rekishi kyōiku* 歴 史 教 育 (History education), IX (1961), 10, 53–59.

_____. "Kansei kaikaku to kanjōsho goyōtachi no seiritsu 寛 政 改 革 と 勘 定 所 御 用 達 の 成 立 (The Kansei Reform and the establishment of the financial purveyors)," *Nihon rekishi* 日 本 歴 史 (Japanese history), 128 (February 1959), 23–32; 129 (March 1959), 49–56.

Tamaoka Mitsuo 玉 岡 三 男. "Kansei no kien ni tsuite 寛 政 の 棄 捐

に 就 て(On the cancelation of debts of the Kansei era)," *Shigaku kenkyū*史 学 研 究(Historical studies), V (1933), 2, 235–48.

"Tamarizume on-rei ōseagerare sōrō setsu溜 詰 御 礼 被 仰 上 ト 節 (Note on the ordered gifts in relation to the Antechamber seat)." Manuscript. Sukagawa, Fukushima prefecture: Ichihara Tadashiichi 市 原 正 一.

Tamura Eitarō田 村 栄 太 郎 . *Yonaoshi*世 直 し (Rectification of the world). Tokyo: Yūzankaku, 1960.

————. "Shirakawa-han seisō to nōmin ikki白 河 藩 政 争 と 農 民 一 揆(Political struggle in Shirakawa han and peasant uprisings)," *idem, Ikki, kumosuke, bakuto* 一 揆 、 雲 助 , 博 徒 (Uprisings, coolies, gambling). Tokyo: Obatake shoten, 1933, pp. 251–401.

Tanaka Kōjiro田 中 幸 二 郎 . "Songo mondai ni okeru Matsudaira Sadanobu no fushin 尊 号 問 題 に 於 け る 松 平 定 信 の 不 臣 (Matsudaira Sadanobu's disloyalty in relation to the Title Incident)," *Chūō shidan* 中 央 史 談 (Central history review), XIII (1927), 9, 104–06.

*Tanuma shudono gashiradono e ōse-wataserare sho*田 沼 主 殿 頭 殿 ～ 被 仰 渡 書(Memorial to Lord Tanuma). *Rekkō shimpiroku* 列 侯 深 秘 録 (Secret records of the daimyo). Edited by Hayakawa Junsaburō早 川 処 三 郎. Tokyo: Kokusho kankōkai, 1914, pp. 522–27.

Tatsui Matsunosuke龍 居 松 之 助. *Edo jidai-shi*江 戸 時 代 史 (History of the Edo period). Vols. XX–XXI in *Sōgō Nihon-shi taikei* 綜 合 日 本 史 大 系 (Comprehensive outline of Japanese history). 26 vols. Tokyo: Naigai shoseki, 1939–40.

Tauchi Chikasuke田 内 親 輔 . *Go-gyōjō kiryō*御 行 状 記 料 (Materials and records of illustrious deeds). In Vol. XVII of *Nihon ijin genkō shiryō*日 本 偉 人 言 行 資 料 (Materials on words and deeds of exceptional Japanese). Tokyo: Kokushi kenkyūkai, 1916. pp. 65–198.

"Tenmei kōsetsu 天 明 巷 説 (Rumors of the Tenmei era)." Manuscript. 1786. Tokyo: Keio University.

*Tenmei shichi hinoto hitsuji nen Edo kikin sōdō no koto*天 明 七 丁 未 年 江 戸 飢 饉 騒 動 之 事(The disturbance of the famine in Edo in the seventh year of Tenmei). In Vol. XVII of *Katei shiseki shūran* 改 定 史 籍 集 覧 (Revised edition of a collection of historical works). Compiled by Kondō Heijō 近 藤 瓶 城 . 42 vols. Tokyo: Kondō shuppanbu, 1912–19, pp. 644–49.

Tokugawa jikki 徳 川 実 紀 (Official records of the Tokugawa house). Vols. 38–47 of *Kokushi taikei* 国 史 大 系 (Outline of Japanese history). Edited by Kuroita Katsumi 黒 板 勝 美 . 63 vols.

2d ed. Tokyo: Yoshikawa kōbunkan, 1966–67.

Tokutomi Iichirō 徳 富 猪 一 郎 . *Matsudaira Sadanobu jidai* 松 平 定 信 時 代 (The era of Matsudaira Sadanobu). Vol. XXIV of *Kinsei Nihon kokumin-shi* 近 世 日 本 国 民 史 (History of the Japanese people in the early modern period). 100 vols. Tokyo: Jiji tsūshinsha, 1964.

Tsuda Hideo 津 田 秀 夫. *Hōkenshakai kaitaikatei kenkyūjosetsu* 封 建 社 会 解 体 過 程 研 究 序 説 (Introduction to the study of the disintegrative process of feudal society). Tokyo: Kōshobō, 1970.

_____. "Kansei kaikaku 寛 政 改 革 (The Kansei Reform)," *Nihon rekishi: kinsei* 日 本 歴 史 近 世 (Japanese history: The early modern period), IV. Vol. XII of IKNR, 233–82.

Tsuda Sōkichi 津 田 左 右 吉. *Nihon no Shinto* 日 本 の 神 道 (Japanese Shinto). Vol. IX of *Tsuda Sōkichi zenshū* 津 田 左 右 吉 全 集 (Complete works of Tsuda Sōkichi). Tokyo: Iwanami shoten, 1964.

Tsuji Zennosuke 辻 善 之 助 . *Tanuma jidai* 田 沼 時 代 (The Tanuma era). Tokyo: Nihon gakujutsu fuyūkai, 1936.

Uezaki Kyūhachirō 植 崎 九 八 郎 . *Sensaku zasshū* 穿 鑿 雑 収 (August plan). In Vol. XX of NKT, 505–39.

Umehara Takeru 梅 原 猛. *Bi to shūkyō no hakken: sōzōteki Nihon bunkaron* 美 と 宗 教 の 発 見 : 創 造 的 日 本 文 化 論 (The discovery of the beautiful and of religion: An original theory of Japanese culture). Tokyo: Chikuma shobō, 1967.

Wajima Yoshio 和 島 芳 男. "Kansei igaku no kin no kaishaku: Kinsei no Sung gaku-shi no shūmatsu 寛 政 異 学 の 禁 の 解 釈 : 近 世 宋 学 史 の 終 末 (An interpretation of the Kansei ban on heterodoxy: the end of the history of Sung learning during the Kansei era)," *Kobe Jogakuin Daigaku ronshū* 神 戸 女 学 院 大 学 論 集 (Collection of essays of the Jogakuin University of Kobe), III (1957), 3, 43–63.

Watanabe Seyū 渡 辺 世 祐 . *Daimyo-hen* 大 名 篇 (Daimyo). Vol. III of *Denki dainihonshi* 伝 記 大 日 本 史 (Biographical history of Japan). Tokyo: Yūzankaku, 1934.

Watanabe Toshimasa 渡 辺 年 応 . *Fukko shisō to Kansei igaku no kin* 復 古 思 想 と 寛 政 異 学 の 禁 (Restoration thought and the Kansei ban on heterodoxy). Vol. XXX of *Kokumin seishin bunka kenkyū* 国 民 精 神 文 化 研 究 (Study of the spiritual culture of the people). Tokyo: n.p., 1937.

Yamada Tadao 山 田 忠 雄. "Tanuma Okitsugu no seiken dokusen o megutte 田 沼 意 次 の 政 権 独 占 を め ぐ っ て (On the monopolization of political power by Tanuma Okitsugu)," *Shigaku* 史 学

(History), XLIV, 3 (April 1972), 91–114).

_____. "Tanuma Okitsugu no shikkyaku to Tenmei matsunen no seiji jōkyō田沼意次の失脚と天明末年の政治状況(The fall of Tanuma Okitsugu and the political situation at the last year of the Tenmei era)," *Shigaku*史学(History), XLIII (1970), 1–2, 241–57.

_____. "Tenmei no Edo uchikowashi天明の江戸うちこわし (The destructive riot in Edo during the Tenmei period)," *Shigaku* 史学(History), XXXVI (1963), 2–3, 243–58.

Yamaguchi Keiji山口啓二. "Shiryō shūshū fukumeisho: Shiga-ken 史料蒐集復命書：滋賀県(Report on the collection of historical materials: Shiga prefecture)." Vol. II. Tokyo: Tokyo Daigaku Shiryō hensanjo, November, 1967. (Mimeographed.)

"Yōikukin kankei bunsho養育金関係文書(Documents concerning education allowances)," in "Sukagawa-shi shihenshū shiryō: XII. Sukagawa-machi daikan Naitō-ke bunsho須賀川市史編集 資料第12集須賀川町代官内藤家文書 (Materials for the compilation of the history of the town of Sukagawa: XII. Documents of the Naitō family of deputies of the town of Sukagawa)." Compiled by Sukagawa-shi shihenshū iinkai須賀川市史 編集委員会 (Committee for the compilation of the history of the town of Sukagawa). Fukushima prefecture: Sukagawa-shi, 1970. (Mimeographed.)

*Zoku Tokugawa jikki*続徳川実紀(Official records of the Tokugawa house. Continued.). Vols. 48–52 of *Kokushi taikei*国史大系 (Outline of Japanese history). Edited by Kuroita Katsumi黒板勝美. 63 vols. 2d ed. Tokyo: Yoshikawa kōbunkan, 1966–67.

Character List

This is a list of special terms and proper nouns referred to in the text and in the notes; it includes also titles of works mentioned in the text.

Abe Masatomo 阿部正倫
Abukuma gawa 阿武隈川
Aizu 会津
Akaezo fūsetsu kō
　赤蝦夷風説考
Akai Tadaakira 赤井忠晶
Akamatsu Sōshū 赤松滄州
Akita 秋田
Akō 赤穂
Amagasaki 尼崎
Andō Nobunari 安藤信明
Aoyama Yoshisada 青山幸道
Arai Hakuseki 新井白石
Arima Shigesumi 有馬誉純
Asakawa 浅川
Asakusa 浅草
Asama 浅間
ashi 葦
bakufu 幕府
bakuhan 幕藩
bakumatsu 幕末
betsudawara 別俵
Bitchū 備中
Bitō Nishū 尾藤二州
Bōjō Toshiyasu 坊城俊逸
Bokumin kōhan 牧民後判
Bōsō 房総
bu 分
Bubisai 武備祭
bugyō 奉行
buke densō 武家伝奏
Buke shohatto 武家諸法度
Bukkaron 物価論
bumbu 文武

Ch'en Fan 陳蕃
Ch'en Yüan-pin 陳元贇
chiki 地気
chikoku-anmin 治国安民
chinkoku 鎮国
Chiyoda 千代田
chū 忠
Chu Hsi 朱子
chū-kō 忠孝
chū-shin 忠信
Confucius 孔子
daigaku no kami 大学頭
Daigakuengi 大学衍義
Daigaku keibun kōgi
　大学軽文講義
Daijō-e 大嘗会
daikan 代官
daimyo 大名
daimyōjin 大明神
Dai Nihon-shi 大日本史
Dajō-tennō 太上天皇
Date 伊達
Dazai Shundai 太宰春台
Dentsū-in 伝通院
Dewa 出羽
Doki Hannokyoku 土岐半之丞
Echigo 越後
Edo 江戸
eedjanaika ええじゃないか
Ezo 蝦夷
fudai 譜代
fudasashi 札差
fudasashi kabunakama
　札差株仲間

209

Fujii Umon 藤井右門
Fujiwara Seika 藤原惺窩
fukiage goden 吹上御殿
fukin 夫金
Fukui 福井
Fukuoka 福岡
Fukushima 福島
Furuya Tsunetaka 古屋昔陽
fusen 筆銭
Fushimi 伏見
fushinkata 筆請方
fuyōigi 不容易義
gakumon gimmi 學問吟味
gakumonjo 學問所
gannoma 雁之間
Genshishū 言志集
Getaya Jimbei 下駄屋甚兵衛
gi 義
gisō 議奏
gō 合
Go-Hanazono 後花園
Go-Horikawa 後堀河
Go-kaisei yakusho 御改正役所
go-kenin 御家人
gōkō 郷校
Go-Mizunoo 後水尾
gosekke 五摂家
Gotō Nuinosuke 後藤縫殿助
Gotō Shibayama 後藤芝山
goyōtachi 御用達
gundai 郡代
Hagi 萩
Haguro Yōsen 羽黒養潜
Hakurokudō-shōin keiji
　　白鹿洞書院掲示
hamaoka dono 浜岡殿
han 藩
harigami nedan 張紙値段
Harima 播磨
hatamoto 旗本
Hatchōbori 八丁堀
Hatsugano Nobutomo
　　初鹿野信興

Hatta 八田
Hattori Nankaku 服部南郭
Hayakawa Mozaeimon
　　早川茂佐衛門
Hayashi 林
Hayashi Baisai 林塔斎
Hayashi Fukusai 林復斎
Hayashi Gahō 林鵞峯
Hayashi Gakusai 林学斎
Hayashi Hōkō 林鳳岡
Hayashi Hōkoku 林鳳谷
Hayashi Hōtan 林鳳潭
Hayashi Jussai 林述斎
Hayashi Kansai 林侗斎
Hayashi Kimpō 林錦峯
Hayashi Razan 林羅山
Hayashi Ryūkō 林榴岡
Hayashi Shihei 林子平
Heian 平安
Higashi honganji 東本願寺
Hikone 彦根
Himeji 姫路
hino-e uma 丙午
Hirado 平戸
Hirobashi Katsutane 広橋勝胤
Hirobashi Koremitsu 広橋伊光
Hiroshima 広島
Hisamatsu 久松
Hisamatsu Sadakatsu 久松定勝
Hisamatsu Sadatsuna 久松定綱
Hitachi 日立
Hitotsubashi 一橋
Hitotsubashi Harusada
　　一橋治済
Hitotsubashi Munemasa
　　一橋宗尹
Hitotsubashi Narimasa
　　一橋斉匡
Hizen 肥前
Hokkaido 北海道
Hokujō Genyō 北条立善
Honchō 本町
Honda Tadahira 本多忠平

Honda Tadakazu 本多忠籌
Honda Tadayoshi 本多忠義
Honda Tadayoshi 本多忠可
honden 本田
Hongō Yasuyuki 本郷泰行
Honmaru 本丸
Hōreki 宝暦
Horidaira Saeimon 堀平左衛門
Hoshina Masayuki 保科正之
Hosoi Heishū 細井平州
Hosokawa Shigekata 細川重賢
Hotta Masaari 堀田正順
Hotta Masaatsu 堀田正敦
Hotta Masamori 堀田正盛
Hotta Masayoshi 堀田正毅
Hou Han shu 後漢書
hyō 俵
Hyōgo 兵庫
Ibaragi 茨城
Ichigaya 市ヶ谷
Ichijō Terunaga 一條輝良
Ichikawa Kakumei 市川鶴鳴
igaku no kin 異学禁
Ii Naoaki 井伊直亮
Ii Naoakira 井伊直朗
Ii Naohide 井伊直幸
Ii Naosuke 井伊直弼
Iioka Yoshinari 飯岡義斉
Ikeda Osae 池田長恵
Imaji 今治
Ina Hanzaeimon Tadakata
　伊奈半左衛門忠尊
Inaba 因幡
Inaba Masaakira 稲葉正明
Inagaki Sadagazu 稲垣定計
Isezaki 伊勢崎
Ishikawa 石川
Ishikawa Tadatomi 石川忠房
Itō 伊藤
Itō Jinsai 伊藤仁斎
Itō Randen 伊藤藍田
Iwaki 磐城
Iwamura 岩村

Iwase 岩瀬
Iwatsuki 岩槻
Iyo 伊予
Izumi 泉
jikatatori 地方取
Jikyōkan 自敬鑑
jin 仁
jinsei 仁政
jisei 時勢
jitsugi 実義
Jōdo shinshū 浄土真宗
Jōkyū 承久
jōruri 浄瑠璃
jūdō 柔道
jūhachi daitsū 十八大通
jūjutsu 柔術
katchi metsuke 徒目付
Kada no Arimaro 荷田在満
Kada no Azumamaro 荷田春満
Kagetsutei hikki 花月亭筆記
Kagoshima 鹿児島
Kaikoku heidan 海国兵談
Kainan 海南
kaisho 会所
kakemai 欠米
Kamakura 鎌倉
Kameda Hōsai 亀田鵬斎
Kamei Nanmei 亀井南冥
Kameoka 亀岡
Kameyama 亀山
Kaminoyama 上山
kammon 貫文
Kamo no Mabuchi 賀茂真淵
kamon 家門
kampaku 関白
kan 疋
Kangiten 歓喜天
K'ang Yu-wei 康有為
Kan'in no miya 閑院宮
kanjōgashira 勘定頭
kanjōkata 勘定方
Kanjo ronsetsu 漢書論説
kanjōsho goyōtachi

勘定所御用達
Kanko-dōri 諫鼓鳥
Kanō Hisachika 加納久周
Kansai 関西
Kansei 寛政
Kanto 関東
karō 家老
Kashiwasaki 柏崎
Kasumi no tomo 霞の友
Katayama Hokkai 片山北海
Katō 加藤
kaya 茅
kei 敬
Keian 薩南
Keichō 慶長
keigi naigai 敬義内外
ki 起
Kitō 起倒
kien-ryō 棄捐令
Kii 紀伊
Kimon 崎門
Kinkaishū 金槐集
Kinoshita Jun'an 木下順庵
Kinoshita Kikutan 木下菊潭
Kinshiroku 近思録
Kitamura 喜多村
Kitsushōin 吉祥院
kō 公
kō 孝
Kōchi 高知
Kōchi 河内
Kochū 古註
Koga Seiri 古賀精里
Kojiki 古事記
Kōkaku 光格
koku 石
Kokugaku 国学
kokuhō 国法
Kokuhonron 国本論
kokutai 国体
komekata 米方
kome-nakagaishō 米仲買商
komeurikata 米売方
Konoe 近衛
Konoe Uchisaki 近衛内前
Kontonsha 混沌社
kōrizukai 郡使
Koshi-itsu 古史逸
Kossendan 滑川談
Kubota Masakuni 久保田政邦
kuchimai 口米
Kudō Heisuke 工藤平助
Kujō Naozane 九條尚実
Kumamoto 熊本
Kumazawa Banzan 熊沢蕃山
kumigashira 組頭
kuramaitori 蔵米取
Kuroda 黒田
Kurosawa Chikō 黒沢雉岡
Kuwana 桑名
Kuze Hirotami 久世広民
Kyōgoku Takahisa 京極高久
Kyōhō 享保
Kyoto 京都
Kyoto shoshidai 京都所司代
Kyūgen roku 求言録
Kyūji-saku 救時策
Kyūshū 九州
Magabuchi Kagetsugu 曲渕景漸
magokoro 真心
mai 枚
makanaikata 賄方
Makino Fusashige 牧野宣成
Makino Sadanaga 牧野貞長
Makino Tadakiyo 牧野忠精
Manyōshū 万葉集
manrinokoji dono 万里小路殿
Manrinokoji Masafusa
万里小路政房
Maruoka 丸岡
masuraoburi 益荒男振
Matsudaira Katanobu 松平容頌
Matsudaira Michi 松平猷
Matsudaira Nobuaki 松平信明
Matsudaira Nobuhide 松平信豪
Matsudaira Nobumichi

松平信道
Matsudaira Nobuyuki 松平信享
Matsudaira Norimori 松平乗薀
Matsudaira Norimura 松平乗邑
Matsudaira Norisada 松平乗完
Matsudaira Noritada 松平乗尹
Matsudaira Sadafumi 松平定奉
Matsudaira Sadakazu 松平定和
Matsudaira Sadakuni 松平定邦
Matsudaira Sadakuni 松平定国
Matsudaira Sadanaga 松平定永
Matsudaira Sadanobu 松平定信
Matsudaira Tadatomi 松平忠福
Matsudaira Tadatsugu
　松平忠告
Matsudaira Yasuji 松平康致
Matsudaira Yasutomi 松平康福
Matsudaira Yoshinori 松平義知
Matsue 松江
Matsumae 松前
Matsumoto Hidemochi
　松本秀持
Matsushiro 松代
Matsuura 松浦
Matsuyama 松山
mawari kome-osamekata
　廻米納方
Meiji 明治
Meishō 明正
meitoku 明徳
Meiwa 明和
meyasubako 目安箱
Mie 三重
Migiri no yanagi 砌の柳
Minamoto Sanetomo 源実朝
Minogawa Kien 皆川淇園
Mitani Sankurō 三谷三九郎
Mito 水戸
Miura Baien 三浦梅園
Miyagawa 宮川
Mizuno Tadakuni 水野忠邦
Mizuno Tadatomo 水野忠友
Mizuno Tamenaga 水野為長

momme 匁
Momozono 桃園
mon 文
Moriyama 森山
Moriyama Takamori 森山孝盛
Motoori Norinaga 本居宣長
Muraji Gyokusui 村士玉水
Murakami 村上
Muro Kyūsō 室鳩巣
Mutsu 陸奥
Myōhōin 妙法院
Nabeshima Harushige 鍋島治茂
Nabeshima Shigemochi
　鍋島重茂
Nagame 灘目
Nagaoka 長岡
Nagasaki 長崎
Nagato 長門
Nagoya 名古屋
Naidaijin 内大臣
naisekisama kata 内席様方
Naitō Heizaemon
　内藤平左衛門
Nakae Tōju 中江藤樹
Nakai Chikuzan 中井竹山
nakama 仲間
Nakamura Ranrin 中村蘭林
Nakanoin Michimura 中院通村
Nakatsu 中津
Nakayama Yoshichika
　中山愛親
Namikawa Tenmin 並河天民
Naniwa-e 難波江
Nara 奈良
Naraya 奈良屋
Nemuro 根室
Nihonmatsu 二本松
Nihon gaishi 日本外史
Nihongi 日本紀
Niigata 新潟
Niinamesai 新嘗祭
Nikkō 日光
ninjō 人情

Nishimaru 西丸
Nishinomiya 西宮
Nishio 西尾
Nishiyama Sessai 西山拙斉
Nishiyori Bokuzan 西依墨山
Nishiyori Seisai 西依成斉
Niwa 丹羽
Nochimigusa 後見草
O-ana-muchi 大己貴
Obama 小浜
ōbangashira 大番頭
ōbiroma 大広間
Odawara 小田原
Ōgaki 大垣
Ōgimachi Kin'aki 正親町公明
Ōgosho 大御所
Ogyū Hokkei 荻生北渓
Ogyū Sorai 荻生徂徠
ōjōya 大庄屋
Okada Kanzen 岡田寒泉
Okina mondō 翁問答
Okudaira Masatoki 奥平昌男
Okudaira Tadahiro 奥平忠弘
Okudono 奥殿
Ōmae Sombei 大前孫兵衛
ōmetsuke 大目付
Ōmiya Kizaeimon
　　近江屋喜左衛門
omote yaku 表役
omotezukaishū 表使衆
Ōmu no kotoba 鸚鵡詞
Ōnin 応仁
Ōoka Chūyō 大岡忠貫
Ōoka Tadamitsu 大岡忠光
osa hyakushō 長百姓
Osaka 大坂
Osamekata kaisho 納方会所
osameyado 納宿
Oshi 忍
Ōshūkaidō 奥州街道
Ōsu 大州
Ōta Nampo 大田南畝
Ōta Sukechika 太田資愛

Ōtsuka Kōi 大塚孝成
Ōtsuka Kōtaku 大塚孝绰
Owari 尾張
oyakata 親方
Ōzaki 大崎
Rai Sanyō 頼山陽
Rai Shunzui 頼春水
Rakuō-kō 楽翁公
Rakutei hikki 楽亭筆記
Reiganjima 霊巌島
ri 利
ri 理
Rintoku-ki 麟徳記
rizai 理財
rōjo 老女
rōjoshū 老女衆
rōnin 浪人
ryō 両
Saga 佐賀
Sagami 相模
Sakai Tadamitsu 酒井忠貫
Sakakibara 榊原
Sanada Yukitsura 真田幸貫
sanke 三家
sankyō 三卿
Sano Masakoto 佐野政言
Santō Kyōden 山東京伝
Saruya-machi kashikin kaisho
　　猿屋町貸金会所
Satō Issai 佐藤一斎
Satsuma 薩摩
sei 正
Seidō 聖堂
Seigaku 正学 聖学
Seigo 政語
seijikata 政治方
seijimuki no gi 政治向の義
seishin-shūshin 正心修身
Sekizenshū 責善集
Sendai 仙台
Sentō 仙洞
sesshō 摂政
Settsu 摂津

shi 私
Shibano Ritsuzan 柴野栗山
Shibata 新発田
Shibayama Mochitoyo
　芝山持豊
Shichibu kintsumetate Edochō
　kaisho
　七分金積立江戸町会所
Shiji seiyō 資治清要
Shiki 史記
Shikoku 四国
Shimbu no michi 神武道
Shimizu 清水
Shimizu Shigeyoshi 清水重好
shimpan 親藩
shinden 新田
Shingaku 心学
shinjutsu 心術
shinki 神気
Shinobu 信夫
Shirakawa 白河
shishirashii 志士らしい
shissei jaro 執政邪路
shita yokome 下横目
Shōdō-ki 升堂記
Shōgaku 小学
Shōhei 昌平
Shōhei-zaka gakumonjo
　昌平坂学問所
Shōnai 庄内
shōshō 少将
shōtenchi 小天地
Shōtoku 正徳
shōya 庄屋
Shoyū hen 庶有編
shu 朱
Shugendō 修験道
Shugyō roku 修行録
shukoku 守国
Shun 舜
Shundai zatsuwa 駿台雑話
Shūshin roku 修身録
sobayōnin 側用人

sobayōtoritsugi 側用取次
Sōbō kigen 草茅危言
sodoku gimmi 素読吟味
Sōma 相馬
Songo jiken 尊号事件
Sōrishū 双鯉集
sōshaban 奏者番
Sugawara Michizane 菅原道真
Sugita Gempaku 杉田玄白
Suika reisha 垂加霊社
Sukagawa 須賀川
sukegō 助郷
Sukehito 典仁
Suwa 諏訪
Suzuki Kunitaka 鈴木邦教
Takatsukasa Sukehira 鷹司輔平
taigi meibun 大儀名分
Taira 平
tairō 大老
Takakura 高倉
Takamatsu 高松
Takashima 高島
Takata 高田
Takenouchi Shikibu 竹内式部
tamarinoma 溜之間
tamarinoma onrei 溜之間御礼
Tamura 田村
Tanabe 田辺
Tanaka 田中
Tanaka Kurokami 田中玄宰
Tanakura 棚倉
Tanuma Okimune 田沼意致
Tanuma Okitomo 田沼意知
Tanuma Okitsugu 田沼意次
taoyameburi 手弱女振
Taruya go-yakusho 樽屋御役所
Taruya Yozaemon
　樽屋与左衛門
Tatebayashi 館林
Tayasu 田安
Tayasu Haruaki 田安治察
Tayasu Munetake 田安宗武
Tayasu Tanehime 田安種姫

teikannoma 帝鑑之間
Tempō 天保
tenjin ichiri 天人一理
tenki 天気
Tenmei 天明
Tenmei kōsetsu 天明巷説
Tenri 天理
tō 倒
Toda Ujinori 戸田氏教
tokonoma 床の間
Tokugawa 徳川
Tokugawa Harusada 徳川治済
Tokugawa Ieharu 徳川家治
Tokugawa Iemitsu 徳川家光
Tokugawa Iemoto 徳川家基
Tokugawa Ienobu 徳川家宣
Tokugawa Ieshige 徳川家重
Tokugawa Ietsugu 徳川家継
Tokugawa Ietsuna 徳川家綱
Tokugawa Ieyasu 徳川家康
Tokugawa jikki 徳川実紀
Tokugawa Munechika 徳川宗睦
Tokugawa Tsunayoshi
　　徳川綱吉
Tokugawa Yoshimune 徳川吉宗
Tokuhitsu yokyō 禿筆餘興
Torii Tadaoki 鳥居忠意
toritsugi 取次
Tosa 土佐
Tosaki Tanen 戸崎淡園
Toshima Hōshū 豊島豊洲
toshiyori 年寄
Tōtōmikakagawa 遠江掛川
Tottori 鳥取
tozama 外様
Tōzen manpitsu 燈前漫筆
tsubushi 潰
Tsuchiyama Sōjūrō 土山宗十郎
Tsukada Taihō 塚田大峰
tsukiban 月番
Tsuyama 津山
uchikowashi 打毀

Uesugi Harunori (Yōzan)
　　上杉治憲（鷹山）
Uezaki Kyūhachirō 植崎九八郎
Uge no hito koto 宇下人言
Usa mondō 宇佐問答
Utsunomiya 宇都宮
waka 和歌
Wakayama 和歌山
Wang Yang-ming 王陽明
Yagyū Shuzennokami Hisamichi
　　柳生主膳正久道
yamabushi 山伏
Yamaga Sokō 山鹿素行
Yamagata 山形
Yamagata Daini 山県大弐
Yamamoto Hokusan 山本北山
Yamamura Yoshio 山村良旺
Yamazaki 山崎
Yamazaki Ansai 山崎闇斎
Yao 堯
Yokoi Chiaki 横井千秋
yokome 横目
Yokota Noritoshi 横田準松
Yōkun hōshi kokoroe
　　幼君奉仕心得
yonaikin 余内金
yonaoshi 世直
Yonezawa 米沢
yōnin 用人
yoseba 寄場
Yoshida 吉田
Yoshikawa Koretaru 吉川惟足
Yoshimura Matazaeimon
　　吉村又右衛門
Yoshio Kōgyū 吉雄耕牛
yūhitsu 祐筆
Yūki 結城
Yūki naonori 結城直矩
Yūki Yoshinori 結城義知
Yumoto 湯本
Yūshoku kojitsu 有職故実

Index